CAREER DIRECTIONS

W9-BXW-126

CAREER DIRECTIONS

New Paths to Your Ideal Career

Sixth Edition

Donna J. Yena
Johnson & Wales University

Mc
Graw
Hill
Education

CAREER DIRECTIONS: NEW PATHS TO YOUR IDEAL CAREER, SIXTH EDITION

Published by McGraw-Hill Education, 2 Penn Plaza, New York, NY 10121. Copyright © 2015 by McGraw-Hill Education. All rights reserved. Printed in the United States of America. Previous editions © 2011, 2007, and 1997. No part of this publication may be reproduced or distributed in any form or by any means, or stored in a database or retrieval system, without the prior written consent of McGraw-Hill Education, including, but not limited to, in any network or other electronic storage or transmission, or broadcast for distance learning.

Some ancillaries, including electronic and print components, may not be available to customers outside the United States.

This book is printed on acid-free paper.

1 2 3 4 5 6 7 8 9 0 DOW/DOW 1 0 9 8 7 6 5 4

ISBN 978-0-07-352250-0
MHID 0-07-352250-3

Senior Vice President, Products & Markets: *Kurt L. Strand*
Vice President, Content Production & Technology Services: *Kimberly Meriwether David*
Director: *Scott Davidson*
Executive Director of Development: *Ann Torbert*
Development Editor II: *Alaina G. Tucker*
Digital Development Editor II: *Kevin White*
Digital Product Analyst: *Thuan Vinh*
Executive Marketing Manager: *Keari Green*
Marketing Specialist: *Lindsay Pawlik*
Director, Content Production: *Terri Schiesl*
Content Project Manager: *Jean R. Starr*
Senior Buyer: *Debra R. Sylvester*
Design: *Lisa King*
Cover Image: © *artvea/Getty Images*
Content Licensing Specialist: *Shawntel Schmitt*
Typeface: *10/12 Times LT Std Roman*
Compositor: *Laserwords Private Limited*
Printer: *R. R. Donnelley*

All credits appearing on page or at the end of the book are considered to be an extension of the copyright page.

Library of Congress Cataloging-in-Publication Data

Yena, Donna J.
    Career directions : new paths to your ideal career / Donna J. Yena, Johnson & Wales University.–
Sixth edition.
        pages cm
    Includes index.
    ISBN 978-0-07-352250-0 (alk. paper)—ISBN 0-07-352250-3 (alk. paper)
    1. Vocational guidance. 2. Career development. I. Title.
    HF5381.Y46 2015
650.1—dc23
                                                            2013047147

The Internet addresses listed in the text were accurate at the time of publication. The inclusion of a website does not indicate an endorsement by the authors or McGraw-Hill Education, and McGraw-Hill Education does not guarantee the accuracy of the information presented at these sites.

Dedication

This book is dedicated to the thousands of students and teachers who have applied the techniques in this book as a tool for planning and launching successful careers for the past 30 years. Along with employers, they have provided me valuable guidance, support, and inspiration to ensure this text continues to benefit the career success of the students it serves. Thank you!

About the Author

With over thirty years of experience in career services and human resources, Donna Yena brings a practitioner's perspective to this book. Her experience as Vice President of Career Services at Johnson and Wales University, along with her background as manager, instructor, and curriculum designer, contribute to the advice and techniques found in *Career Directions: New Paths to Your Ideal Career* and the *Career Directions Handbook.*

Yena developed and implemented a series of career management education courses for students at Johnson and Wales University, while responsible for experiential education programs for more than 4,000 students at four campuses. For thirty consecutive years, 98 percent of Johnson and Wales graduates were employed within sixty days of graduation. As a certified DACUM (Developing a Curriculum) facilitator, Yena worked with employers and faculty to formalize employer input into the university curriculum and, with select employers, coordinated the DACUM process as input into corporate training and development programs and as a tool to refine screening and interviewing processes.

At Johnson and Wales University, Yena also served as a classroom teacher of career management and student success courses, director of university planning, coordinator of employee development programs, and Director of Career Development before assuming the roles of Vice President of Career Services and Alumni Relations and Vice President of Employer Relations. In her various roles, Yena traveled to Thailand, Israel, Hungary, Turkey, Austria, Germany, Switzerland, France, South America, and the Caribbean to facilitate relationships with university alumni and employers.

She currently serves as a member of the Johnson and Wales University Corporation and has previously served as a member of the Board of Governors for the World Association of Cooperative Education and a member of the Society of Human Resource Management; the Women's Foodservice Forum; and the National Association of Colleges and Employers (NACE).

Yena is a nationally recognized speaker on career services, graduate employment, student success, and employer relations. She has led workshops for school professionals and their students and has been a speaker at numerous state and national association meetings across the country.

Over 100,000 students have used this textbook in its previous editions to help launch and propel their careers. Yena continues to receive feedback from students and alumni regarding its utility throughout their careers.

Brief Contents

Contents

Part 1: Explore Your Potential 1

1 Connecting to Today's Workplace 3

2 Self-Assessment 19

3 Goal Setting and Career Decision Making 39

4 Personal Development 53

10 Resumes and Job Applications   171

11 Letters   209

12 Successful Interviews   235

Preface

WELCOME TO *CAREER DIRECTIONS: NEW PATHS TO YOUR IDEAL CAREER*

Career Directions: New Paths to Your Ideal Career has been adapted to combine the use of modern job search technology with time-tested, traditional strategies found in previous editions. Today's savvy job seeker or career professional is able to strike the right balance using a digital job search, professional online identity, and face-to-face connections to network the way to career success. Striking that right balance enables you to develop and present the best version of you, effectively telling YOUR STORY to prospective employers. The ultimate objective of this text is for you to distinguish yourself in today's highly competitive employment market in ways that lead you to successful interviews resulting in the best possible outcome for you.

Armed with the material in this text, you will be better able to create a distinct personal brand, think of it as "YOU Inc.," which will elevate your application to the top of the pile, in effect, enabling you to begin and manage your career from day one.

This sixth edition of *Career Directions* focuses on *new paths* to your ideal career that include:

- Social media profiles
- Online Career Portfolios
- Multiple resume versions
- Maximization of the use of keywords

New to this edition is a chapter exclusively devoted to the increasingly important use of social media in the job search and the world of work, including the importance of managing your professional online identity. Focus includes readying social media profiles for a job search.

The development of your Career Portfolio is a central theme throughout the text. By completing Career Portfolio Entry activities, you will build your Career Portfolio. The updated Career Portfolio chapter focuses on effectively showcasing examples of your work. Employers are relying more on Career Portfolios to screen job applicants because evidence of best work and accomplishments validate claims made on your resume and provide a more complete picture of what you can do.

Today's resume is prepared in multiple versions ranging from a PDF or edit-ready version, to web, video, social, or even infographic resume options to target specific employers. All new examples of these different resume options are provided along with advice on their best use in your job search.

You will learn the effective use of keywords and their impact on getting the attention of hiring managers. The newly organized *Career Directions Handbook* has been updated to include a wide range of industry- and job-specific keywords to help strengthen your job search and online presence.

Career Directions, sixth edition, contains updated content on career management essentials found in previous editions.

- **Part 1: Explore Your Potential** Includes the most current strategies for self-assessment, goal setting, personal development, communication skills, and career research. Tips for professional online communication are included.

- **Part 2: Brand Your Potential** Focuses on your Career Portfolio, social media profiles, career networking, and internship and co-op programs, multiple resume versions, letters, and successful interviews.
- **Part 3: Career Management** Focuses on strategies for growing your career and contemporary issues in the workplace.

CAREER DIRECTIONS HANDBOOK

The *Career Directions Handbook* is a current and comprehensive tool that can be used as a companion to the textbook or as a stand-alone product. It is available both in print and online. Packed with valuable information, the *Career Directions Handbook* arms you with knowledge of keywords important to your job search and the latest career paths, job titles, and salary ranges and hundreds of specific job descriptions spanning a multitude of industries. Included industries range from technology to health care to business, and everything in between!

This edition of the *Career Directions Handbook* contains a new section of industry keywords and keyword phrases along with other keyword examples throughout. Ideas are presented on how to use keywords to strengthen your job search online and offline.

The information on keywords and career paths found in the handbook is a helpful resource for completing many activities in the textbook including goal setting, career research, content development for social media profiles, resumes, and job search letters, and for practicing salary negotiation.

The all-new textbook *Career Directions: New Paths to Your Ideal Career* and updated *Career Directions Handbook* are your complete career management reference tools for preparing to enter and succeed in today's workplace. You will find yourself referring back to them at different points in your career to explore new opportunities or affirm the course you are on. Enjoy your journey!

Acknowledgments

I would like to acknowledge the tremendous efforts and guidance of the entire McGraw-Hill Higher Education team whose vision, partnership, and expertise contributed to the development of this sixth edition. Particular thanks go to Alaina Tucker for the talent, commitment, and diligence demonstrated in shepherding this new edition to completion. I would also like to extend my gratitude to Scott Davidson for your continued support and belief in this book; to Keari Green for your marketing efforts in ensuring the value of this book is communicated to students and instructors alike; to Jean Starr for your efforts behind the scenes regarding schedule coordination and production; to Lisa King for your work on the cover and interior design; and to Destiny Hadley and Marcy Lunetta for your work on citations and permissions, respectively.

McGraw-Hill and Donna Yena would like to acknowledge all the instructors who reviewed this and previous editions. Their continued insight and input contribute directly to the development and success of this text.

6th Edition Reviewers

Chris Cobian, *Blue Ridge Community and Technical College*

Jean DeVenney, *Clackamas Community College*

Darren Aldred, *Tennessee College of Applied Technology*

Wilma Kerns, *Allegany College of Maryland*

Kris Bloos, *Indiana University Southeast*

Cathy Combs, *Tennessee College of Applied Technology—Morristown*

Kathleen Kesser, *New England Culinary Institute*

Richard Smith, *Valley College of Technology—Martinsburg*

Vicky Keller-Schleeter, *Rochester Community and Technical College*

James Bruce, *Metropolitan Learning Institute*

Paul Dexter, *University of Southern Maine*

Terri L. Moore, *South Central Louisiana Technical College—Lafourche*

Ann Henry, *ServiceSource—Delaware*

Philip Campbell, *McCann School of Business & Technology*

Damarcus Smith, *Pensacola State College*

Cindy Bennett, *Chesapeake College*

Heather Stone, *Bethel University*

Josh Burgess, *McCann School of Business*

Kathy Powell, *Colorado Northwestern Community College*

Belen Torres-Gil, *Rio Hondo College*

Carole Mackewich, *Clark College*

Valarie Robinson, *University of North Florida*

Shar Sharusan, *Everest College*

Linda Helmers, *Iowa Lakes Community College*

Howard Roose, *Southwest Institute of Technology*
Kitty Spires, *Midlands Technical College*
Eva Johnson, *Pacific Lutheran University*
Miranda Miller, *Tennessee College of Applied Technology*
Tony Anderson, *Hartnell College*
Dr. Ronald Harmon, *Metropolitan Learning Institute*

The sixth edition of *Career Directions: New Paths to Your Ideal Career* is designed to ensure that students will not only learn fundamental strategies of career success, but also will be able to put those basics into action through real-world cases, examples, and a multitude of activities.

Career Directions is

"A refreshing change from my current textbook, with more contemporary topics."

Belen Torres-Gil, Rio Hondo College

---

learning outcomes

After completing this chapter, you will:

1 **Learn** how to build your Career Portfolio

2 **Plan** your Career Portfolio

3 **Collect** Career Portfolio materials

4 **Organize** and assemble your Career Portfolio

5 **Practice** and present your Career Portfolio

6 **Reflect,** refine, and edit your Career Portfolio

7 **Create** a Career Portfolio entry

Your Career Portfolio is a tool you can use to present your unique employment skills to a potential employer on a job interview. Your Career Portfolio should contain samples of work and other documentation of your skills and credentials that employers in your career field are interested in. This will be an enhancement to using only a resume to present yourself professionally. While certain fields, such as advertising and public relations, have

LEARNING OUTCOMES outline the focus of the chapter and provide a roadmap for the material ahead. Each is tied to a main heading in the chapter, as well as to the chapter summary, to help reiterate important topics throughout.

CASE STUDIES located at the beginning of each chapter introduce students to chapter topics through real-world scenarios. Related Discussion Questions are provided at the end of each case to encourage classroom discussion.

"It encompasses real world application, engages active learners, and is at an appropriately rigorous level."

Maria E. Sofia, Bryant & Stratton College

CASE STUDY

Linda's Tool Kit—People and Technology

Linda completed her nursing degree and wanted to gain some work experience before applying for a full-time nursing position. She was working full time as an office manager for an insurance company, a position she held for the last 10 years while raising her daughter and attending nursing school part time. Linda was open to working in a variety of settings. She searched the Internet for job postings in her area to keep informed about the various types of nursing jobs available. She knew from fellow adult students, also making a career change, that it was sometimes difficult to find a job in a new field without some work experience. Even though the job market was very good for nurses in the state she lived in, Linda deCded to work for a temporary services agency that speCalized in plaCng nurses and obtained a weekend job as a visiting nurse.

Discussion Questions

1. Can you identify direct and indirect sources of job information available to Linda?
2. What other resources could Linda have used to further explore the hidden job market?
3. What do think are some advantages to an employee referral program for a company?

... a comprehensive and engaging way for students to explore, identify, and achieve their ideal career paths.

REAL LIFE STORIES exemplify chapter topics, and allow students to connect the material to current businesses, well-known individuals, and their own lives. These stories range from companies like American Girl, LLC, to everyday individuals such as Steve Jobs, who have had experiences similar to those that students might face.

Real Life Stories

Sean and Lori: Handling Unemployment Status in Social Media Profiles

Sean was having trouble finding a job for some time after he graduated. He did not know how to refer to his unemployment status on his LinkedIn profile. He decided to use this as an opportunity to reach out to his LinkedIn network. In the Professional Headline section of his profile he wrote, "Recent College Grad Seeking Entry Level Accounting Position. Would appreciate appropriate referrals." In the Current Position section he wrote, "Recent Grad at (name of college).edu." He went one step further and shared the same with his college's LinkedIn Alumni Community Group and received three referrals within seven days.

Lori was laid off from her job after working for three years as a certified nursing assistant (CNA). In her LinkedIn profile she listed her Professional Headline as "Experienced CNA in transition." In the Summary section of her LinkedIn profile she mentioned her availability for work and contact information. She thought she was taking a risk exposing her unemployment status, but she knew that she had to be truthful. It is easy for employers to read through vague statements and to verify a questionable employment status. It's better to be truthful, and like Sean, work your LinkedIn and other career networks for leads to new opportunities.

ACTIVITIES provided throughout each chapter encourage immediate application and practice of the topics covered.

"Easy to read; full of activities to make students begin thinking."
Debbie Liddel, Pinnacle Career Institute

"I like the variety of exercises. They are thought-provoking and allow the student to personally connect with the content."
Earl Wiggins, Miller-Motte College

IVITY 6.4
marize Your
s and Role-Play

Work with another person, who will play the role of an interviewer. Summarize the skills and accomplishments you want to highlight to an employer, and select the evidence you have to demonstrate. Have the "interviewer" ask you about your skills, and role-play your response to each question and the presentation of your portfolio.

It may take a few practice sessions to become familiar with promoting yourself this way, but it will be worth it when you convince a prospective employer you are a highly qualified candidate for the job.

EXAMPLE

Interviewer Asks: Can you give me an example of a situation in which you displayed leadership skills?

Sample Response 1: Yes. As an offcer of Future Business Leaders of America, I was responsible for motivating the membership to initiate an annual fund-raiser for the homeless in our community. Let me show you some letters of appreciation from the mayor and the homeless shelter we worked with.

Sample Response 2: Yes. In my research and design class, I led our work group in presenting our marketing proposal to a local business firm. Here is a copy of our proposal, which was accepted and implemented.

PROGRESS CHECK QUESTIONS

facilitate class discussion and encourage students to pause and reflect on key topics as they progress through each chapter.

· ▶

"The Progress Check Questions are on target, thought-provoking, and can be used effectively as the basis for classroom (or online) discussion."

David M. Leuser, Plymouth State University

Progress Check Questions

1. How would you describe the current job market where you live?
2. How might current conditions in the job market influence your career decisions?

· ·

DIVERSITY

Workforce diversity is described by a variety of dimensions such as ethnicity, race, or gender as well as by secondary influences such as religion, socioeconomics, and ed tion. For companies that compete globally, a diverse workforce has distinct advant Work teams with different backgrounds and experiences bring different views on p lem solving, team building, marketing, and a variety of other areas that are importar enhancing individual and company performance.

NOTES | Awareness of the World around You

Topics	Sources of Information
Economic trends	Internet
Job trends	*Wall Street Journal*
Major political events	*USA Today*
Cultural issues in your community	Community groups and organizations
Health-related issues	Professional associations
Bills being voted on that may affect you	Local and national political representatives
Cost-of-living trends	Trade journals
Sports-related news	Television
Cultural activities	Social network (movies, plays, events)

NOTES BOXES highlight material directly related to chapter topics, providing reinforcement and enhancement of the subject matter.

◀ ·

CAREER PORTFOLIO ACTIVITIES

The development of your Career Portfolio is a central theme throughout the text. By completing Career Portfolio activities you will learn to effectively showcase examples of your work, validating claims made on your resume and providing a complete picture of what you can do.

CAREER PORTFOLIO 4.1

DEMONSTRATE COMMUNICATION SKILLS

Demonstrate your written and verbal communication skills with samples of your work. If done well, a writing sample and a visual sample of your communication skills can help distinguish you in your job search. Choose one or both of the options below, depending on what you know you can do best. Work with an instructor to ensure the quality of your samples. Save your samples to include in your Career Portfolio.

1. Written communication skills—writing sample
   Write a one- or two-page description of one of the following:
   - Class project
   - Work or community service experience related to your career goal
   - Special distinction you earned (award, honor, etc.) related to your career goal
2. Verbal communication skills—visual sample
   Create a video of yourself describing what you wrote about.
   You can use Vine, Vimeo, or any other platform you are comfortable with.
   Your video can be posted online and used to become part of your online Career Portfolio, or you can simply upload it to your iPad to show your targeted audience—for example, an employer during a job interview.

REFLECTION EXERCISES at the end
of each chapter allow students to think critically about what they have learned and respond through an application-based exercise.

"The exercises are very useful and lend themselves to group discussion or activity."

James Rubin, Paradise Valley Community College

REFLECTION EXERCISE

CAREER PORTFOLIOS AND CAREER DECISION MAKING
Based on what you learned about portfolios in this chapter, think about what decisions you need to make about developing your Career Portfolio.

1. What am I trying to decide?

_____

_____

2. What do I need to know?

_____

_____

3. How will it help me make a more informed decision?

_____

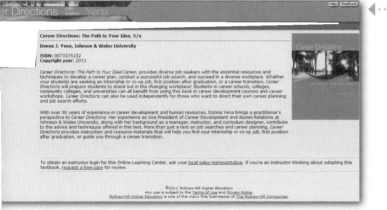

ONLINE LEARNING CENTER

The Online Learning Center (OLC) is a website that follows the text chapter by chapter with digital supplementary content. The instructor's side of the OLC contains useful resources to aid in planning and teaching the course, including the Instructor's Manual, PowerPoint presentations for each chapter, a Test Bank, and Retention Kit, containing:

- Facilitator's Guide
- Tools for Time Management
- Establishing Peer Support Groups
- Involving the Faculty Strategy
- Capitalizing on Your School's Graduates

As students read the book, they can go to the student side of the OLC to take self-grading quizzes, review material, access relevant Web links, and view and print examples and relevant forms. The information center includes the book's table of contents, preface, sample chapter, description of supplements available, and information about the author. The OLC for *Career Directions* is located at **www.mhhe.com/yena6e**.

WHAT'S NEW

NEW THROUGHOUT THE TEXT!

NEW to this edition: Case Studies
NEW to this edition: Real Life Stories
NEW to this edition: Progress Check questions in each chapter
UPDATED Chapter Summaries throughout

CHAPTER 1: CONNECTING TO TODAY'S WORKPLACE

- TRENDS AFFECTING YOU IN THE WORKPLACE
  - Social Media
  - Digital Job Search
    - Public Image and Your Reputation
    - Job Search Documents
    - Specific Skills
    - Quality, Not Quantity
  - Face-to-Face Connections
  - Jobs and the Economy
    - Employment Rates
    - Underemployment
    - "Rusty" Job Search Skills
    - Transition Opportunities
    - Technology

CHAPTER 2: SELF-ASSESSMENT

- NEW REAL LIFE STORY: Steve Jobs
- The Myers-Briggs Temperament Indicator (MBTI)
- List of Transferable/Functional Skills and Technical Skills

CHAPTER 3: GOAL SETTING AND CAREER DECISION MAKING

- TYPES OF GOALS
  - Inspirational Goals
  - Planning Goals
  - Milestone Goals
  - Bridge Goals (expanded discussion of SMART Goals)

CHAPTER 4: PERSONAL DEVELOPMENT

- Communicate Your Message
- Professional Online Communication
  - Effective Online Messages (E-mails, Texts, and Tweets)
  - Visual Communication Skills
  - Career Portfolio Preview
  - Career Portfolio Entry Examples
  - CAREER PORTFOLIO ENTRY ACTIVITY: Demonstrate Communication Skills
  - Expanded discussion of business dress for women and men and business casual dress

CHAPTER 5: CAREER AND JOB RESEARCH TOOLS

- INDUSTRY CAREER TRENDS
  - High-Growth Careers
  - Fast-Growing Industries by Percentage of Change through 2020
  - Steady-Growth Careers
- INDUSTRY, COMPANY, AND JOB RESEARCH
  - Your Research Toolkit
- Activity 5.3 Industry Research
- Activity 5.4 Company Research
- Activity 5.5 Researching Job Information and Leads
- INFORMATIONAL INTERVIEWS
- JOB SEARCH ENGINES
  - Advanced Search Feature
- KEYWORDS IN JOB DESCRIPTIONS

CHAPTER 6: YOUR CAREER PORTFOLIO

- YOUR CAREER PORTFOLIO
  - Building Career Portfolio Entries
  - CAREER PORTFOLIO ENTRY ACTIVITIES BY CHAPTER
  - Types of Career Portfolio Entries by Chapter
  - Amanda's Career Portfolio
  - Derek's Digital Career Portfolio

Explore Your Potential

"The best thing you're ever going to do, you haven't even thought of yet. You're just getting started"

Ann Curry, former co-anchor, *The Today Show*[1]

[1]Retrieved April 4, 2013, from www.lhj.com/style/covers/ann-curry/.

Connecting to Today's Workplace

After completing this chapter, you will:

1 **Identify** how trends affect you in the workplace

2 **List** the 21st century skills employers consider critical to career success

3 **Recognize** the value of your education in the workplace

It is important for you to have an awareness of the world around you as you prepare for today's workplace. Societal and economic trends will affect your job and work environment. This chapter discusses how trends are reshaping your world of work by focusing on the major challenges today's workers face and how businesses and people are responding to these changes. The chapter also focuses on the skills you will need for success in today's workplace. A major part of your career success will depend on your ability to respond and adapt to these changes.

CASE STUDY

Maria's Career Launch

Maria attended community college immediately following her graduation from high school. While pursuing her degree in communications, Maria completed an internship at a local hospital in the public relations office. As an intern, Maria was part of a team that helped develop a local ad campaign to recruit more members of the community into the hospital's volunteer program. Her work included meeting with college students and local business groups to explain the importance of the volunteer program and share the positive feedback about the experience from current volunteers. Her goal after graduation was to work in a small advertising firm where she could further develop her writing and presentation skills and learn more about how to promote a variety of different products and services.

When Maria graduated, the job market was extremely tough. She spread the word about her qualifications and skills by posting her Web resume online and was contacted by three employers whom she was unfamiliar with for interviews. Her first choice was to obtain a position with an agency she applied to that had a well-established reputation in the large Hispanic community where she lived. Maria took Spanish courses while at the community college and felt confident speaking the language Maria was offered the job. Many of the employees who worked with her were older than Maria and had more knowledge and experience. There were four other recent college graduates. Her fellow workers came from various ethnic backgrounds, and most had been with the firm for some time. One of her assignments was developing an advertising plan for a line of nutrition products that she did not know a lot about. Maria had built an online network to keep in touch with friends, teachers, and colleagues from the hospital and the community college. She used her network to reach out to a few former teachers and colleagues at the hospital to gain advice on how to go about the project and to learn more about the product. Jim, one of her older colleagues at the firm, knew a little about the product but had never created an ad campaign targeted to a Hispanic community.

Maria involved Jim in the project along with two other colleagues who had experience with creating ad campaigns targeted to different ethnic groups. When the project was near completion, she was able to test the ad campaign with members of the community by conducting focus groups in Spanish. The product was very successful, and Maria was assigned to work with Jim and several other more experienced colleagues to develop an online community of contacts who could either provide leads or product information for future projects.

Discussion Questions

1. What skills did Maria need to apply to work successfully with her coworkers who were so different from her?
2. Why do you think Maria was selected to create the campaign for the nutrition products?
3. What else could Jim do to increase his value to the firm in a competitive job market?

⦿ 1.1 TRENDS AFFECTING YOU IN THE WORKPLACE

The workplace constantly changes in response to world events and trends. In the past few years, social media, emerging job search technology, and the economy have had the most dramatic impact. An aging and diverse population and growth in entrepreneurial opportunities are other examples. Being aware of how these trends are shaping the workplace can help you better prepare for and manage your career.

SOCIAL MEDIA

The growth of social media in the last 10 years has reinvented career and job search management and how we connect to the workplace.

Employers have a presence on LinkedIn, Facebook, and Twitter to promote their company and attract qualified applicants. More employers are including review of candidates' online profiles as part of the screening process when hiring (Figure 1.1).

A new survey by Bullhorn, a company that makes technology products for employers and recruiters, shows how powerfully LinkedIn dominates the world of job search and recruitment. Of a poll of 1,848 staffing professionals, 98.2 percent of respondents said they tapped some form of social media for recruiting in 2012. Almost as many—97.3 percent—said they used LinkedIn as a recruiting tool in the same year.[2]

LinkedIn and Twitter are used to build professional networks including linking employers and job candidates. In the past, Facebook was used primarily to build social networks, but has evolved into a professional and job search tool. Social media have become such worldwide job search resources that, if ignored, can leave someone far behind in the job market.

[2]Retrieved April 9, 2013, from www.forbes.com/sites/susanadams/2013/02/05/new-survey-linked-in-more-dominant-than-ever-among-job-seekers-and-recruiters-but-facebook-poised-to-gain/.

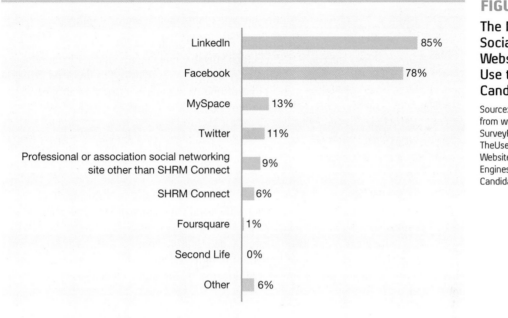

FIGURE 1.1

The Most Common Social Networking Websites Organizations Use to Screen Job Candidates

Source: Retrieved April 5, 2013, from www.shrm.org/Research/SurveyFindings/Articles/Pages/TheUseofSocialNetworkingWebsitesandOnlineSearchEnginesinScreeningJobCandidates.aspx.

If managed well, use of social media can be an asset to a job search and career. Having a strong online profile is one way to promote yourself and gain access to potential job leads. This makes it important to pay attention to the quality of online profiles, particularly when searching for a job.

DIGITAL JOB SEARCH

In addition to the use of social media, employers have stepped up the use of other digital tools. Job search engines, resume boards, and company websites that include job boards, blogs, chat rooms, online videos, and links to industry networking groups are the most commonly used. The more employers rely on these resources, the more important it is for job searchers to know how to use these digital tools effectively. How well you manage your digital job search impacts your success with each step of the process from planning, searching, and being hired. The rate at which new job search technology is emerging can make an online job search seem confusing. Staying focused on managing the following four key areas helps prioritize your online job search efforts.

Public Image and Reputation   On the Internet, your image is public. When you post an online profile or resume, participate in a blog or a chat room, virtually anything you do on the Internet can be viewed by others. Every comment, every status, and every response is captured and stored on a server so Google and other search engines can link to it. Being mindful of the image you build online puts you in control of one of your most important career assets—your reputation.

Job Search Documents   Knowing how to prepare and distribute job search documents and supporting materials in various formats is important to a successful digital job search. This includes preparing an online resume, creating an online profile on social media sites, completing online job applications, and preparing an online Career Portfolio.

"Proficiency in social media is a differentiator now, but will soon be a qualifier."

Dan Schawbel, managing partner, Millennial Branding[3]

---

[3]Retrieved April 17, 2013, from http://danschawbel.com/quotes/.

Personal websites are growing in use and provide another option for you to distinguish yourself online.

Specific Skills   Employers focus first on searching for specific skills that match particular job requirements. Paying attention to keywords used to describe skills on an online profile or resume is critical to linking to the right employers and jobs online.

Quality, Not Quantity   The ease of accessing job information online often leads to an overreliance on the Internet in a job search. Employers find it difficult to wade through the mass number of applications received online, and candidates can spend more time at the computer than making valuable face-to-face connections. Targeting your job search helps focus on the quality of jobs you connect with versus the quantity.

Each of these areas is discussed in greater detail throughout the text. As changes occur in job search technology, the most important thing is to stay current on the basic tools to manage your reputation, create job search documents, highlight special skills, and target your search.

FACE-TO-FACE CONNECTION

With all of the focus on social media, it is important to remember that online tools play only one important part in a successful job search and career. They help you get your foot in the door. With or without an online presence, managing face-to-face connections is one of the most powerful ways to set you apart. When you network or interview for a job, face to face, you have the opportunity to demonstrate those intangible qualities not always obvious online; for example, social skills, body language, one-on-one communication skills, listening skills, high energy level, positive attitude, genuineness, and personal appearance. Face-to-face connections tell how well you might relate to others in a particular company culture. By building personal relationships, you can win the trust of others who can help you in more meaningful ways than your online connections. As more day-to-day interaction is done online, there is renewed importance in the role face-to-face connections play in distinguishing yourself in today's job market and workplace. Successfully combining online and offline strategies is the best approach to convince an employer you are the total package. Techniques for building strong face-to-face relationships are discussed in Chapter 4.

JOBS AND THE ECONOMY

Employment Rates

Getting and keeping a job throughout fluctuations in the economy requires focus and skill in both good and poor job markets. If you develop the right mindset, you can be successful under most circumstances. Look beyond the unemployment rate. A high unemployment rate does not always equate to a lack of jobs, but almost always equates to more people competing for fewer jobs. In February 2013, the number of jobs available was 3.9 million. That's about three people available for every job opening—an improvement from seven people available for every job in 2009. Developing the right job search skills can help you successfully compete in most any job market.[4]

Understanding some reasons for unemployment below can also help you overcome associated challenges in your job search.

[4]Retrieved April 28, 2013, from http://money.msn.com/now/post.aspx?post=d766374f-88b3-4e66-b963-ac025136fca0.

Unemployment Rates

Business Closings and Downsizing When people have less money to spend, some industries are negatively impacted. The entertainment and retail industries are two examples. When there is a loss of jobs in an industry you are interested in, it is important to be knowledgeable about industries that continue to thrive even in a weak economy. Accounting, finance, health care, and technology are just a few examples.

Mismatch of Skills, Education, and Experience A recent survey from the Society for Human Resource Management (SHRM) shows that 66 percent of hiring firms have trouble finding workers for specific positions. Yet, the number of unemployed remains high.[5]

Skills Gap The skills gap refers to the difference between skills needed to perform a job and the skills possessed by applicants. Applicants are either underqualified or overqualified for available positions. Wide differences in education and experience levels contribute to this imbalance.

Changes from Job to Job Some short periods of unemployment occur when someone is between jobs moving from one position to another. This may occur because of the need to relocate or just the difference in timing between ending and starting a new job. This type of unemployment can be beneficial to others in a job search since there are positions being left vacant as a result of moves to other positions.

"Rusty" Job Search Skills Some unemployed people are not conducting effective job searches because they are not up to speed on technological changes that have occurred in the job search process.

Underemployment

Underemployment increases during periods of high unemployment. This includes people working in a lower capacity than they are qualified for including in lower-paid jobs or for fewer hours than they would like to work.

Transition Opportunities Transition opportunities are job opportunities that become available to job seekers during their job search. Although a transition job might not meet a person's criteria for an ideal job, it might provide experience, contacts, or income that can move the individual closer to his or her goal.

Transition opportunities and other strategies for dealing with unemployment are discussed in greater detail in Chapter 13. As you can see from this discussion of employment rates, the good news is that even in periods of high unemployment there are jobs available. You need the job search skills to uncover them and the vision to see long-term value in the opportunities that present themselves.

Globalization and Outsourcing U.S. companies are doing more business in other countries to compete in the global marketplace. One outcome is outsourcing work outside the United States. The complicated U.S. visa system makes it difficult and expensive for employers to hire foreign workers in this country. The advantage to outsourcing is keeping costs low because firms can pay lower wages to workers in other countries and minimize visa issues. Call center outsourcing to India is an example. The disadvantage to the United States is a loss of jobs.

Financial Markets Financial markets grow and create jobs. Gains in financial markets cause consumers to be more confident and increase spending. When spending goes up, the number of jobs increases. The housing market is an example. A housing recovery drives job growth in a number of industries including construction, real estate, banking, utilities, and home goods retail. During a housing market crisis, defaults on mortgage payments and home foreclosures rise. Credit counselors are in greater demand to help people manage resulting debt. Financial counselors, sometimes called prevention counselors, help people create a financial plan to avoid home foreclosures.

[5]Danielle Kurtzlebe. (March 28, 2013). "Surveys Find Employers Have Too Few and Too Many Qualified Workers." *U.S. News*. Retrieved April 16, 2013, from www.usnews.com/news/articles/2013/03/28/surveys-find-employers-have-too-few-and-too-many-qualified-workers.

Technology   Technology reduces the dependence on labor in many sectors. It is common for jobs to be divided into simpler, routine tasks that can be handled by technology. Online shopping and online banking are examples. When technology either replaces or reduces jobs, new technology jobs are created usually resulting in net job creation requiring different skills. For example, cloud computing and social networking provide low-cost resources for new business development and create new jobs. Application software developers (apps developers) create new applications for computers, phones, and other electronic devices. Social media consultants advise businesses on how to optimize use of social media to grow business.

ACTIVITY 1.1

Researching Job Growth Trends

Working with a group, create a plan for how to research trends in job growth based on economic conditions. List three sources of information that you think are the most informative (e.g., *Occupational Outlook Handbook*, local newspaper, financial reports online similar to Moodyseconomy.com).

1. _____

2. _____

3. _____

List some key economic indicators of job growth to follow and why they are important (e.g., stock market, housing market, outsourcing).

_____

_____

_____

_____

Progress Check Questions

1. How would you describe the current job market where you live?

2. How might current conditions in the job market influence your career decisions?

DIVERSITY

Workforce diversity is described by a variety of dimensions such as ethnicity, race, age, or gender as well as by secondary influences such as religion, socioeconomics, and education. For companies that compete globally, a diverse workforce has distinct advantages. Work teams with different backgrounds and experiences bring different views on problem solving, team building, marketing, and a variety of other areas that are important to enhancing individual and company performance.

"By 2050, there will be no majority race."

America's Career Resource Network (ACRN)[6]

Different groups have different needs, and they want their needs to be recognized and met as much as possible. Employers that provide more customized approaches to employee recruitment and training, coaching, retention, and benefits plans are able to attract and retain a diverse workforce.

Ethnicity and Race   A landmark study, Workforce 2020,[7] points to the impact that ethnic diversity in the labor force has on changing the workplace. Kraft Foods is an example of

[6]America's Career Resource Network. (2009). "The Economic Challenge." Retrieved March 12, 2009, from http://cte.ed.gov/acrn/econchal.htm.

[7]R. W. Judy and C. D'Amico. (1997). "Workforce 2020: Work and Workers in the 21st Century." Retrieved September 1, 2009, from www.eric.ed.gov/ERICDocs/data/ericdocs2sql/content_storage_01/0000019b/80/16/bb/41.pdf.

a company responding effectively to its diverse workforce. Through the development of diversity network groups, Kraft uses employee councils to build employee development.

Through 10 employee councils (African-American Council, Hispanic Council, Asian-American Council, Women in Sales Council, Black Sales Council, Women in Operations, Hispanic-Asian Sales Council, Rainbow Council, Professional Support Council, and the African-American in Operations Council) Kraft takes an active role in mentoring and supporting its diverse workforce.[8] One example of its work includes outreach to college and university internship programs to source new talent in addition to internal professional development programs.

Companies that are open to creating formal and informal opportunities for workers to network in groups with both similar and different ethnic backgrounds build better communication channels among employees and a sense of community that can enhance employee satisfaction and retention.

Age   Age diversity is the inclusion of employees of all age groups in the workplace. Each age group brings diverse skills and strengths. Older workers bring historical perspective on traditional approaches to workplace issues. Younger workers who bring an understanding of the modern market may better identify and apply technology solutions and may be more flexible in considering multiple viewpoints and solutions to business problems. All age groups can learn new ideas and new ways of thinking from each other (Figure 1.2).

Although there are advantages to age diversity in the workplace, there is also the potential for some unique challenges. Older workers may need more technology training, while younger workers may need more training in product knowledge. Different age groups may have different attitudes toward their work environment. For example, older workers may see the corner office as a sign of status. Younger workers typically prefer more open team work spaces or informal meetings at offsite locations like Starbucks.

Older workers who choose to work beyond their planned retirement age may find themselves working for recent college graduates. There are many ways in which companies can customize programs and services to maximize the strengths of each age group.

Gender   Gender diversity refers to the proportion of males to females in the workplace. The number of females in the workplace continues to grow. By 2016–17, women are projected to earn more doctorate degrees as well as first professional degrees than men.[9] Companies continue to find progressive ways to attract and retain women to build gender diversity. The Deloitte Diversity External Advisory Council provides a national network of people to support women in a variety of ways. A women-to-women mentoring program supports efforts to attract women to the firm.[10]

---

[8]Diversity Careers (December 2010/January 2011). "Kraft Foods Provide Millions of Products for Consumers Worldwide." Retrieved October 21, 2013 from www.diversitycareers.com/articles/pro/10-decjan/dia_kraft.html.

[9]Catalyst Inc. (2009). "U.S. Labor Force, Population & Education." Retrieved September 1, 2009, from www.catalyst.org/file/143/qt_us_percent20labor_force_pop_ed.pdf.

[10]Deloitte and Touche USA LLP. (2009). "Championing Diverse Workplaces." Retrieved August 27, 2009, from www.deloitte.com/view/en_CA/ca/about/diversity/article/4052388a90ffd110VgnVCM100000ba42f00aRCRD.htm.

FIGURE 1.2

The Aging Workforce

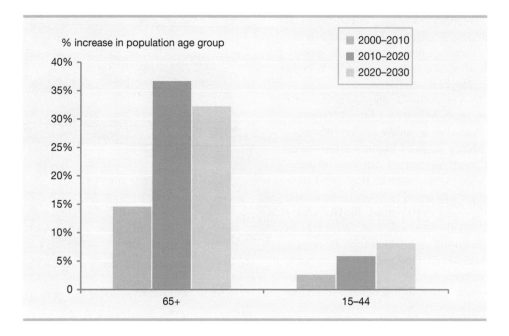

Focus on career advancement opportunities is designed to support the growth and retention of talented women within the company. Another network provides information sharing for female professionals who are also mothers.

In addition to mentoring programs for women, many companies offer coaching and mentoring to men who may be adapting to working with and for more female executives. There are still gender gaps in mid- and upper-level management in many companies. One reason is that many women choose to leave and reenter the workplace at different points in their lives to care for their children or parents. This often slows down the career advancement that may have occurred with steady employment. A survey of U.S. college graduates by *Harvard Business Review* showed that 37 percent of women voluntarily stopped working at some point in their career as opposed to 24 percent of men. Voluntary decisions to take a break during one's career is a major cause of the gender gaps that still exist today.[11]

GENERATIONAL DIFFERENCES

Employers are concerned about the loss of talent that will come with the retirement of the baby boomers in their companies. At the same time, more baby boomers and some Generation X'ers are rethinking their retirement age and seeking out opportunities to continue to work and be productive at their jobs. In response, some employers provide incentives for employees to continue working beyond their planned retirement age. More employers also rehire retirees from other companies recognizing the benefit of their knowledge and experience.

With older workers remaining active at work, companies are addressing ways to connect the four generations of workers that now comprise their workplace. Each generation has a different definition of success based on the value they place on family, work, personal fulfillment, and the use of technology. In progressive organizations, training and development integrates the talents each group brings and mentoring occurs up, down, and across the organization to maximize everyone's talent.

[11]S. A. Hewlett, C. B. Luce, P. Shiller, and S. Southwell. (February 24, 2005). "Hidden Brain Drain: Off-Ramps and On-Ramps in Women's Careers." S.A. Hewett, C.B. Luce (March 2005). "Off-Ramps and On-Ramps: Keeping Talented Women on the Road to Success." *Harvard Business Review*. Retrieved October 21, 2013, from http://hbr.org./2005/03/off-ramps-and-on-ramps-keeping-talented-women-on-the-road-to success/ar/1.

Progress Check Questions

1. How would you describe the type of experiences you have had interacting with diverse groups, and what did you learn from those experiences?

2. How many generations are living in your family? What are some things that all the generations have in common?

ENTREPRENEURSHIP

Entrepreneurial careers are projected to grow as large corporations downsize and demand increases for more customized services to meet the needs of diverse populations. Young entrepreneurs are frequently motivated to achieve work–life balance and contribute to the community, which often drives them to own and operate their own businesses. Older workers often choose owning and operating their own business as an alternative career path after gaining experiences and accumulating the financial resources needed to start a company. Being able to apply knowledge and skills acquired over years of work experience in new and creative ways can provide increased career and personal satisfaction.

Those choosing this career path must be prepared to meet internal and external challenges. Internal challenges include supporting product development, hiring and training the right employees, managing cash flow, and ultimately making a profit. External challenges include financing and government regulations. Technology makes it easier to start and manage new start-up companies. Online tools provide resources such as articles, forums, blogs, on-demand seminars, podcasts, and professional advisors to provide prospective entrepreneurs with the preparation and networks needed to be successful. Entrepreneurs must have a strong knowledge base of the field, an extensive network inside and outside the field, a strong commitment, and a willingness to take risks.

Real Life Stories

The American Girl Doll

The American Girl doll was founded by Pleasant T. Rowland. Rowland was an elementary school teacher who developed innovative teaching materials focused on the integration of reading with other language arts. Her interest in creative and educational toys for her own children led her to writing children's books. She had a vision that she could create educational products that would make learning fun for children. She expanded her work to developing other educational products including dolls and toys that successfully integrated learning with play. Her first attempt to present a new doll with clothing representing an era in history and a children's book that told the story of that era was not successful. She persisted in believing that her product had value. Her repeated efforts finally resulted in mothers embracing the new product line. Its appeal as an educational product led to a rapid success of the American Girl Doll throughout the country and later around the world. Rowland started with a concept that she believed in and applied her teaching and writing skills and her experience as a mother in a new and creative way. Rowland has been honored as one of the 12 outstanding entrepreneurs in the United States by the Institute of American Entrepreneurs.[12]

SitePoint.com

At the age of 15, Matt Mickiewicz launched SitePoint.com, which grew to become one of the best-known resources for Webmaster/Web developers on the Internet. Matt started SitePoint.com with the goal of providing educational resources to Web

[12]FundingUniverse. (2005). American Girl, Inc. Retrieved September 1, 2009, from www.fundinguniverse.com/company-histories/American-Girl-Inc-Company-History.html.

developers to help them grow their businesses and careers. SitePoint.com publishes e-mail newsletters focusing on design and development and a wide range of business topics. One newsletter targets a community of developers who participate in online forums.

Matt began his career by building a one-page resource site that outlined useful tools and software for building a website. The demand for the information grew rapidly, and Matt saw an opportunity to build a full-service online educational site for developing and improving websites. Matt noticed the trend for viewers to print tutorials they were most interested in. Matt saw this as an opportunity to publish tutorials in print-on-demand books on the website. He added a feature called the Marketplace where websites can be bought and sold. The website has become a leading resource for Web developers throughout the world and has received up to 4 million unique visitors and 27 million page views each month.

When opening your own business, Matt advises it is important to set modest goals at the start and be patient. Finding investors that believe in your product and building a customer base can be tedious and requires perseverance. He stresses the importance of creating value for your product and services and creating a niche by focusing on something you know you can consistently do well. Finally, he notes the importance of being constantly tuned in to new opportunities and being prepared to act on them to stay current and sustain long-term success.[13]

Kinko's

Paul Orfalea, founder of Kinko's Inc., realized as a student that he had the ability to see the big picture when presented with challenging situations. He enjoyed analyzing and thinking creatively about ways to solve problems. He developed a self-confidence that enabled him to feel comfortable taking risks and learning from his successes or failures. When Paul discovered that he had dyslexia and attention deficit hyperactivity disorder (ADHD), he understood his need to learn more from hands-on experience and networking than from reading or writing about how to do things. In college, he noticed that the copier machine in the library was in constant demand and that copy machines were not easily available to the public. Paul saw an opportunity to create his own copy service and started his business at a stand near a college campus. Paul developed a steady customer base of college students but did not have financial resources to grow his business.

He encouraged local investors to share ownership with him, and within 10 years, established a network of 80 stores. Keeping his eye open to customer demand, he started a 24-hour service that enabled students, businesses, and travelers to access his service when they needed it. Kinko's grew to 1,200 locations and 23,000 employees in 10 different countries. When advising college students about becoming an entrepreneur, he does not attribute his success to any particular type of copy machine or technology. Instead, he talks about how he focused on his strengths and saw his disabilities as learning opportunities.[14]

Progress Check Questions

1. What are some traits that Pleasant T. Rowland, Matt Mickiewicz, and Paul Orfalea share that make them successful entrepreneurs?

2. Do you currently possess any of these traits?

---

[13]Lou Dubois (November 3, 2010). "Chronicles of a Young Serial Entrepreneur." INC Magazine. Retrieved October 21, 2013, from www.inc.com/articles/2010/11/interview-with-matt-mickiewicz.html.

[14]FundingUniverse. (1997). Kinko's Inc. Retrieved September 1, 2009, from www.fundinguniverse.com/company-histories/Kinkos-Inc-Company-History.html.

1.2 WORKPLACE KNOW-HOW AND 21ST CENTURY SKILLS

The relationship between the employment community and educators is extremely important. Companies need graduates who have the skills necessary to make positive contributions to their business. When employers hire, they expect you to have basic workplace skills. Being able to demonstrate those skills to employers will be a great advantage to you when applying for a job. These skills also help you stand out when being considered for a new position or promotion. The Partnership for 21st Century Skills is an example of one way the business community and educational leaders are working together to improve the success of graduates in the workplace (Figure 1.3).

THE PARTNERSHIP FOR 21ST CENTURY SKILLS

The Department of Education and the business community conducted a survey of 431 employers to identify the critical workplace skills graduates need.[15] Employers cited the knowledge, applied skills, and emerging content areas necessary for graduates to succeed in the workplace. While a wide range of knowledge and skills were cited, employers ranked the following four skill areas as most important:

- Professionalism and work ethic
- Oral and written communications
- Teamwork and collaboration
- Critical thinking and problem solving

NOTES | Knowledge

English language (spoken)
Reading comprehension (in English)
Writing in English (grammar, spelling, etc.)
Mathematics
Science

Government/economics
Humanities/arts
Foreign languages
History/geography

FIGURE 1.3
21st Century Skills

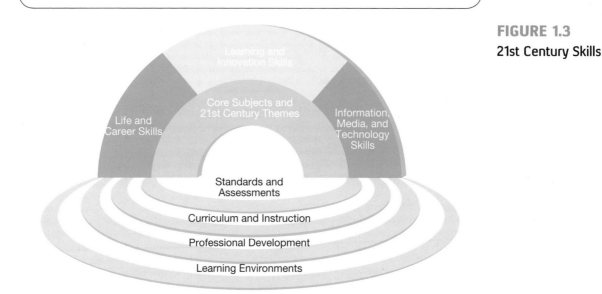

---

[15]Partnership for 21st Century Skills (March 2011). "Framework for 21st Century Learning." Retrieved October 21, 2013, from www.p21.org/storage/documents/1._p21_framework_2-pager.pdf.

NOTES | Applied and Transferable Skills*

Critical thinking   Leadership
Oral communications   Creativity/innovation
Written communications   Lifelong learning/self-direction
Teamwork/collaboration   Professionalism/work ethic
Diversity   Ethics/social responsibility
Information technology application

Applied skills refer to those skills that enable entrants to use the basic knowledge acquired in school to perform in the workplace. *Transferable skills* refer to those skills, acquired in a variety of settings, to new or different workplace settings.

NOTES | Emerging Content Areas

Expectations of personal responsibility for health, finances, and career on the rise:

Health and wellness choices
Personal financial responsibility
Entrepreneurial skills
Economic issues and the role of the U.S. and global economy
Economic and cultural effects of globalization
Informed citizenship
Importance of non-English skills[16]

> "Education is transformational. It changes lives. That is why people work so hard to become educated."
>
> *Condoleezza Rice,* 66th U.S. Secretary of State[17]

> "In today's knowledge based economy, what you earn depends on what you learn."
>
> *William J. Clinton,* 41st President of the United States[18]

In Chapter 2 you will assess your knowledge and applied skills and preparedness in emerging content areas. In Chapter 3 you will set goals for self-improvement.

In Chapter 12 you will learn about interview questions that target particular 21st century skills and practice suggested answers to these questions.

Progress Check Questions

1. Why do you think applied and transferable skills are so important to employers?

2. Why do you think there is an increase in the importance of personal responsibility for finances, health, and career?

---

[16]Partnership for 21st Century Skills (2006). "Are They Really Ready To Work?" Retrieved October 21, 2013 from www.p21.org/storage/documents/FINAL_REPORT_PDF09-29-06.pdf.

[17]www.searchquotes.com/quotation/Education_is_transformational._It_changes_lives._That_is_why_people_work_so_hard_to_become_educated./319872/

[18]Retrieved October 21, 2013 from www.brainyquote.com/quotes/w/williamjc173256.html.

1.3 EDUCATION AND THE WORKPLACE

America's Career Resource Network (ACRN) has reported that 65 percent of the fastest-growing occupations in the United States require some form of postsecondary education including either an associate's degree, vocational certification, or bachelor's degree.[19] In most career fields there are incremental earnings per year as a result of degree attainment. Typically, associate's degree graduates earn more per year than high school graduates. That annual additional salary grows for bachelor's degree and master's degree graduates. The U.S. Census Bureau website is a reliable source for the most current information on earnings by degree attainment (Figure 1.4).

The value of a college degree holds strong through fluctuations in the economy. In fact, college graduates have been reported to have a much lower unemployment rate than the nation as a whole. For example, in March 2013 the national unemployment rate was 7.7 percent while the unemployment rate for college graduates with a bachelor's degree was 3.8 percent.[20]

ACTIVITY 1.2

Understanding the Value of Your Degree

You can do research using the Bureau of Labor Statistics website, which provides information about your possible earning potential for three different jobs that you might be interested in that utilize the degree you will earn. List (1) the job title, (2) potential earnings, and (3) required education.

1. _____

2. _____

3. _____

Based on what you found, are you interested in one job more than another? _____
Did you become interested in any other jobs with greater earning potential if you pursued an additional degree? _____

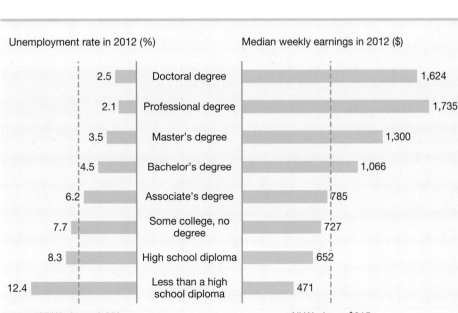

FIGURE 1.4

Education Pays

Source: Bureau of Labor Statistics, Current Population Survey. Retrieved October 21, 2013 from www.bls.gov/emp/ep_chart_001.htm.

Unemployment rate in 2012 (%)		Median weekly earnings in 2012 ($)
2.5	Doctoral degree	1,624
2.1	Professional degree	1,735
3.5	Master's degree	1,300
4.5	Bachelor's degree	1,066
6.2	Associate's degree	785
7.7	Some college, no degree	727
8.3	High school diploma	652
12.4	Less than a high school diploma	471
All Workers: 6.8%		All Workers: $815

[19]America's Career Resource Network. (2009). "The Economic Challenge." Retrieved March 12, 2009, from http://cte.ed.gov/acrn/econchal.htm.

[20]Nelson D. Schwartz and Binyamin Applebaum. (2013). "Unemployment at 4-Year Low as U.S. Hiring Gains Steam." *The New York Times.* Retrieved April 10, 2013, from www.nytimes.com/2013/03/09/business/economy/us-added-236000-jobs-in-february.html?pagewanted=all&_r=0.

When unemployment is high, many return to school to retrain for new or better jobs. What this means for you is the investment you are currently making in your education has the potential to increase your earning power over your lifetime. A spread between college graduates' and overall unemployment has held constant through every recession since at least the 1970s.

Progress Check Questions

1. How can your education impact your career success in the field you have chosen?
2. If your field requires any special certifications or licenses, do you know what will be needed to keep them current as you progress through your career?

There will always be external factors that change the workplace and the skills and experiences needed to be successful in your career. We have seen how swings in various aspects of the economy, from the stock market to the housing market, can significantly impact the career opportunities available to you at any given time. Make it a habit to monitor these trends so that you can anticipate ups and downs in the job market and in particular career areas.

Your ability to work with individuals from diverse backgrounds is essential for you to be effective in whatever role you play in your company. Whether members of your work groups differ by ethnicity or race, age, or gender, you will need to be open to different ways of solving problems, working through processes, and accommodating work–life situations and different learning and management styles.

Developing entrepreneurial skills can help you succeed in a large corporation as well as in starting your own business. In the global market in which so many U.S. companies compete, companies that perform best often do so on their ability to think and market creatively, take risks, develop strategic partnerships, and stay closely aligned with customer needs. Learning these skills can be important to your ability to add value to your company in a way that stands out from others.

The importance of developing relevant workplace skills and keeping them current is critical to your career success in both good and bad economic times. Stay knowledgeable about the skills employers say they need. Plan on constantly developing and growing those skills in school, at work, or through other life experiences. In Chapter 2, you will assess how well prepared you are to demonstrate the skills important to employers. In Chapter 2, you will also learn to assess yourself in other areas important to your career success. Understanding the process of self-assessment is very important because it is something that you will need to do periodically to successfully manage your career.

TODAY'S WORKPLACE IMPACT ON YOUR CAREER DECISIONS

Based on what you learned in Chapter 1, what level of influence do you think each of the following will have on your career decisions? Mark an "X" on the line under your choice.

	None	Somewhat	High
Affecting You in the Workplace Trends			
Social media			
Digital job search			
Economy			
Diversity			
Generational differences			
Entrepreneurship			
Workplace Know-How and 21st Century Skills			
Knowledge			
Applied skills			
Emerging content areas			
Education and the Workplace			
Employment rates and your degree			
Earnings and your degree			

1. Which of these are most in your control? Discuss why.

2. How do those that you consider not in your control affect your career decisions?

"If we all did the things we are capable of, we would literally astound ourselves."

Thomas A. Edison[1]

[1]Retrieved April 5, 2013, from www.brainyquote.com/quotes/authors/t/thomas_a_edison.html.

Self-Assessment

After completing this chapter, you will:

1   **Identify** the factors involved in understanding yourself

2   **Determine** how your values influence your career choice

3   **Recognize** interests that influence your career choice

4   **Define** how your personality traits relate to your career choice

5   **Describe** how well your skills compare with 21st century skills employers want

6   **Explain** how emotional intelligence is related to your self-assessment

This chapter focuses on helping you better understand yourself in relation to your career planning. Knowing yourself is an important first step toward a successful career because your job should be compatible with who you are. When you choose a job that is a good match, you are likely to stay in the job longer and be more satisfied with your decision. Self-assessment is the process of identifying your values, interests, personality traits, knowledge, and skills. Once you have a better understanding of yourself in each of these areas, you can think about how each of them can influence the career choices you make now and in the future. In this chapter, you will identify your values, interests, personality traits, and skills. In the process, you will focus on the 21st century skills employers have identified as important for career success in the workplace, and you will learn what emotional intelligence is and the role it can play in your career success.

CASE STUDY

Carlos Dreams Bigger

Carlos enrolled in a paralegal studies program at the nearby community college. He had graduated with honors from high school. He thought he chose the right college program, but wasn't really sure. His father was a police officer, and Carlos admired the work that he did. He often talked to Carlos about going to college and how important it was to follow a career in which you could make a difference to others.

One of his instructors referred Carlos to a professional career counselor in the nearby area who could help him assess whether he was choosing the right career field. The counselor was trained to administer and interpret a variety of career assessment tests. When he met the counselor after completing his tests, Carlos learned some things about himself that would help him feel more comfortable with his career choice now and in the future.

The tests basically confirmed that Carlos had the personality and skills to be successful as a paralegal. He also learned about other career options that matched his personality and skills. The personality test revealed that Carlos was self-directed, motivated, reliable, and had characteristics that indicated a good work ethic. It also revealed that Carlos was a compassionate person and often put others' needs before his own. Carlos agreed with this, telling his counselor that he often had difficulty saying no to others.

His skills tests showed that Carlos had above-average writing skills and strong analytical and problem-solving skills. That was aligned with his interest in and skill with researching and processing complex information.

His counselor told Carlos that his test results supported his choice to pursue a career as a paralegal, but reminded Carlos that he need not limit his thinking to that career field.

During their discussion, Carlos talked about his strong desire to do work that would help improve the local community and make it a more attractive place for people to live and work. He also said that he thought he would enjoy learning more about the law, how cases were prepared and presented, and how legal decisions were made. His counselor asked Carlos if he had ever considered being a lawyer. Carlos was surprised by the suggestion at first. He later did not rule out the possibility as a long-term career goal. His counselor advised him to get started as a paralegal and use that experience to further develop his verbal presentation skills, legal knowledge, and ability to persuade and influence others. Carlos would also need to practice being firm and decisive in his professional dealings with others. He was now convinced that his career choice as a paralegal was the right decision and that someday he might consider other career paths that maximized his professional skills and interest in the law.

Discussion Questions

1. What personal values influenced Carlos's career choice?
2. In what areas did Carlos need to improve if he wanted to consider a career as a lawyer? Do you believe that these are areas he could improve in through experience as a paralegal? Why or why not?
3. How do you think that your values, interests, personality, and skills will determine your long-term career path?

2.1 UNDERSTANDING YOURSELF

Knowing what you enjoy doing, how you like to spend your free time, or what motivates you to accomplish your goals is part of understanding who you are. As you consider what your values are, what interests you, and what some of your personality traits are, you can begin to build your own career profile which will help you market yourself to employers during your job search. Adding a list of your workplace skills and your education and experience will ensure your career profile is complete. You will find the information about yourself that you keep in your career profile to be helpful when you prepare to network, write your resume, promote yourself during an interview, or decide whether a job offer is a good match for you.

NOTES	My Career Profile
My **V**alues	
My **I**nterests	
My **P**ersonality traits	= VIPS
My **S**kills	

2.2 YOUR VALUES

Your values are the standards you choose to live by. Your values affect most of the choices you make every day. The sum total of your personal values or standards make up your value system. Values themselves are not right or wrong. What is an acceptable choice for one person may be unacceptable for you because of your value system. For example, one person may feel little or no obligation to spend time helping others through some sort of community work. For you, community service may be very important because one of the standards you have set for yourself is helping others. The following are some examples of values:

- Time with family
- Financial reward
- Community service
- Professional position
- Personal relationships
- Social status

One way to identify your values is to ask yourself, What is important in my life? The answer may tell you a lot about the values you have. The examples listed may reflect some of your values. There are probably some you would like to add or subtract from the list. Knowing what is important to you makes you aware of your own value system.

"Stick to your values, they are your foundation."

Howard Schultz,
CEO, Starbucks[2]

ACTIVITY 2.1

Choosing Values

Values affect most of the choices we make every day. The career you choose should be compatible with your values. The following words describe some common values. From the list, select 10 that are most important to you and then rank them 1 to 10, with 1 being the most important.

Values	Most Important	Rank (1 = most important)
Achievement		
Authority		
Caring		
Contribution		
Commitment		
Diversity		
Fairness		
Freedom		
Independence		
Individuality		
Integrity		
Justice		
Making a difference		
Membership		
Openness		
Power		
Professionalism		

[2]Retrieved April 5, 2013, from www.businessinsider.com/howard-schultz-quotes-2012-11#on-trusting-yourself-1.

Values	Most Important	Rank (1 = most important)
Reputation		
Respect		
Service		
Teamwork		
Wealth		

VALUES AND YOUR CAREER CHOICE

Your values can influence your career choices in many ways. For example, if you value independence and individuality, you may decide to work with a small, entrepreneurial company where you might have more freedom to work in a less structured environment. If you value teamwork and diversity, you may be better suited for a larger company. You can also choose companies in your job search that match your values. Service to the community or diversity are two examples of company values that might match your own personal values.

Not only do your values influence the type of company you may choose, but they can also influence your choice of job. If you value nights and weekends with your family, you will probably require a job that does not include much overtime or weekend work. Frequent travel may be something you prefer to avoid. If your job choice is to be a loan officer in a bank, you will generally find spending time with your family will be possible because this job typically has a standard workweek and little, if any, travel.

Try not to make a career choice that conflicts with your values. For example, if you are considering a career in sales, you may need to travel and work some nights and weekends. Perhaps if you rethink what is important to you, you may realize that time with your family, rather than a standard schedule, is what really counts and that good planning gives you the free time you want while you pursue a sales career.

Progress Check Questions

1. How do you think your values affect your career choice?
2. Do you think your values will change at different stages of your life and career? Why or why not?

Real Life Stories

Laura Murphy

Dissatisfaction with several entry-level positions and work for a car rental company led Laura Murphy to pursue a more rewarding career. She went back to school and obtained an associate's degree in nursing. She became a travel nurse and eventually assumed a nursing position at a medical center's high-risk and delivery center. She also worked with new mothers, like herself, to adjust to parenthood.

Laura moved on to work as a full-time school nurse which allows her to spend time with her two children. She believes nursing offers a wide variety of career paths for those seeking a personally rewarding career with many opportunities.[3]

[3]T. Riemer Jones et al. (Winter 2005). "Values-Based Career Moves." Alpha Phi Quarterly 117(1). Retrieved from http://issuu.com/alphaphiintl/docs/2005_winter/1.Page4

⬤ 2.3 YOUR INTERESTS

Interests are the activities you choose because you enjoy them. Your interests may lean toward individual or group activities. Most people enjoy some combination of the two. Some of the interests you enjoy the most may become hobbies. Having a variety of interests and hobbies helps you grow and develop, while, at the same time, providing a good source of fun and relaxation.

INTERESTS AND YOUR CAREER CHOICE

How you spend your free time says a lot about you—your likes, dislikes, and motivation. This information can provide you with leads to the career that is best for you. For example, if you spend free time as an officer in a club or organization, you may have an interest in a job that puts your leadership skills to work.

ACTIVITY 2.2

Identifying Your Interests and Hobbies

Interests affect most of the choices we make every day. The career you choose should be compatible with your interests. The following words describe some common interests and hobbies. From the list, select 10 that are most important to you and rank them 1 to 10, with 1 being the most important.

Interests/Hobbies	Most Important	Rank (1 = most important)
Collecting		
Computer games		
Cooking		
Dancing		
Drawing/sketching		
Exercise/fitness		
History		
Listening to music		
Movies		
Painting		
Photography		
Playing a musical instrument		
Reading		
Sports		
Theater		
Traveling		
Writing		
Writing a journal		

An interest in writing while pursuing a career in culinary arts may mean that you are suited for a career as a food writer. Pay attention to what you enjoy doing, and you may discover interests that apply to a variety of career areas. Career interest inventories can help you find out more about yourself and how your interests relate to different careers, including making matches with occupational groups and specific occupations.

Progress Check Questions

1. How do you think your interests affect your career choice?
2. Do you think the current career you are considering matches your interests?

Real Life Stories

Denzel Washington

The American actor Denzel Washington is an example of a person who launched a successful career based on his longtime interest in acting.

As a camp counselor for the American Boys and Girls Club of America, Denzel had his first experience with acting, appearing in a small theater production for kids. As an adult, his interest in acting did not surface again until he went to college and explored a few different career interests. He started in a premed program and then switched his major to political science. Finally, he decided that neither of these career paths interested him. He then majored in journalism, thinking that he would pursue a writing career. While in college, his acting abilities became apparent after appearing in two student productions. After receiving his degree in journalism, he immediately pursued acting roles that eventually led to his successful acting career. Denzel says that although it took him a while to discover what he really wanted to do while he was in college, he learned a lot about himself in the process.

"I found what I liked and what I didn't like. I became aware of my own study habits and I eventually found the thing I loved."[4]

Denzel Washington's story demonstrates how your interests can play a major role in your career decisions. His story also demonstrates the importance of learning from the decisions you make along the way, even if they do not turn out to be the final path you take.

NOTES | Values and Interests Tests

DiSC profile tests are often used in career planning to assess behavior, personal interests, attitudes, and values. DiSC is an assessment tool to help you learn your behavior patterns and to what degree you use each dimension of behavior in a situation. The DiSC tests allow you to discover your general behavioral style in regard to four dimensions: dominance, influence, steadiness, and conscientiousness.

DiSC profiles can tell you a lot about your own communication style, how you relate to others, and how you might respond to different situations.

DiSC profiles evaluate how you respond (according to four behavioral dimensions) to the four *Ps*:

Problems (dominance)
People (influence)
Pace (steadiness)
Procedures (conscientiousness)

DiSC testing does not detect right or wrong behaviors; rather, it helps you understand how you instinctually react when confronted with conflict or challenges. DiSC attitudes, personal interests, and values reports can help you discover your strengths.

Source: www.discprofile.com.

---

[4]R. Hazell. (October 2000). "Education Is the Pathway for Success in the Mind of Denzel Washington." *The Black Collegian Online.* Retrieved September 1, 2009, from www.black-collegian.com/issues/1stsem00/denzel2000-1st.shtml.

2.4 YOUR PERSONALITY TRAITS

A personality trait is a distinguishing quality or characteristic that belongs to you. The sum total of your unique personality traits makes up your personality. Developing an effective personality is critical to your career success.

The career you choose should be compatible with your personality traits.

ACTIVITY 2.3

Identify Your Personality Traits

From the list, select 10 that you think best describe you and then rank them 1 to 10, with 1 being what you consider to be your strongest personality trait. Your strongest personality trait may be either an asset or a drawback to your career success.

Personality Traits	Your Strongest	Ranking (1 = your strongest)
Adaptive		
Aggressive		
Artistic		
Compassionate		
Confident		
Consistent		
Creative		
Curious		
Defensive		
Empathetic		
Enterprising		
Extrovert		
Honest		
Humble		
Impulsive		
Inspiring		
Loyal		
Moody		
Objective		
Private		
Passionate		
Perseverance		
Passive		
Persistent		
Positive		
Realistic		
Risk taker		
Selfish		
Serious		
Social		
Tolerant		

Progress Check Questions

1. Do you think your strongest personality traits are always an advantage to you? Why or why not?

2. How do you think your personality traits affect your career choice?

Real Life Stories

Steve Jobs

Steve Jobs's extraordinary career is an example of how to draw on strong personality traits to set ambitious goals and overcome obstacles. As a boy, Jobs and his father took apart and reconstructed electronics in the family garage. This hobby helped Jobs develop self-confidence, determination, and mechanical skill that led him to realize his vision to make computers accessible to everyone. Jobs thought broadly and constantly set higher goals. He observed a new technology designed by Xerox to make a new copy machine. Although Xerox's thinking about the new technology limited it to copy machines, Jobs visualized how The technology could be applied to different uses to eventually achieve his vision. He co-founded Apple Computers pioneering revolutionary technologies. After much success, Jobs experienced failure marked by a series of unsuccessful products causing Apple to plummet and Jobs to resign. While he battled cancer for over nine years, Jobs kept focused and maintained a passion for invention. He started Pixar Animation Studios which later merged with Disney to produce popular animated films including *Finding Nemo, The Incredibles,* and the *Toy Story.* Disney asked Jobs how to turn around a period of declining profits. Jobs's simple response was "dream bigger." Jobs later returned to Apple and brought it back to success with a series of new products, including the iPhone and iPad. He attributed his continued success to his focus on working hard and never giving up on his belief that he could turn Apple Computers into a world leader. Steve Jobs's story is filled with examples of personality traits that helped him stay focused on his goals despite personal and professional setbacks and achieve career success.[5]

ACTIVITY 2.4

Develop Your Personality Traits

List five of the preceding personality traits you would like to develop, and write a goal to develop them.

Example	Plan
Confidence	*I will offer my opinions more often in class even when they are different from those of others.*
1. _____	_____
2. _____	_____
3. _____	_____

---

[5]www.biography.com/people/steve-jobs-9354805; www.forbes.com/sites/carminegallo/2010/12/14/steve-jobs-advice-dream-bigger/.

4. _____   _____
_____
_____

5. _____   _____
_____
_____

PERSONALITY AND YOUR CAREER CHOICE

The best way to understand the connection between your personality and your career choice is to complete a personality assessment with the help of a career counselor, to see how closely your choice matches your personality. The Myers-Briggs Type Indicator, the Keirsey Temperament Sorter, and the DiSC inventory are the more common personality assessment tools used.

The Myers-Briggs Type Indicator   The Myers-Briggs Type Indicator (MBTI) organizes four sets of attributes into a matrix of different personality types. Each type is indicated by a four-letter code.

- E I Extroversion/Introversion
- S N Sensing/Intuiting
- T F Thinking/Feeling
- J P Judging/Perceiving

For each personality type, the MBTI system includes a profile that describes the characteristics common to people who fit into that category. The MBTI focuses on how what people think and feel affects the way they make decisions. The Myers-Briggs personality types follow, with a few examples of careers that fit each type.

Guardians

ISTJ and ESTJ; Inspector and Supervisor

Accountant, administrator, advisor, bank officer, computer programmer, detective, financial advisor, military leader, police officer, sales representative, systems analyst, trade and technical teacher

ISFJ and ESFJ; Protector and Provider

Administrative assistant, childcare worker, counselor, designer, healthcare professional, nurse, office manager, paralegal, preschool teacher, real estate agent, retail manager

---

Artisans

ISTP and ESTP; Artisan and Dynamo

Computer technical support, detective, engineer, entrepreneur, law enforcement, marketing representative, paramedic, pilot, police officer, sales representative, stockbroker

ISFP and ESFP; Composer and Performer

Actor, artist, chef, composer, consultant, event planner, fashion designer, interior decorator, musician, photographer, politician, public speaker

---

Rationals

INTJ and ENTJ; Mastermind and Commander

Business manager, computer consultant, corporate strategist, credit investigator, dentist, doctor, entrepreneur, environmental planner, inventor, mortgage broker, researcher

INTP and ENTP; Architect and Inventor

Advertising agent, artist, entertainer, computer systems analyst, financial analyst, journalist, marketing specialist, public relations specialist, research assistant, sports agent, strategic planner, technical writer

Idealists

INFJ and ENFJ; Counselor and Teacher

Childcare worker, corporate trainer, counselor, fundraiser, fitness instructor, high school teacher, human resource specialist, massage therapist, nonprofit agency worker, nutritionist, workshop facilitator

INFP and ENFP; Healer and Champion

Account executive, advertising account representative, counselor, editor, inventor, librarian, publicist, restaurateur, social worker, television reporter, writer

Exploring these profiles can help guide you toward a career fit that best matches your personality. Keep in mind that these are examples and that they do not represent the entire spectrum of careers associated with each personality type.[6]

The Keirsey Temperament Sorter   The Keirsey Temperament Sorter (KTS) describes four basic temperament groups subdivided into character types. The terminology used to describe the temperament groups and character types is similar to Myer-Briggs terminology, but these two instruments are different. Unlike the MBTI, which focuses on how people think and feel, the KTS focuses on understanding long-term behavior patterns.[7]

These instruments help you better identify careers and jobs that might be best suited for your personality type. Employers often use these instruments in the hiring process, to develop training programs, and to coach and evaluate job performance.

Once you complete either the MBTI or KTS, you can obtain a report that describes how your results relate to career paths that you might be well suited for. This information provides a solid foundation for your career planning and can help you feel more confident as you make your career decisions.

[6]www.myersbriggs.org/my-mbti-personality-type/mbti-basics/.

[7]http://marlissmelton.com/PDF/CareerchoicesMBTIandKeirsey.pdf.

If you decide that you are interested in taking one of these assessments, be sure to work with a qualified professional who can help you through the process of taking the assessment and interpreting your results. Check with your career services department, or an instructor, for guidance on individuals at your school who may be qualified to administer and interpret the assessments. You may also consider working with a private career counselor.

In Chapter 5 you will become aware of career trends and major areas of projected job growth. The *Career Directions Handbook* contains detailed information on career paths and related jobs in a wide range of career fields. You can use the results of your assessment with the information in the *Career Directions Handbook* to research and consider career paths that might best match your personality.

2.5 YOUR SKILLS

Skills are abilities that have been acquired by training or experience. An ability is something you are able to do and is usually innate as opposed to learned. You can learn skills in the classroom, at work, or through a variety of life experiences. As you are career planning and conducting a job search, you will want to focus on assessing how many skills you have developed that are important to employers. The most important workplace skills are transferable or functional skills and technical skills.

Transferable or functional skills are skills that can be transferred from one job to another. Your transferable skills will enable you to explore a wider variety of career choices and will help you stand out with employers whether you are applying for your first job, changing careers, or interested in career advancement. You should think about transferable skills as the key to career mobility throughout various phases of your career. Technical skills are the knowledge and capability to perform specific operational tasks related to a job.

It is important to know your transferable/functional and technical skills as you build your career profile. You will refer back to the list of skills you identify for yourself when you write your resume, search for jobs online using keywords, and communicate your strengths in an interview or cover letter. Skills may build throughout your career as you acquire more experience. Some skills you will use right away; some you will use in the future.

The following are examples of transferable/functional and technical skills.

Transferable or Functional Skills

Abstracted	Approved	Calculated	Conceived
Achieved	Arranged	Charged	Conducted
Acquired	Ascertained	Chartered	Conferred
Acted	Assembled	Checked	Conserved
Adapted	Assessed	Clarified	Consolidated
Addressed	Assigned	Classified	Consulted
Administered	Assisted	Coached	Contracted
Advertised	Assured	Collaborated	Contributed
Advocated	Attained	Collected	Controlled
Aided	Audited	Comforted	Converted
Allocated	Augmented	Communicated	Cooperated
Analyzed	Authored	Compared	Coordinated
Answered	Authorized	Completed	Counseled
Anticipated	Briefed	Compiled	Decided
Applied	Budgeted	Composed	Defended
Appraised	Built	Computed	Defined

Delegated	Helped	Observed	Requested
Delivered	Identified	Obtained	Researched
Designed	Illustrated	Operated	Responded
Detected	Imagined	Ordered	Restored
Determined	Implemented	Organized	Revamped
Developed	Improved	Overcame	Reviewed
Devised	Improvised	Oversaw	Scanned
Diagnosed	Inaugurated	Participated	Scheduled
Directed	Increased	Perceived	Schemed
Discovered	Influenced	Perfected	Screened
Discriminated	Initiated	Performed	Selected
Discussed	Innovated	Persuaded	Self-monitored
Displayed	Integrated	Planned	Set goals
Dissected	Inspected	Practiced	Shaped
Disseminated	Instituted	Predetermined	Skilled
Documented	Integrated	Predicted	Sold
Drafted	Interpreted	Prepared	Solicited
Drove	Interviewed	Presented	Solved
Edited	Introduced	Prioritized	Specialized
Eliminated	Invented	Problem-solved	Stimulated
Enabled	Inventoried	Produced	Strategized
Endorsed	Investigated	Programmed	Streamlined
Enforced	Judged	Projected	Strengthened
Enlisted	Languages	Promoted	Studied
Ensured	Launched	Proposed	Substantiated
Established	Learned	Protected	Succeeded
Estimated	Lectured	Proved	Summarized
Evaluated	Led	Provided	Supported
Exceeded	Listened	Publicized	Synthesized
Executed	Located	Published	Supervised
Expanded	Made	Purchased	Supported
Expedited	Maintained	Questioned	Surveyed
Experimented	Managed	Raised	Sustained
Explained	Manipulated	Ran	Taught
Explored	Mapped	Ranked	Theorized
Extracted	Mastered	Rationalized	Trained
Facilitated	Maximized	Read	Translated
Financed	Mediated	Reassured	Updated
Fixed	Memorized	Reasoned	Upgraded
Followed-up	Mentored	Recommended	Utilized
Formulated	Met	Recorded	Validated
Founded	Minimized	Recruited	Valued
Gained	Modeled	Received	Verified
Generated	Modified	Reduced	Visualized
Governed	Monitored	Referred	Won
Guided	Narrated	Related	Wrote
Headed	Negotiated	Reported	Yielded

Technical Skills

Adobe systems
Analyzing
Assembling
Auditing
Autocad
Biometrics device applications
Blueprints
Bookkeeping
Budgeting
Calculating
Communication tools and equipment
Computer graphics
Computing
Content development and management
Correlating
Costing
Databases
Designing
Devising
Drafting
Drawing
Extrapolating
Forecasting
Google Drive
Graphic design
Identity management tools
Inspecting
Interpolating
Finishing
Job boards
Job search engines
Keyword analysis
Kitchen equipment
Lab skills
Layout design
Logistics
Math skills
Medical equipment
Microsoft Excel
Microsoft Outlook
Microsoft PowerPoint
Microsoft Publisher
Microsoft Word
Mobile device applications
Modeling
Multiple formatting
Operating systems
Online courseware
Phototyping
Portfolio software
Privacy settings
Project management tools
Programming
Quality control
Repairing
Reservations systems
Restoring
Resume software
Safety systems
Search engine optimization (SEO)
Security systems
Sketching
Software development
Sorting
Spreadsheets
Staging
Storyboarding
Tabulating
Taxonomy design
Technology security tools
Tracking systems
Transcribing
Typesetting
Typing
Video software
Web conferencing
Web design
Web technologies

21ST CENTURY SKILLS

The results of a study, conducted by four organizations with over 400 employers, provides relevant information about the key skills needed to succeed in the emerging, 21st century workplace. The four organizations that conducted the study include The Conference Board, Corporate Voices for Working Families, Partnership for 21st Century Skills, and the Society for Human Resource Management. The main summary of the findings indicate that, by far, employers rated transferable/functional skills as very important to career success.[8]

> "Our nation's long-term ability to succeed in exporting to the growing global marketplace hinges on the abilities of today's students."
>
> *J. Willard Marriott Jr.*, chair and CEO, Marriott International, Inc.[9]

[8]The Conference Board. (2009). Retrieved August 31, 2009, from www.conference-board.org/Publications/describes.cfm?id.

[9]Corporate Voices for Working Families. (July 2008). "Tomorrow's Workforce Ready or Not–It's a Choice the Business Community Must Make Now." Retrieved June 20, 2009, from www.cvworkingfamilies.org/system/files/2008WorkforceReadiness-ReadyorNot.pdf.

> **NOTES** | 21st Century Transferable/Functional Skills
>
> Critical thinking/problem solving
> Oral communication
> Written communication
> Teamwork/collaboration
> Diversity
> Information technology application
>
> Leadership
> Creativity/innovation
> Lifelong learning/self-direction
> Professionalism/work ethic
> Ethics/social responsibility
>
> **Emerging Content Areas**
> Health and wellness choices
> Personal financial responsibility
> Entrepreneurial skills
> Economic issues
>
> Globalization
> Informed citizenship
> Non-English language skills

The degree to which you have already developed many of the 21st century skills employers need depends on your age and the amount of experience you have had. Even if you are younger and have limited experience, you will find that you have applied many of the preceding skills to some degree. By completing the inventory of the following skills, you will recognize skills you have applied and target the skills you still need to develop.

ACTIVITY 2.5

21st Century Skills Inventory

> From the list of skills provided, give examples of times when you applied one or more functional skills.
>
> Once you have written your examples, choose three to five functional skills you think you still need to develop. You will refer back to this list later in Chapter 3 when you practice goal setting for self-improvement.
>
> | Skills | Examples of Times When You Applied These Skills |
> |---|---|
> | *Critical Thinking/Problem Solving* | |
> | Exercised sound reasoning and analytical thinking to solve problems | _____ |
> | Applied math and science concepts to problem solving | _____ |
> | *Oral Communication* | |
> | Articulated thoughts and ideas clearly and effectively | _____ |
> | Demonstrated public speaking skills | _____ |
> | *Written Communication* | |
> | Wrote memos or letters clearly and effectively | _____ |
> | Wrote complex technical reports clearly and effectively | _____ |
> | *Teamwork/Collaboration* | |
> | Built collaborative relationships with classmates, colleagues, or customers | _____ |
> | Worked with diverse teams | _____ |

Diversity

Learned from and worked collaboratively with
individuals representing different cultures, races,
ages, gender, religions, lifestyles, and viewpoints

Information Technology Application

Selected and used appropriate technology to
accomplish a given task

Applied computing skills to problem solving

Leadership

Leveraged the strengths of others to achieve
common goals

Used interpersonal skills to coach and develop
others

Creativity/Innovation

Demonstrated creativity and inventiveness

Integrated knowledge across different disciplines

Lifelong Learning/Self-Direction

Continuously acquire new knowledge and skills

Monitor my own learning needs

Learn from my mistakes

Professionalism/Work Ethic

Demonstrated personal accountability

Demonstrated effective work habits, e.g.,

Punctuality

Working productively with others

Time management

Workload management

Ethics/Social Responsibility

Demonstrated integrity and ethical behavior

Acted responsibly with the interest of the greater
community in mind

Emerging Content Areas

Health and Wellness Choices

Made appropriate choices concerning health
and wellness, e.g.,

Nutrition

Exercise

Stress reduction

Work–life effectiveness

Personal Financial Responsibility

Exercised personal financial responsibility, e.g.,

Balancing a checkbook

Budgeting skills

Retirement planning

Entrepreneurial Skills

Used entrepreneurial skills to enhance workplace
    productivity and create career options   _____

Economic Issues

Understand economic issues and the role of
    business in the U.S. and global economy   _____

Globalization

Demonstrated understanding of global markets
    and the cultural effects of globalization   _____

Informed Citizenship

Participated effectively in government and com-
    munity as an informed citizen   _____

Non-English Language Skills

Used non-English language skills as a tool for
    understanding other nations, markets, and
    cultures   _____

Go back and circle three to five of the functional skills and three emerging content areas you
    think you still need to develop.

21ST CENTURY SKILLS AND YOUR CAREER CHOICE

You may find that you are interested in a career that uses the skills you already have, or you may wish to develop new skills that will set you in a different career direction. For example, if you have good listening skills and interpersonal skills, you may have what it takes to be a front desk manager at a hotel. You may learn specific computer skills for the hotel's reservation system. By combining the skills you already have and the ones you want to develop, you can begin to make yourself a stronger job candidate. If you are unsure about whether you will fit into a career field that interests you, remember there is a wide range of jobs that may suit you within each field.

If you tend to have many hands-on technical skills, such as programming or graphic design, you may enjoy a variety of positions in the technology industry. If you have great social skills, such as working well as a team member or teaching, and prefer using them on a daily basis, you may enjoy a job that focuses more on dealing with people. Within every career field, jobs range from high people orientation to high task orientation. The travel/tourism field is a good example. If you are in a travel/tourism program in school and you find that many of your good skills are interpersonal ones, you will probably enjoy a job as a tour escort, where you are dealing with people a lot. If you find your personal and technical skills to be stronger than your interpersonal skills, you may enjoy a job as a data analyst in the travel industry. The tour escort spends most of his or her time working with the public, individually and in groups, while the data analyst may independently review population trends in a city and write recommendations on whether or not to build a new hotel or restaurant there. Both jobs are in the travel/tourism industry, but each requires a different type of person.

Progress Check Questions

1. Which functional/transferable skills do you think are the most difficult to develop?

2. Which of the emerging content areas do you currently have under your control?

2.6 EMOTIONAL INTELLIGENCE

Emotional intelligence is your ability to identify, assess, and manage your emotions. An important part of your self-assessment is being aware of how your emotional intelligence impacts your career success. People who manage their emotional intelligence well are better able to work productively in teams, take a logical approach to problem solving, manage stress, and build positive relationships. Emotional intelligence is important to working with and managing a diverse workforce. While your emotional intelligence is influenced by your values, interests, and personality, it is your value system that primarily drives the behavior associated with emotional intelligence.

ACTIVITY 2.6

Understanding Your Emotional Intelligence

Assessing how you think about and react to a variety of situations can help you better understand your own emotional intelligence. Once you have an overall sense of your emotional intelligence, you can work on improving areas you need to develop to enhance your performance in the workplace.

Provide answers to each of the following questions.

1. How well do I take criticism?

2. How well do I communicate constructive criticism to others?

3. How well do I tolerate uncertainty?

4. Do I control my negative emotions well?

5. Am I open to suggestions from others?

6. Do I see opportunity in diffcult situations?

7. Do I demonstrate confidence in most situations?

8. Am I dependable in an emergency?

9. Am I comfortable in most new situations?

10. Do I exercise self-discipline in most aspects of my life?

11. Can I usually control my anger?

12. How well do I deal with disappointment?

_____

_____

13. Am I concerned about disappointing others?

_____

_____

14. Do I think about the long-term consequences of my decisions and/or behavior?

_____

_____

15. Do I consider opinions that differ from mine when making decisions?

_____

_____

MANAGING YOUR EMOTIONAL INTELLIGENCE

The two key areas to focus on to manage your emotional intelligence are self-management and relationship management.

Self-management includes awareness of what emotions you are feeling and why and how your feelings may affect what you do, think, or say. Relationship management includes sensing and understanding what others feel and think and managing your response to them.

Being aware of what you are feeling and thinking can help you control your emotions. Try to think about situations you are dealing with, and ask yourself the following questions:

- What am I thinking right now?
- What am I saying to myself?
- What am I feeling about the situation?

By pausing before acting on a situation, you can better understand the emotions that might positively or negatively impact your behavior.

Progress Check Questions

1. In what kinds of situations do you need to manage your emotional intelligence the most?
2. Was there a time when your use of emotional intelligence determined a positive outcome for you?

The foundation of a successful career plan and job search is understanding who you are.

We have seen that there are a variety of self-assessment resources that you can use to gain a clearer picture of your likes and dislikes, strengths and weaknesses, and the careers you might best be suited for. By completing a number of activities to learn more about yourself, you have identified key characteristics that you can now use to determine your best career paths. You have seen how matching your values, interests, personality traits, and skills is key to your career success and satisfaction.

Your skills are integral to your ability to perform your job well. By exploring skills that range from technical to functional and transferable, you are better aware of how different types of skills contribute to your career growth. When you develop a wide range of skills, you expand your career choices and prepare yourself for career advancement opportunities and for changing your career, should you decide to do so. You should constantly assess your skills and set goals to improve them or learn new skills to ensure your skills are always relevant to changes in the job market. This is also one of the best ways to recession-proof your career during an unstable economy.

SELF-ASSESSMENT AND CAREER DECISION MAKING

Take time to reflect on each of the following items based on the work you have completed in Chapter 2.

Make two or three entries in each section that best represent you at the current time. This will be a start of your career profile that you should regularly review and update as your priorities change and you learn new skills. You can refer to your profile throughout various phases of your job search as you prepare your resume or online profile or prepare for a job interview.

MY CAREER PROFILE

My career goals: _____
_____
_____

My values: _____
_____
_____

My interests: _____
_____
_____

My personality traits: _____
_____
_____

My skills: _____
_____
_____

"I believe that everyone is the keeper of a dream."

Oprah Winfrey[1]

[1]Retrieved May 6, 2013, from www.quotationspage.com/quotes/Oprah_Winfrey/31.

Goal Setting and Career Decision Making

After completing this chapter, you will:

1   **Develop** your definition of career success

2   **Identify** and write goals for self-improvement

3   **Apply** career decision-making skills

Successful careers are built on setting goals and making effective career decisions on an ongoing basis.

Your goals and decisions need to be directed toward your larger definition of what career success means to you. Career success means something different to everyone. Your personal definition will be influenced by your values, interests, personality traits, and skills. Your age, gender, or ethnicity may also play a role.

Once you personalize your vision of career success, you can set specific goals for self-improvement. The goal of your self-improvement plan should be to close any gaps between your qualifications and employers' expectations. Applying effective career decision-making skills will help keep you on track to reach your goals and achieve success. In this chapter, you will develop your own definition of career success, practice goal setting for self-improvement, and learn a process for making career decisions that you can practice with each career topic in this book now and throughout your career.

CASE STUDY

Derek's Goals Create Opportunities

Derek was always interested in learning more about how websites are developed and how they have emerged as such a powerful source of communication, education, and promotion throughout the world. While enrolled in a degree program for Web development, Derek spent his free time organizing events and programs to help educate low-income families about how to manage their personal finances. He enjoyed his community service work and often thought about establishing his own nonprofit organization to help educate more communities about how to become more self-sufficient. Derek grew up thinking that he would be a teacher, following in the footsteps of family members.

When he was close to graduation, he interviewed with several companies interested in graduates with his technological background and experience. Before interviewing, Derek decided to speak to a career counselor at his school about how to weigh his strong sense of service with his interest in Web development in his career decision.

His career counselor advised him to take a self-assessment test that might help him find out more about career choices that best fit his values, interests, and personality. Derek scored high in areas that matched a career in the technology field, though he also scored fairly high in some social service career areas. Derek's counselor explained that no career assessment can tell you all the careers for which you are best suited. She also explained that there is not a perfect occupation for everyone and that Derek's first career decision was not a career choice for life. In fact, she explained that most people change jobs five to seven times throughout their lives. Career assessment is a continuous process that does not stop with the first job.

After thinking through his options, he decided to start his career as a Web developer with a *Fortune* 500 company that offered a competitive salary and an opportunity for Derek to continue his education when he was ready. Part of the company's core values was service to the community. Employees were able to volunteer on behalf of the company, one day per month, with an organization of their choice. Derek decided that his short-term decision made the most sense. He was doing work he loved and was in an environment where he could learn and continue to develop his skills. He knew that by taking this route, he would one day have the financial resources to open his own business if he still wanted to and have enough financial security for his retirement down the road.

Discussion Questions

1. How did Derek's view of success influence his career choice?
2. Do you think Derek made the right choice? Why or why not?
3. Can you describe the career decision-making skills Derek applied?

3.1 YOUR DEFINITION OF CAREER SUCCESS

Your career plan will be built on your personal definition of career success. Now that you have thought about your own values, interests, personality traits, and skills, you can better describe what career success means to you.

Over the years, your view of career success changes. Talk with some successful people, and ask them what their definition of career success was when they first started their careers. They might say something like:

"I'd like to be earning six figures at age 40."

"I'd prefer to work independently, owning my own business."

"I'd want to be able to afford a second home to enjoy more leisure time."

"I'd like to be published in my field."

Then ask if that definition of success has changed over the years. In almost all cases, the answer will be yes. People who are more established in their careers will probably give some very different answers. Some examples are:

"I'd like to balance my time with family, friends, and my career."

"I'd like to be challenged in my work."

"I am concerned about the legacy I will leave once I retire."

"I'd enjoy mentoring others to reach their career goals."

"I'd like to be debt free."

The first group of responses tends to focus on achievement, status, and financial success. The second group of responses tends to focus on lifestyle, interesting work, and developing others. To get started, thinking about your own definition of success, think about some factors that influence individual definitions of success. For example, some research has shown that your age, gender, or ethnic background may influence your thinking.

CAREER SUCCESS AND AGE

Different age groups traditionally have varying viewpoints on career success. A look at how different generations think about success might help you develop your own definition of career success now and in the future. Review the basic profiles of four generations and then think about how each differs in their thinking about their career success.

⊙NOTES	Four Generations in Today's Workforce
Baby boomers	Born between 1946 and 1964 Heavy emphasis on work and climbing the corporate ladder
Gen X	Born between 1965 and 1980 More concerned about work–life balance
Millennials/Gen Y	Born between 1981 and 1994 Emphasis on family and personal time over career ambition
Gen Z	Born between 1995 and 2010 Emphasis on personal freedom, frequent job changes, promotion

Baby Boomers   The career environment for this generation is characterized by

1. "Workaholics"
2. Flexibility
3. Achievement
4. Focus on individual priorities

Career success for many baby boomers is driven by work as one's identity, broader interests beyond work, achievement, and choice to climb the corporate ladder or lateral career advancement.

Gen Xers   The career environment for this generation is characterized by

1. More work–life balance
2. Less formal work environments
3. Stronger relationships with coworkers
4. Workplace learning

Career success for this generation is driven by quality of life, valuing others, and learning new skills.

Gen Yers   The career environment for this generation is characterized by

1. Autonomy
2. Flexibility
3. Stronger relationships at multiple levels at work
4. Customized career paths

Career success for this generation is driven by work–life balance, contributing to community, specialization, and entrepreneurship. Gen Yers rank their top work priorities as (1) realizing their full potential,

(2) working for an ethical organization, (3) performing interesting work, (4) making money, and (5) having good colleagues.

Gen Zers   The career environment for this generation is characterized by

1. Technology tools and gadgets
2. Multitasking
3. Multiple careers
4. Virtual employers/coworkers

ACTIVITY 3.1

Career Success and Age

> Write down three or four ways you think your age might influence your definition of career success now and in the future.
>
> _____
> _____
> _____
> _____

CAREER SUCCESS AND GENDER

Some men and women think differently about career success. Different priorities about personal values and lifestyle goals seem to be the biggest influences on how men and women might think differently about career success. One study revealed that middle-aged men tend to value achievement and material success higher than life balance or relationships.[2]

One of their major priorities was to live without financial burden. Women valued life balance and relationships more than material success. In fact, only 3 in 20 women mentioned money as part of how they define success for themselves. Some women saw group achievement as more important than individual achievement, and most valued being recognized for what they accomplish at work very highly.[3]

Some of this is changing as more Gen X and Y women care more about income levels and opportunities for career advancement than those in previous generations.

ACTIVITY 3.2

Career Success and Gender

> Write down three to four ways you think your gender might influence your definition of career success now and in the future.
>
> _____
> _____
> _____
> _____

CAREER SUCCESS AND ETHNICITY

Some studies show that there is a difference between how people with different ethnic backgrounds think about career success. Your ethnic background and experiences can shape how you develop your career goals and envision personal and professional success.[4]

[2]L. Dyke and A. Murphy. (September 1, 2006). "How We Define Success: A Qualitative Study of What Matters Most to Women and Men." Retrieved August 31, 2009, from www.accessmylibrary.com/article-1G1-157839547/we-define-success-qualitative.html.

[3]Ibid.

[4]K. M. Perrone, W. E. Sedlacek, and C. M. Alexander. (December 2001). "Gender and Ethnic Differences in Goal Attainment." *Career Development Quarterly.*

Two main influences are socioeconomic background and access to mentoring and assessment. For example, some ethnic groups have more individuals with higher socioeconomic backgrounds. Those groups solely focus on the financial aspect of their career and choose work that interests them over work that simply pays more. Seeking help in setting and achieving career goals is important to career success. Members of some ethnic groups tend to initiate a request for help from a career counselor or mentor more often than others.

> Write down three to four ways you think your ethnic background might influence your definition of career success now and in the future.
> _____
> _____
> _____
> _____

ACTIVITY 3.3

Career Success and Ethnicity

CAREER SUCCESS AND CAREER CHOICE

As you decide on the career you will pursue, think about how well it will allow you to meet your individual definition of success. For example, will it provide you the level of financial stability you are looking for? Will promotion eventually require a higher level of education than you are currently pursuing? Will it enable you to satisfactorily maintain your relationships with family and friends? Ultimately, you need to ask yourself if your career choice will allow you to have the overall lifestyle you want. A successful career helps you lead a successful life.

QUALITIES OF SUCCESSFUL PEOPLE

Your career plan should include your action plan for developing qualities of successful people. Here are 10 common characteristics shared by many successful people:

Goal oriented: take small successes and use them to build bigger successes in the future.

Positive attitude: prevent disappointments and obstacles from becoming setbacks.

Risk taker: willing to accept both failure and success as a learning experience.

Enthusiastic: build spirit around an idea or a cause that motivates others.

Self-motivated: work well independently and drive own direction and results; believe they are in control.

Trusting: trust and believe in self and in others.

Informed and aware: interested and interesting because knowledgeable of current events.

Creative: create something of value that is original or the result of combining something that exists.

Curious: willing to explore new avenues of information.

Applied knowledge: solve problems, create and market products, manage people and systems.

These qualities of success come from within and are very much in your control to develop and manage.

Above all, success is an attitude. It is your choice to respond to problems as opportunities and to see alternative routes to your goals when others see only a dead end.

Real Life Stories

Sonia Sotomayor

President Barack Obama nominated Sonia Sotomayor to the U.S. Supreme Court. She was born of Puerto Rican descent in the Bronx. Sotomayor was raised by her mother after her father died when she was only nine years old. Her father had a third-grade education and did not speak English. After her father died, Justice Sotomayor became fluent in English. She was a good student with an excellent attendance record and also worked to support her own education. Justice Sotomayor worked at a retail store and then a hospital. Even though she was accepted to Princeton University, she struggled with her writing and vocabulary skills. She asked for help and worked with a teacher over the summer to improve her skills. This helped her increase her self-confidence.

When she attended law school, Justice Sotomayor was co-chair of a group for Latin, Asian, and Native American students. After law school, she held a variety of positions to build her credentials. Justice Sotomayor often talks about times throughout her career when she was challenged by what she considered to be stereotyping. Some expressed concern about her ability to render objective decisions without the influence of her ethnic background and experiences. She worked to overcome their objections openly by addressing these concerns directly in many of her presentations, ensuring her commitment to bring an objective viewpoint to her work. Justice Sotomayor successfully addressed this question one more time during her confirmation hearings. In 2009, she went on to become the first Hispanic and the third woman to serve as a Supreme Court justice.

Source: Accessed September 10, 2009, from www.whitehouse.gov/the_press_offce/Background-on-Judge-Sonia-Sotomayor/.

ACTIVITY 3.4

Your Career Success Statement

Now that you are able to consider how age, gender, ethnicity, and qualities of successful people may influence your own definition of career success, practice writing your personal career success statement. Because your definition of career success may still be developing and you may not be able to express your thoughts in a single statement, start by practicing two or three different statements that best express your thoughts at this time.

_____

_____

_____

3.2 SETTING AND WRITING GOALS FOR SELF-IMPROVEMENT

Throughout this self-assessment process, you have identified your own values, interests, personality traits, skills, and ideas of success. You have also reviewed those qualifications that employers prefer when deciding to hire a candidate.

TYPES OF CAREER GOALS

Career goals with the right start have a great finish. When you start by developing career goals that reflect what inspires you, it is easier to develop and implement planning goals

with an action plan you believe in. This includes setting self-improvement goals to better prepare you for your career.

Inspirational Goals Inspirational goals express how what you are passionate about can translate to a dream career. Inspirational goals ignore obstacles and constraints and allow you to focus on *what, not how.* Successful people have goals that create a vision for the future. To make your goals real to you, try to imagine the successful outcome of your work or actions.

A successful chef imagines how the dish being created will look and taste before preparing it.

A successful athlete imagines winning the game before the game begins.

A successful Web developer imagines the look and functionality of a website before it is developed.

Planning Goals Planning goals are a combination of short-term and long-term goals that help you create a plan to achieve career success. They identify steps along the way which are the *how* to your success.

Milestone Goals Milestone goals fuel motivation by identifying *major accomplishments* along the way.

Bridge Goals Bridge goals help *close the gap* between skills or experience you have and those needed for the job you want.

SMART Goals SMART goals are actionable goals with a time line. Your planning goals can be broken into smaller pieces each with its own time line and resources. SMART goals identify specific steps for reaching individual planning goals.

It is important to know how to write effective goal statements. Writing effective goal statements will help you stay focused on achieving your goals because you will have a more specific road outlined for achieving your goal. Writing effective goal statements is also important when communicating your career goals to prospective employers.

The best way to learn to write effective career goals is to practice writing some using the SMART approach. The SMART approach to writing goals incorporates goals that are specific, measurable, achievable, realistic, and timely.

> "What would you do if you weren't afraid?"
> *Sheryl Sandberg,*
> COO, Facebook[5]

> "A dream is a goal with a deadline."
> *Napoleon Hil[6]*

---

[5]Retrieved April 15, 2013, from www.goodreads.com/quotes/749767-what-would-you-do-if-you-weren-t-afraid.

[6]Retrieved March 4, 2013, from www.brainyquote.com/quotes/quotes/n/napoleonhi152852.html.

NOTES | SMART Goals Worksheet

Goal _____

Today's Date _____ Target Date _____ Start Date _____

Date Achieved _____

*S*pecific: Are your goals focused and clearly understood?

*M*easurable: How will you know when you have reached your goal?

*A*chievable: Is achieving this goal realistic?

        Will it take much effort?

        Will it take extraordinary commitment?

        Do you have the resources to achieve the goal?

        If not, how will you get them?

*R*ealistic: Why is this goal important to you?

*T*imely: When will it be achieved?

Before you practice how to write effective goal statements using the SMART approach, it might be useful to review some good goal statements compared to the vague statements that are commonly used.

NOTES | Sample Goal Statements

Vague Goal Statements	SMART Goal Statements
1. I want to save my money.	1. I will save 10 percent of my income to pay for my professional certification test to be taken next spring.
2. I want to be happy with my job.	2. By January, I will have my resume updated with the eight transferable skills from my current job with the goal of having a new job by April.
3. I want to work for a progressive company.	3. I want to work for a company that has customized career paths that will allow me to move to a senior financial analyst's position in five years.
4. I want to find an internship in my field.	4. I want a teaching internship to earn the 13.5 credits I need to qualify me for my student teaching by September.
5. I want to improve my skills.	5. I have registered for a six-week course in public speaking to learn how to present at my first management meeting in eight weeks.
6. I want a raise.	6. I will ask for an 8 percent increase during my performance review based on the 10 percent increase in sales I led over the last six months.
7. I want to start my own company.	7. My first financial services business will open in January, and by June we will have $200,000 in profits.
8. I want work–life balance.	8. My wife and I will dine at home four nights per week, and I will play basketball one night a week with my son.
9. I want a job using my education and experience.	9. I only apply for jobs that require an associate's degree in health services and hospital volunteer experience.
10. I want to improve my appearance for my next job interview.	10. I will lose five pounds in the next six weeks to be better prepared to present a professional appearance during my five interviews scheduled at Career Conference.

Review each of the following general goals. For each of these goals, create a SMART goal statement.

1. I will find a part-time job.

_____

2. I will stick to my budget.

_____

3. I will join a club.

_____

4. I will learn a new language.

_____

5. I will study harder.

_____

6. I will learn a new skill.

_____

7. I will win my next race.

_____

8. I will do volunteer work.

_____

9. I will work with my career counselor.

_____

10. I will graduate.

_____

ACTIVITY 3.5

Practice Writing SMART Goal Statements

Using the SMART approach to writing goal statements, practice writing three goals important to you now and three future goals.

Choose from the gaps you identified in values, interests, personality traits, skills, education, or experience, and set goals for self-improvement. When you use the SMART method, you will include actionable steps and timetables that describe how you intend to reach your goal.

Write three goals important to you now.

1. _____

2. _____

3. _____

Write three future goals.

1. _____

2. _____

3. _____

ACTIVITY 3.6

Write Three Goals

OVERCOMING OBSTACLES

Making progress toward your goals is an ongoing process. When you think you are getting stuck, take time to evaluate what you perceive as obstacles that could stop you from reaching your goal. There are many reasons why people don't reach their goals. By being aware of some, you can plan not to let any setbacks stop your progress. Some ways to stay on track include the following:

- Break larger goals into manageable chunks.
- Take the first step, and then plan the next step.
- Believe that your goals are nonnegotiable.
- Create a daily routine that you can stick to.
- Fit new goals into your current lifestyle; don't try to change everything.
- Have patience with yourself.
- Don't try to do too much too soon.
- Have a plan to get back on track when setbacks happen.
- Keep your goals at the top of your mind.
- Reassess your goals.

Progress Check Questions

1. How often do you set and review your goals?
2. Can you give an example of when you overcame an obstacle to achieving a goal to use as a future reference when an important goal is difficult to achieve?

3.3 CAREER DECISION-MAKING SKILLS

Simply put, decision making is the act of making up your mind about something. Good career decision-making skills are important because when you take the time to think through your career decisions carefully, you have a greater chance of being more successful and satisfied with your career. Learning the process of making good career decisions enables you to apply it many times in your career.

Start by better understanding the basics of the decision-making process and then applying that process to decisions about your career. Decision making is the result of a mental process leading to the selection of a course of action among a number of alternatives or choices. The alternatives you choose will be based on your values and preferences. When you follow a good decision-making process, you are better able to decide which alternatives have the greatest probability of success and best fit your goals, values, and lifestyle. It is important to realize that very few, if any, decisions are certain. But a good decision-making process will minimize most uncertainty.

The following discusses two different approaches to consider as good decision-making processes.

THE DECISION-MAKING PROCESS

You should follow this five-step approach when making an important decision:

1. Set a goal or reason for the decision.
2. Get the facts.
3. Establish criteria.
4. Develop alternatives.
5. Make the decision.

"When your values are clear to you, making decisions becomes easier."

Roy E. Disney[7]

---

[7]Retrieved April 6, 2013, from www.brainyquote.com/quotes/authors/r/roy_e_disney.html.

Set a goal or reason for the decision. Why is the decision you are making important to you? Most major decisions can have long-term consequences, so you want to make sure that the decision you make is purposeful in your life. For example, the reason for making an important financial decision may be to ensure that you will have enough funds to support yourself in your retirement.

Get the facts. It is important to get as many facts as possible that are important to your decision. Take into consideration that you may not have all the information you want at the time of your decision. This is when you need to weigh the risk of making the decision with limited information. For example, if you want to save your money for retirement in a particular type of savings account or investment fund, you probably will not know what the actual value of your money will be over time because you cannot precisely predict the ups and downs of the financial market over the years. You can, however, obtain expert advice on expected trends and make a reasonable decision knowing there will be some uncertainty in the outcome. In this case, you use information to minimize the risk of the outcome of your decision.

Establish criteria. Identify any criteria for the decision you are making. The criteria are the requirements that each alternative must possess to some degree in your opinion. An example of a criterion in your job search might be salary. Some job offers may meet your salary requirement, but not your choice of location or position. Location and position can impact your salary. If you have selected salary as a criterion for your decision on a job offer, then you are deciding to be more flexible with location and the type of position. It does not mean that it is not possible to have all three preferences available to you at the time of your job offer, but it does mean that if all three preferences are not available to you at the time, you will be prepared to base your decision on the salary.

Develop alternatives. Once you have set your goal and established your criteria, you will be able to explore alternatives that you are willing to consider. The alternatives that you choose should be those that have the greatest possibility for success and best fit your goals, lifestyle, and values. Each alternative will have advantages and disadvantages.

Make the decision. Once you think through the possible outcomes of your alternatives, you should feel better prepared to make a good decision. Going through this type of decision-making process will increase your confidence in the decisions you make and increase your chances of your decision leading to a successful outcome.

CAREER DECISION-MAKING QUESTIONS

Another way to approach making your decisions is to ask yourself a series of questions about the decision you are making. By doing so, you create a plan for making the most informed decision you can.

1. What am I trying to decide?

   Example: I want to decide between applying for a position as a teacher and as a training assistant with a company.

2. What do I need to know?

   Example: I need to know several things about both positions before I am able to decide including:

   Current job market

   Typical level of education required

   How my skills match the job requirements

3. How will it help me make a more informed decision?

   Example: By knowing the preferred education for different levels of these positions, I will know whether or not I will need to further my education or need additional training.

4. How can I obtain what I need to know?

People

Example: Are there people that I can observe, interview, or network with to obtain the information I am looking for?

Experience

Example: Will my internship, community service experience, or part-time job help me learn more about how my education and skills match the job requirements?

Research

Example: What websites, trade journals, or professional associations are available to me to find more information?

5. Who are my best resources for the information I need?

Example: Is my teacher, coworker, spouse, parent, career counselor, or current employer the best resource for me right now to discuss the information I need?

Progress Check Questions

1. What do you think is the best career decision you have made to date?
2. What is the next career decision you think you will need to make?

CHAPTER SUMMARY

Because self-assessment and career planning are continuous processes, you have learned the importance of knowing how to make good career decisions and set career goals periodically. By practicing career decision-making skills, you can apply the process over and over again as you need to at any point in your career. You will also find that you write and rewrite your goals as often as you make new career decisions.

You have learned the 21st century skills that employers have identified as important to go beyond the traditional technical and transferable skills to include important life skills such as managing your health and wellness. In Chapter 4, you will explore how to manage these important life skills that are important to both your personal life and your career. For example, you will learn time and stress management skills. You will further build your career profile to include a review of your education and training and your experiences.

GOAL SETTING AND CAREER DECISION MAKING

Based on what you learned about the career decision-making process in this chapter, choose a career decision you are currently trying to make and practice the decision-making process by answering each of the following questions:

1. What am I trying to decide?

_____

_____

2. What do I need to know?

_____

_____

3. How will it help me make a more informed decision?

_____

_____

4. How can I obtain what I need to know?

_____

_____

People _____

Experience _____

Research _____

5. Who are the best resources for the information I need?

_____

_____

"I always did something I was a little not ready to do. I think that's how you grow."

Marisa Mayer, CEO, Yahoo[1]

[1]Retrieved April 20, 2013, from www.cnn.com/2012/07/17/tech/mayer-yahoo-career-advice.

Personal Development

After completing this chapter, you will:

1 **Understand** the importance of good communication skills

2 **Develop** time and stress management techniques

3 **Identify** the importance of personal care and personal appearance

4 **Recognize** the importance of managing your personal finances

5 **Create** a Career Portfolio entry

This chapter focuses on four areas of development that have a major impact on both your personal and professional success. These include learning to better manage your communication skills and your time, reduce stress, present a professional image, and manage your personal finances. In Chapters 1 and 2, you learned that employers listed these as critical workplace skills. Of all the necessary skills, good communication skills may be your greatest asset as you develop your career in almost any field you choose. Good time and stress management skills are evidence of effective self-management skills.

Your appearance and overall image tells a lot about you to a prospective employer. Good grooming and appropriate interview and workplace dress are two essential components of your overall image. Knowing what to wear on an interview and how workplace dress may vary by type of industry or geographic region can help you dress appropriately for different situations. Management of personal finances is important to your career, as well as personal success. Having a personal financial plan helps you evaluate job offers. The financial reputation of job candidates has become increasingly more important to employers who look for evidence of personal responsibility before agreeing to give individuals roles involving authority and decision making within their companies.

All of these self-management skills are the first step to demonstrating your career readiness.

CASE STUDY

Cameron and Michelle: Making Positive Changes

Cameron was very active in extracurricular activities while studying for her degree in criminal justice. She volunteered two days a week at a local agency, worked 25 to 30 hours a week at the mall to earn extra money, and was vice president of a national student organization on campus. She felt she was on a good path to building experiences to help her compete for the job she wanted at graduation as a case manager with the local courts.

Her high-energy personality and eagerness to be involved in meaningful work and activities were an asset. Cameron believed that the more she did, the better qualified she would be. Cameron was really passionate about everything she did, but found she had difficulty getting things done. Her grades were very good. Cameron put her studies before her work and other activities. When Cameron was promoted to assistant store manager, she was required to stay to the store closing four nights a week.

She began running late for her early morning classes once her work scheduled changed. She had to cut corners on the volunteer and organization projects she was committed to. She knew she had to make some positive changes, but wasn't sure where to start.

Her roommate, Michelle, was also involved in several activities on and off campus, but seemed to get major projects done on time, keep up her grades, and even have a small amount of free time every week for herself. Two nights a week, Michelle had a routine of keeping two hours open in her schedule.

Although she was involved in a lot of things, she spent those four hours a week working on her business plan for her entrepreneurship class. Michelle planned on opening her own catering business after graduation and was using this class project as her actual business plan with the help of her current boss and her teacher. Part of her project was building a financial plan to include starting small, regularly scheduled investments in a retirement account. Michelle's grandparents advised her to do this after retiring and realizing that it was possible that they could outlive their retirement money. Michelle was grateful to learn how important this one positive change to her business plan would be. While Michelle kept a pretty busy schedule, she decided to hold back from making any extra commitments of her time until she was finished with her business plan.

Discussion Questions

1. How were Cameron and Michelle different from each other?
2. What could Cameron do to better manage her time and still accomplish her work?
3. Was Michelle's business plan realistic? Why or why not?

4.1 COMMUNICATION SKILLS

Employers require good communication skills because they are critical to succeeding at all job levels (Figure 4.1). Good communication skills are necessary for positions dealing with the public. You need good communication skills to work in teams and to mentor and lead others. In the workplace, you will be judged by the impression you make with how you communicate. Demonstrating that you are polished, professional, and knowledgeable in your communication builds credibility in you and in your company. Developing good communication skills is an ongoing process that includes formal learning in the classroom and practice through work and life experiences.

In addition, there are some basic steps you can follow to improve various aspects of your verbal and nonverbal communication skills.

VERBAL SKILLS

Verbal skills include speaking skills you use in one-on-one or group conversations, presentation skills, and phone skills.

Speaking Skills   The spoken word is a powerful tool for your success in school, at work, and in your personal life. The words you choose and how you sound shape how your message will be received. Try to practice thinking before you speak so that you can be sure of what you want to say and how you want to say it. By pausing to do this

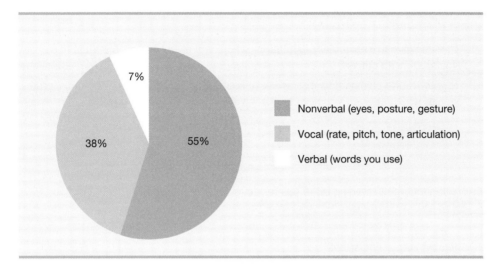

FIGURE 4.1

Communication Skills

first, you will be more confident when you speak and more likely to deliver the message you intend. Factors that may influence how your message is received include how fast you speak (rate), how high or low your voice is (pitch), how positive you sound (tone), and how clear your speech is (articulation). All of these dimensions of speech are learned over time, usually through one or more speech classes or lessons outside the classroom.

In addition to any formal training, you may find the following basic tips to be helpful when preparing to speak one on one, speak in a group, or make a presentation. You can refer back to these speaking skill tips when you learn more about preparing for a successful job interview in Chapter 12.

When speaking, know your audience. Determining the level of formality you should speak with is largely dependent on the makeup of your audience. You may need to be more formal when speaking with those in positions that are senior to yours at work or with people you are meeting for the first time, while you might be less formal with colleagues you have known for some time, and with family and friends.

Tips for Speaking Skills
* Think before you speak.
* Practice if you are unsure of how you will come across.
* Establish and maintain eye contact.
* Pronounce your words clearly.
* Keep a positive and professional or friendly tone depending on the situation.
* Use proper diction, which means correct and effective choice of words.
* Use proper grammar.
* Expand your vocabulary.
* Speak slowly.
* Avoid using jargon, which is terminology that relates to a specific profession, group, or activity.
* Do not use other informal language, including slang words or expressions.
* Try not to repeat yourself.
* Avoid biased or judgmental statements.

Remember that while you might feel more comfortable using informal language with friends and family, these tips are to help you know how to communicate appropriately in more formal or professional situations at school, work, or other situations requiring knowledge of appropriate speaking skills, such as a job interview.

> "Communication skills are ranked FIRST among job candidate's 'must have' skills and qualities."
>
> National Association of Colleges and Employers, 2010 survey: *Mastering Soft Skills for Workplace Success.*
>
> Source: Retrieved November 10, 2013, from www.dol.gov/odep/topics/youth/softskills/Communication.pdf.

. . . .

Progress Check Questions

1. Can you give five examples of situations where you need to be professional in the way you speak with others?

2. If you need to change how you speak in some of these situations to be more professional, what things do you need to change about how you speak now?

. . . .

ACTIVITY 4.1

Set a SMART Goal to Improve a Speaking Skill

Think about the preceding list of tips for developing good speaking skills. List two things you think you currently do well.

EXAMPLE

Thinking before you speak

Using a positive and friendly tone

_____

_____

Identify two areas for improvement.

EXAMPLE

Repeating yourself less

Improving your vocabulary

_____

_____

Using the SMART method for writing goals that you learned in Chapter 3, write a goal for one of the two areas you think you need to improve.

Goal: _____

Write how your goal is:

Specific

_____

Measurable

_____

Achievable

_____

Realistic

_____

Timely

_____

Conversation Skills   In the workplace, good conversation skills help you build a rapport with others and demonstrate your knowledge and interests about and beyond your work. Building rapport with others and being a broad thinker make you a more interesting person for others to be around and can contribute much to your career growth. For example, a nurse with good conversation skills is able to make patients more comfortable if they are stressed. A financial planner may talk with you about the news or encourage you to talk about your interests.

This helps the planner know more about your values and priorities in an informal way, which will influence the advice given to you and also helps establish a level of trust that is important for your work together to be successful. Even at informal events at work, company dinners, or sporting events, your ability to converse well with others will help you be noticed.

"I can walk away from a five-minute conversation and feel their enthusiasm and have a good understanding of what's important to them."

Holly Paul, U.S. recruiting leader, Pricewatershouse Coopers

Source: Retrieved November 18, 2013, from http://online.wsj.com/news/articles/SB10001424127887324735104578118902763095818.

NOTES   Awareness of the World around You

Topics	Sources of Information
Economic trends	Internet
Job trends	*Wall Street Journal*
Major political events	*USA Today*
Cultural issues in your community	Community groups and organizations
Health-related issues	Professional associations
Bills being voted on that may affect you	Local and national political representatives
Cost-of-living trends	Trade journals
Sports-related news	Television
Cultural activities	Social network (movies, plays, events)

Tips for Conversation Skills

- Find out what the other person's interests are.
- Remember something you learned about the person if you have met that person before.
- Give your total attention to the other person you are talking with.
- Let the other person do much of the talking.
- Try not to interrupt or argue with the other person.
- Ask questions.
- Be tactful.
- Be open to different opinions.
- End conversations on a positive note.

Progress Check Questions

1. Can you think about a recent conversation that you really enjoyed?
2. What did the other person do to make the conversation stand out in your mind?

Telephone Skills   Telephone skills are an important part of business communications. Although you are not seen while speaking on the telephone, you are usually heard and judged by how you handle the call.

Tips for Making Business Calls

- Know the name and title of the person you are calling, and the department he or she works in.
- Identify yourself by giving your name and the reason for your call; then ask to be connected to the party you are calling.
- Always refer to the person you are calling by Mr., Ms., or Mrs. and the last name. If you know that the person has a specific title, such as Dr. or Professor, use it.
- Learn the proper pronunciation of the person's name before calling.

IMPORTANT MESSAGE

FOR ___Dr. Smith___

DATE ___10-5-2014___   TIME ___2:15___   AM / PM

WHILE YOU WERE OUT

Mr. ___Allen Jones___

OF ___Cartwright Industries___

PHONE NO. ___(401) 885-6666___

TELEPHONED	✓	PLEASE CALL	✓
CALLED TO SEE YOU		WILL CALL AGAIN	
WANTS TO SEE YOU		RUSH	
RETURNED YOUR CALL			

MESSAGE ___The contract has been received and he has some questions. Please try to call back on Thursday, 10/8 between 2—4pm.___

SIGNED ___Cheryl Anderson___

FIGURE 4.2

Sample Telephone Message

- If you reach your party, greet him or her by the proper name and title, introduce yourself, and state the purpose of your call.
- If your party is unavailable, leave a message asking that the person return your call.
- Always remain pleasant and professional, even when your frustration level is high. You don't want the message to read that you were rude.

Tips for Receiving Calls for Your Company

- No one should ever be left on hold for more than one minute. The first call always has priority.
- Transferring a call within a company requires thorough knowledge of the organization, of the various divisions' duties and responsibilities, and of the names of key people who will handle the call properly.
- If you are not sure where to transfer the call, explain that you are trying to find the proper source to serve the caller's needs; briefly put the caller on hold, and then find out where the call should go. When you are sure you can make the proper transfer, do so.
- If it's your job to screen calls, remember to do so in a professional manner.
- If you are an administrative assistant, you may help an executive return calls by keeping a neat list of calls at your desk and asking the executive if you can place the return call.
- If you must take a message, politely explain that the party being called is unavailable and that you will be sure that the person gets the message. Then be sure to deliver the message (Figure 4.2).

Cell Phones for Business Calls   Cell phone etiquette is much different for business than the rules you may or may not apply for your personal calls.

Tips for Making Business Cell Phone Calls

- Your personal greeting should be clear, concise, and professional.
- Be careful not to have music or noise in the background when recording your message.
- When you record your message, don't use a nickname or the same fun and casual message you might leave for personal callers. You may want to consider having two cell phones, one for business and one for personal use, if you can.
- Turn off your cell phone during interviews and meetings. You should also turn it off during meetings at restaurants. Those you are meeting with should feel that they have your uninterrupted attention.
- Use discretion when having cell phone conversations about business or personal topics in public areas. You do not want to provide access to confidential or sensitive information or discussion to any casual listeners.
- Know the state law about cell phone use while driving in different states. Many states ban cell phone use when you are driving.
- Return cell phone calls promptly.

NONVERBAL SKILLS

Nonverbal skills include writing, listening, and your body language. Developing effective written communication skills is critical to your overall career success.

Writing Skills   Writing effectively can help you gain a competitive edge in your job search when you are composing letters or resumes or completing a job application. Writing samples for your Career Portfolio can be used during interviews. Throughout your career, almost any job will require you to produce written documents. Some examples include writing meeting minutes, PowerPoint presentations, proposals, executive summaries, performance reviews, business correspondence, training materials, and product or process manuals. People form an impression about you through your writing. Well-organized thoughts and good grammar, spelling, and punctuation show the reader that you care about the quality of your work.

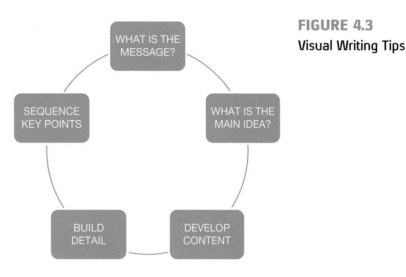

FIGURE 4.3
Visual Writing Tips

Learning how to produce a wide range of writing requires formal instruction and practice. If you are planning to write for business situations or for your job search, you should focus on producing a professional document that has content that is well organized and stated in proper form. The following tips and examples might be useful as review before preparing your written documents (Figure 4.3).

Tips for Writing Skills

- Be clear on the message you want to deliver.

  "I am looking for a *job.*"

- Develop the main idea.

  "I am a *graphic designer specializing in infographics.*"

- Develop content.

  "I completed an *internship* and will graduate with a *bachelor's degree in graphic design.*"

- Build detail.

  "I have *samples* of infographics I designed during my internship and for class projects in my Career Portfolio. Let me describe them."

  "Let me describe my internship experience."

- Sequence key points.

  "I studied graphic design, completed a practice project during my internship, and have samples of my work in my portfolio for my job interview."

  "I am interested in XYZ company because infographics have recently become part of your client services."

  "I am available for work after graduating on May 20th."

Being conscious of how you can improve the impact of what you write and how you write it is the first step. By practicing the tips in the preceding list each time you are preparing an important document, these steps will become a habit and your writing skills can improve.

Progress Check Questions

1. Can you think of examples of how you might apply writing skills in the career field you are interested in?

2. Are you building samples of your writing skills that you can present to an employer if asked during an interview?

"We live in an era of sound bites and 140 character messages, but good writing still matters when it comes to the business world."

Laura Simonds, managing editor, *Small Business Computing*

Source: Retrieved November 13, 2013, from http://business.time.com/2013/04/19/good-writing-can-help-you-succeed/.

ACTIVITY 4.2

Set a SMART Goal to Improve a Writing Skill

Think about the above writing skills tips. List two things you think you currently do well.

EXAMPLE

Concise writing

Proper use of grammar, punctuation, vocabulary

_____

_____

Identify two areas for improvement.

EXAMPLE

Less informal language in e-mails

Proofreading

_____

_____

Using the SMART method for writing goals that you learned in Chapter 3, write a goal for one of the two things you need to improve.

Goal: _____

Write how your goal is

Specific _____

Measurable _____

Achievable _____

Realistic _____

Timely _____

Listening Skills   Listening is an important communication skill that is often overlooked. Listening is paying attention to and understanding what someone is saying. A good listener hears the message being conveyed and evaluates the meaning. Good listening is a form of learning because it reveals a knowledge of others. Hearing what is being said but not concentrating on what it means is called passive listening. In contrast, active listening means hearing what is being said and interpreting its meaning as well. Active listening makes you a more effective communicator because you are able to react to what you have heard.

> "When you listen before you talk, you cause the other party to be interested in you."
>
> *Dan Schwabel,* managing partner, Millennial Branding[2]

As you are planning your career, you will find active listening to be helpful in many ways. Listening to business and personal acquaintances may lead you to a new contact. Listening to how someone talks about a company can tell you a lot about how the company is run and the morale of the employees.

Good listening includes being able to distinguish important from unimportant information, detect inconsistencies in information, and understand the main points of the message. When parts of a message are unclear, the best thing to do is to take notes, jot down your questions, and wait until the entire presentation or discussion is finished before asking questions. It may also be appropriate to provide comments about what was presented or to provide feedback on what was said and how it was said. Remember that many times we have difficulty listening to what is being said because we are distracted by things that are bothering us or by things happening in our environment. Another distraction can be our own emotions about what is being presented or about the speaker.

[2]Retrieved May 13, 2013, from http://danschawbel.com/quotes.

The key to overcoming these distractions is concentration. By developing effective listening skills, you will become more confident in yourself and more effective in your interaction with others.

Tips for Listening Skills

- Make eye contact.
- Listen for the main idea.
- Ask questions.
- Take notes.
- Try to repeat back what you heard to confirm you understood.
- Watch the speaker's body language.
- Appear and be interested.
- Don't interrupt.
- Be open and nonjudgmental.
- Plan your response while the other person is concluding.
- Feel comfortable with silent space.

ACTIVITY 4.3
Active Listening

To understand the importance of active listening, sit across from a partner and, facing each other, prepare to engage in a brief conversation. Decide who will be person A, the listener, and person B, the storyteller. The storyteller should tell a three- to four-minute story about personal interests, family background, and career plans. The listener will repeat the storyteller's story, including as much detail as possible. To determine how accurate person A's listening skills are, you will both assess how effectively person A listened. Place a check (insert a checkmark) in the boxes that describe the listener's behavior while hearing the story.

LISTENING SKILLS CHECKLIST

The Listener's Self-Evaluation

If you were the listener, check the appropriate boxes below.

I Think I

- ❑ maintained eye contact
- ❑ was attentive
- ❑ did not interrupt
- ❑ nodded to show agreement
- ❑ took appropriate notes

The Storyteller's Evaluation of the Listener

If you were the storyteller, check the appropriate boxes below.

I Think Person A

- ❑ maintained eye contact
- ❑ was attentive
- ❑ did not interrupt
- ❑ showed positive acknowledgment
- ❑ took appropriate notes

When you communicate with others, it is important that they perceive you as a good listener. Very often you may think you have appeared to listen, only to find the speaker has a different perception of how well you listened.

PERCEPTIONS OF ACTIVE LISTENING

After each of you has completed your listening skills checklist, discuss how similar or different your responses were. Discuss with each other the behaviors you agreed on and those you did not agree on. By discussing those you did not agree on, person A can gain a better understanding of how well he or she is perceived to be an active listener.

ASSESSING ACTIVE LISTENING

Even though it is important to appear to be an active listener, the true measure of active listening is how well you can recall and interpret what you heard. Discuss how accurate the listener was in relaying the storyteller's story. Were any key points missing? How much detail was repeated? Did the listener provide any interpretation of observations of body language, facial expressions, gestures, or tone of voice?

Real Life Stories

President Clinton

Bill Clinton, the 41st president of the United States, is well known for his exceptional ability to connect with individuals and audiences through his strong communication skills. His active-listening skills are one of his prominent leadership traits. While there are many examples of his listening skills in his interactions with world leaders, there are also examples of his ability to demonstrate his active-listening skills with reporters.

During a press conference following the 2006 Leaders in London Conference a reporter tried to ask President Clinton a question. She could not speak English well and took too much time trying to explain her question. It was obvious that others in the room were frustrated and, because they did not understand her right away, they prejudged her question as unimportant. The conference moderator moved on to the next question. At the end of the press conference, President Clinton asked for the opportunity to respond to her. As it turns out, her question was about families in the developing world and no one, except President Clinton, understood that. The topic was very pertinent to his earlier remarks. Although not apparent at the time, Clinton was concentrating on her question and remained poised during the confusion. By later insisting that he address her individually, he demonstrated to the group that he had a genuine interest in what she said and was able to make her feel that her question was important. His actions provided a leadership example of how active listening can turn a diffcult communication into a productive exchange.

Source: Accessed September 4, 2009, from www.easy-strategy.com/art-of-listening.html.

Body Language   Body language is a form of nonverbal communication conveyed by certain body movements and expressions. Body language includes your facial expression, poise, posture, and mannerisms. When someone looks at you, certain clues can be detected through your body language as to how you feel or what you may be thinking. Facial expressions can show a variety of emotions. Below are just a few simple illustrations of how you communicate with your face, before any words are spoken.

Poise is your ability to act with ease and grace. When you are poised, you appear self-assured and composed in almost every situation. A poised person appears to be in control of most actions and reactions. Posture is one indicator of poise. Standing or sitting straight or still, without appearing tense or uncomfortable, creates an impression that you are confident about the situation you are in. Think about people you know who are noticeable when entering a room just by the way they hold their body. The way a person carries himself or herself indicates that person's level of self-confidence. Poised people can create energy just by walking into a room.

Each of us has certain mannerisms that either add to or detract from our image. Mannerisms are part of our body language and are formed by habits we have developed. They include using your hands a lot when you speak, tapping your foot while you wait or are in a hurry, or rocking back and forth or pacing when standing in front of an audience waiting

Facial Expression	Message to Others
Smile	Acceptance or approval
Frown	Anger, confusion, or disappointment
Wide-open eyes	Interest and confidence
Raised brows	Surprise
Wandering eyes	Boredom or distraction

to make a presentation. While certain mannerisms may have a positive effect, mannerisms like the ones just mentioned may not.

Tips for Good Body Language

- Maintain good posture.
- Maintain good eye contact.
- Nod to show agreement or understanding.
- Use facial expressions to show how you are feeling (smiling, serious, interested, excited).
- Appear to have and take time to listen.
- Appear confident.
- Control nervous habits such as tapping your fingers.
- Be calm.
- Be in control.

Progress Check Questions

1. Can you think of someone you know who takes control of a room as soon as he or she enters? What does the person's body language say that makes such a powerful impression?

2. What do you think others would say about your body language in most situations? What does that say about you?

PROFESSIONAL ONLINE COMMUNICATION

Because it is so easy communicating online, the impact of a message can be strengthened or diminished with the quick press of a button. This is especially true in professional situations such as a job search or work-related setting. Communication is an art that requires thoughtful planning and delivery, particularly online. Knowing the when, why, and how of professional online communication includes the best use of e-mails, texts, and tweets.

Effective Online Messages   These simple steps can help you plan and deliver an effective online message professionally (Figure 4.4).

Timing is everything. Take into consideration the other person's *availability.* Be sensitive to when you send messages if you can. Try to keep your professional communication within business hours.

Make it matter. When planning your message, *relevance* is important. Be sure the content of your message relates to a topic of interest or importance to the recipient.

FIGURE 4.4

Communication Is ART

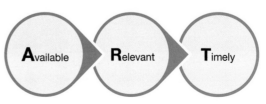

Be in the right place at the right time. A *timely* message captures attention. When a message comes at a good time—not too early and not too late—your impact is the greatest. Providing relevant information prior to a meeting or sending your resume to an employer while the interview process is active are two examples.

Sharpen your tools. Technology continues to provide a steady stream of communication tools. Sharpen your skills using the essential communication tools for professional communication online. These essential tools include Tweets, Texts, E-mails, and Blogs. Other tools may become prominent, depending on changes in technology and specific uses by employers in different industries over time.

> The when, why and how of professional online communication:
>
> Timing is everything
>
> Make it matter
>
> Be in the right place at the right time
>
> Sharpen your tools

E-Mails, Texts, and Tweets

E-Mail. The same professionalism that you bring to face-to-face exchanges or formal writing should be applied to e-mail correspondence. E-mails written for professional use are usually more formal, while e-mails for informal use are more relaxed and incorporate more friendly features like text abbreviations, or updates on personal topics. For professional use, stick to the subject, write short paragraphs separated by blank lines and avoid fancy typefaces. Limit bolding to one or two words and stick to black letter and conservative font. Use complete sentences and capital letters

TWEETS	TEXTS	E-MAILS
less formal	less formal	more formal
share	share	share
opinions	quick updates	quick updates
feedback	messages	messages
information	few details	short details
		information
short		explanations
discussions		concepts
	short content	
		fuller content

beginning each sentence. Unlike Tweets or text messages, E-mail is the right opportunity to use more detail to support your message. Use your professional e-mail address for job search and work-related situations.

Text Messages. Because of the 160 characters limit per text message, texting should be used to pass on simple, informal messages that require little or no detail. It is a very efficient way to provide quick updates, ask simple questions, or make brief comments. Because of the short content, a text message may lack the detail needed to be fully understood. Don't take the chance that your message might be misinterpreted for the sake of efficiency or speed. If you need to, send a more detailed message using e-mail.

Be selective about use of text messaging abbreviations. Use only those that represent words and phrases that you would use in professional settings. Do not use those representing slang, negative opinions, emotions, controversial or unprofessional language. Unless you know if a company allows selective use, don't use text messaging abbreviations. If this causes your message to be too long, consider sending a fuller message using e-mail.

Tweets. Some people limit their use of Twitter to brief messaging. Others make fuller use of the site's features and use it as a social media site.

All tools. With all of these tools, be sure to participate in appropriate discussions with reputable individuals. Communicating online with someone who is criticizing your company or school, a co-worker, others connected to your school or work setting, or job search reflects poorly on you.

You can overuse a good thing. Try not to bombard individuals by sending the same message multiple ways or by sending messages too frequently. If you think you need to resend a message, be sure you have given the other person enough time to respond. Don't get into a 24/7 mindset and expect a response to professional messages outside of business hours unless it has been agreed to ahead of time. There are rare exceptions in critical situations. In these instances you would probably be informed in a more formal way than text messaging.

If a subject is critical, too sensitive or controversial, it is usually best to communicate face-to-face or over the telephone. Be sure to find out and follow the policies on the use of the internet and online communication tools at your school or work setting.

GENERAL GUIDELINES
Tweets, Texts, E-Mails, and Blogs

Avoid	Focus
Unprofessional topics	Concise, clear messages
Sensitive topics or information	Timing
Emotional or confrontational issues	Relevant content
Unprofessional language or tone	Answer messages promptly

Be selective about using new tools professionally until you know if and how they are used by employers.

New tools. Mobile phone applications are among the fastest growing new online communication tools. For example, Whats Apps Messenger, Kik Messenger, and Snapchat are examples of popular mobile phone applications. Monitor their development and watch for growth from their core emphasis on speedy communication to broader use such as professional applications. Remember, Facebook was originally used strictly for social networking before adding a professional networking feature. As a result, employers incorporate Facebook into many aspects of their business communication. Kik Messenger is another example of a similar trend. It's great to know the latest technology, but be selective about using new online communication tools professionally until you know if and how they are used by employers.

VISUAL COMMUNICATION SKILLS

"Whether someone is sending an e-mail or instant message or writing a blog, they are being judged on their communication ability and it must be good to attain success."

Mark Bugaieski, SPHR, HR director, Illinois CancerCare

Source: Retrieved November 18, 2013, from www.weknownext.com/workforce/communication-skills-key-for-young-workers.

Visual communication is done through the use of visual aids such as graphic designs, signs, photos, illustrations, color, or videos. Visual communication has become a prominent part of the job search. For example, infographics and online videos provide more visual ways to present Career Portfolios, resumes, and other job search materials. Online videos can be easily uploaded for personal use or public viewing using video-sharing tools like Vimeo and Vine. Selective visual aids help you build a Career Portfolio for display with potential employers. Like what you write, images you display online contribute to an overall impression about you. Being mindful of your visual communication is important because it can either enhance or tarnish your reputation. Social media and personal websites are forms of visual communication that require care in presentation. A full discussion of both will be handled in Chapter 7.

Career Portfolio Preview   A Career Portfolio is a key tool to showcase skills and accomplishments using visual communication. Employers are more confident in their screening process when there is evidence to support skills and accomplishments presented on a written resume. For this reason, employers have become more reliant on the visual communication provided by Career Portfolios to screen job candidates.

As you work through this text, you will develop Career Portfolio entries using combinations of written, verbal, and visual communication tools to best convey your unique story to potential employers. Career Portfolios are discussed in detail in Chapter 6. You can jumpstart your Career Portfolio by using the information in this chapter to develop a sample of your communication skills.

CAREER PORTFOLIO 4.1

⠿ DEMONSTRATE COMMUNICATION SKILLS

Demonstrate your written and verbal communication skills with samples of your work. If done well, a writing sample and a visual sample of your communication skills can help distinguish you in your job search. Choose one or both of the options below, depending on what you know you can do best. Work with an instructor to ensure the quality of your samples. Save your samples to include in your Career Portfolio.

1. Written communication skills—writing sample

   Write a one- or two-page description of one of the following:

   • Class project
   • Work or community service experience related to your career goal
   • Special distinction you earned (award, honor, etc.) related to your career goal

2. Verbal communication skills—visual sample

   Create a video of yourself describing what you wrote about.
   You can use Vine, Vimeo, or any other platform you are comfortable with.
   Your video can be posted online and used to become part of your online Career Portfolio, or you can simply upload it to your iPad to show your targeted audience—for example, an employer during a job interview.

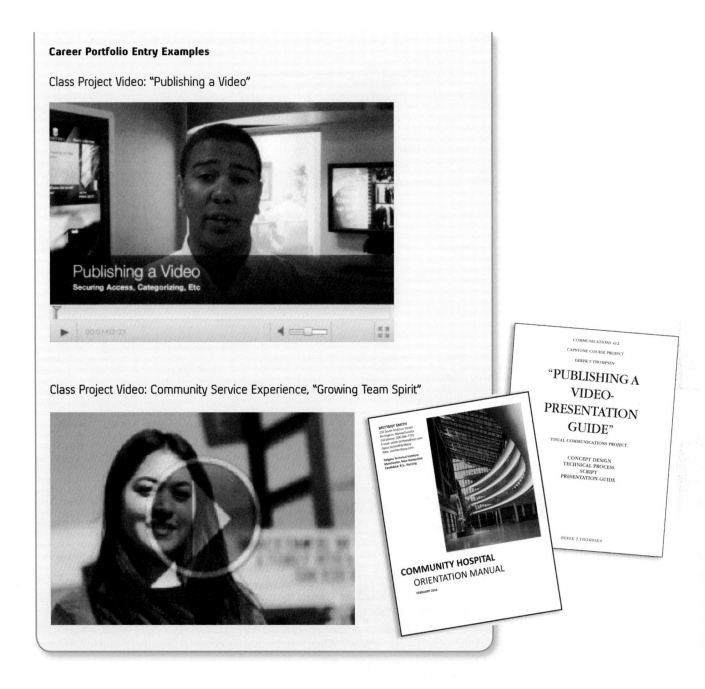

Career Portfolio Entry Examples

Class Project Video: "Publishing a Video"

Class Project Video: Community Service Experience, "Growing Team Spirit"

COMMUNITY HOSPITAL
ORIENTATION MANUAL

"PUBLISHING A VIDEO-PRESENTATION GUIDE"

4.2 TIME AND STRESS MANAGEMENT

Demonstrating effective self-management skills is an important first step to building a positive image and a good reputation as someone who is reliable, dependable, mature, professional, and serious about his or her career.

Time and stress management skills are two examples of important self-management skills. When you manage your time better, you reduce your stress. There are many benefits to learning time and stress management skills, including the ability to be more focused and think clearly, demonstrate that you are able to assume responsibility for yourself and others, and establish work–life balance. Another important benefit is increased productivity.

ACTIVITY 4.4

Time and Stress Management Tips

STAY POSITIVE
- Visualize success.
- Believe you are in control.
- Build confidence.

BE FOCUSED
- Envision your goal.
- Handle interruptions.
- Be patient.
- Be flexible.

STAY FIT
- Exercise: join a fitness club, yoga class or walking group.
- Maintain good diet: eat breakfast, make healthy choices at home and away.
- Sleep.
- Take 10 minute breaks to relax during the day.

CREATE ACTIONABLE ITEMS
- Plan.
- Organize.
- Create systems.

MAKE CHOICES
- Say no.
- Delegate.
- Ask for help.

CELEBRATE MILESTONES

Did these decisions come easily to you? Many people don't practice a decision process to prioritize their tasks; they simply follow a "do whatever comes next" approach. That approach may have worked for you up to now, but what will happen when you receive another important school assignment that must be completed by April 15? When you get sick the second week of May? When your car breaks down on Saturday morning? *Will you still meet your deadlines efficiently?*

Good time management planning is a process that helps you organize your priorities and create an action plan with allocated time for each task, including planned free time so there is still time to complete tasks that become off schedule due to unforeseen circumstances.

The following chart may help you visualize a way to make choices and decisions about the tasks you want to prioritize as part of your time management planning.

Urgent versus Important Tasks

	Important	Not Important
Urgent	1	2
Not Urgent	3	4

Urgent = Urgent tasks are deadline-based without a relation to importance. Here deadlines are often driven by others. Important = How important the task is determines how much time you want to spend on it. Here the quality of the result and the time needed are driven by you.

STRESS MANAGEMENT

Stress is a physical, psychological, or performance-related reaction to internal or external events. Examples of stressful events may include change, health issues, financial debt, or unemployment. Challenges that seem overwhelming to us are a cause of stress. Challenges can range in intensity from schoolwork issues to overcoming a disability to dealing with the sickness or death of someone close to you.

Financial concerns are one of the major sources of stress for many. Determining ways to afford your education is often first on your mind as a student. Poor health habits can create stress. Lack of proper exercise or diet does not provide proper physical energy or mental alertness needed to resist stress.

Overinvolvement in activities that you cannot handle all at once, even if you enjoy them, can leave you frustrated by your inability to do any of them well. Leaving home to go to college or start a new job is often stressful. Not connecting with new friends or coworkers can leave you feeling isolated and anxious. The wrong friend can apply pressure for you to be "like everyone else," leaving you the feeling that you won't belong unless you give in to that pressure. When you feel pressured to be someone you are not, you feel stressed. A lack of goals can leave you unsure of where you are headed and anxious about your future. A lack of confidence or personal problems can cause you to withdraw or internalize feelings, creating anxiety or tension. These are some of the potential causes of stress in your daily life.

Symptoms of stress include procrastinating, rushing or skipping meals, having difficulty listening or sleeping, misplacing things, being forgetful, lacking energy, lacking social time, frequently being late, or experiencing stifled creativity.

The results of prolonged stress may include a lack of productivity, depression, sickness, burnout, chronic tiredness, obesity, headaches, and a general lack of enjoyment or enthusiasm.

Being aware of some of the symptoms of stress will help you determine a plan to reduce your stress. Talk with friends, family members, and teachers, as well as counselors and other professionals trained to help you work through the issues causing you stress. Once you have determined the source of your stress, you can take positive steps to help yourself.

Complete one or both of the following two exercises

ACTIVITY 4.5

Stress Awareness

Check your major sources of stress:

- ❏ Schoolwork
- ❏ Personal problems
- ❏ Finances
- ❏ Lack of goals
- ❏ Poor health habits

- ❏ Involvement in too many activities
- ❏ Lack of friends
- ❏ Family problems
- ❏ Others:

_____

_____

_____

List the strategies you will take to reduce each of the stressors you identified:

_____

_____

_____

_____

Your Action Plan

Goal: _____

Start date: _____

Completion date: _____

When your action is complete, you will be able to manage stress previously caused by _____

_____

_____

_____

ACTIVITY 4.6

Set a SMART Goal to Improve a Time and Stress Management Skill

Think about the preceding tips for improving your time and stress management skills. List two things that you think you currently do well.

EXAMPLE

Create systems.

Stay fit.

_____

_____

Identify two areas for improvement.

EXAMPLE

Make choices and decisions.

Celebrate milestones.

_____

_____

Using the SMART method for setting goals you learned in Chapter 3, write a goal statement for one of the two areas in which you think you need to improve.

Goal: _____

Write how your goal is:

Specific _____

Measurable _____

Achievable _____

Realistic _____

Timely _____

Progress Check Questions

1. How will managing your time be an advantage to you in your career?
2. How will managing your stress be an advantage to you in your career?

🔴 4.3 PERSONAL CARE AND PERSONAL APPEARANCE

Your appearance plays a critical role in the impression you make on an employer during your interview. Good grooming and appropriate dress are the keys to a winning appearance on a job interview. Personal grooming, wellness, and professional dress all help you portray your best professional image.

GROOMING

A professional appearance is a statement of confidence. People are more apt to listen to you if you look like you take your job seriously. In general, basic grooming habits are important to your professional credibility no matter what career field you enter. Many employers follow grooming standards set for their industry.

The health care and food service industries are two good examples. These grooming codes exist not only for you to portray a professional image with the public, but also to meet required sanitation and health codes. A winning appearance begins with good grooming.

NOTES | Good Grooming Tips for Interviews

- Hair should be neatly cut and styled; avoid extreme styles or colors (green or orange). Be sure hair color or highlights are subtle.
- Face should be clean shaven.
- Wear light fragrances, if any at all.
- Nails are best kept short to medium length. Use neutral polish, and save elaborate nail art for more social and casual occasions.
- Makeup should be worn lightly so that it accentuates your features instead of changing your looks.
- Body art (tattoos) should be covered.
- Body piercings should be limited to one earring per ear. Cover any other body piercings.

An important part of good grooming is paying extra attention to your personal hygiene. The confident smile begins with good daily dental care, including freshly brushed teeth and fresh breath. When you shower, fresh, clean fragrances are better than strong fragrances that can be overpowering. There are different opinions about whether beards or mustaches are acceptable for interviews. The answer can vary by industry and company. The general rule is to be clean shaven and remove your facial hair. Women should also take care to be clean shaven to ensure a crisp appearance.

These efforts to create a well-groomed look are all critical to your credibility with a prospective employer. Too many times, job applicants fail to build a well-groomed image by addressing only one area rather than concentrating on the total look. For example, time after time students have arrived for interviews with a new, well-fitted suit and old or casual shoes or long hair that is not properly maintained. Unless you commit to your whole look, employers may not view you seriously as a professional.

WELLNESS

Proper exercise and diet can help you better manage your time, stress, and overall energy and wellness. Diet and exercise are often neglected because of constantly changing work or school schedules. Here are some guidelines for building healthy habits:

- Control total fat and salt intake. It is recommended that total fat intake not exceed 30 percent of caloric intake. Reading food labels can help you be aware of how much fat and salt are in the foods you eat.

- Avoid substance abuse that can result in overuse or misuse of alcoholic beverages, drugs, or tobacco.

- Drink plenty of water. If you find eight glasses excessive for you, be sure to incorporate at least five to six glasses of water in your diet per day.

- When dining in a restaurant, choose the healthy choices on the menu. Most restaurants offer a variety of leaner foods (pasta, chicken, fish, and salads) and a choice of how food is prepared (baked, broiled, poached, steamed, or grilled).

- If you can, exercise moderately every day. You may decide to join a fitness center or take a yoga class, or you may want to develop your own walking routine.

ACTIVITY 4.7

Strengthen Your Image

What things can you work on to present a better image to others?

❏ Exercise

❏ Lose weight

❏ Update your wardrobe

❏ Improve grooming

❏ Practice facial expressions

❏ Smile

❏ Walk with more confidence

❏ Make more direct eye contact

❏ Hear yourself as others do

❏ Listen to your voice samples

❏ Project your voice better

❏ Modify your language (choice of words, organization, and support of your ideas)

STRATEGIES

❏ Do it yourself

❏ Hire an expert

❏ Work with a group

Which strategy will you choose?

_____

INTERVIEW AND WORKPLACE DRESS

Dressing appropriately for an interview and for work today can mean lots of different things. The type of work you do and the work setting define your work dress policies. Most jobs require a professional look appropriate to the job setting. Projecting a good image, no matter what work you do or with whom you interview, tells others that you know what is appropriate and have pride in yourself.

NOTES   Choose a Professional Look

While you should be aware of typical workplace dress in different industries, when you interview, you should go for the professional look. Once you get the job, you can adjust your style to the norm of the company.

NOTES   Workplace Dress by Industry Examples

This is just a sample of how workplace dress may vary by industry:

Uniforms	Health care, food service, hospitality, airline, law enforcement, cosmetology
Casual and artistic and business casual	Outdoor work such as recreation and leisure, tourism, technology, advertising, acting, teaching, retail
Professional	Accounting, financial services, law firms, banking, insurance companies

Dress codes can vary from business professional to business casual to wearing uniforms.

Business Professional Dress   Some examples of industries that typically require business professional dress are accounting, financial services, banking, insurance, and legal services. There are many more work environments that have this more formal dress code. If you are not sure what a company's dress code is, you are always safe to take the more conservative approach and then make appropriate changes down the road. When you go on a job interview, your dress should be business professional. You can't go wrong following the basic business dress guidelines for men and women presented below.

Business Casual Dress   While business casual dress is less formal, you should still be concerned about looking appropriate for a business environment. High-tech firms, retail stores, social service agencies, and some educational systems are good examples of industries where business casual is more the norm. While the purpose of business casual dress is to create a more relaxed work environment, you are still representing the business during work hours and you are still being judged on your appearance.

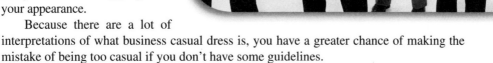

Because there are a lot of interpretations of what business casual dress is, you have a greater chance of making the mistake of being too casual if you don't have some guidelines.

Uniforms   Jobs in many fields of work require uniforms, especially in the health care, technical, food service, and hospitality industries. If your profession requires you to wear a uniform, don't assume that you can be lazy about your professional attire. When uniforms are required for work or the classroom, treat them as you would any other good clothing you would buy. Keep them clean, pressed, and new-looking at all times. Buy a good number of uniforms to be sure you always have a clean one available. Wear only uniforms that look crisp and clean. Replace a uniform when the fabric or color begins to wear. Wear shoes that are appropriate for the uniform. Do not overaccessorize a uniform with scarves, jewelry, and so on.

Business Dress for Women

Business Professional

- Suits
  - Business skirt or dress and jacket
  - Business pantsuit
  - Dark colors (black, navy blue, or gray)
  - Knee-length dresses and skirts
- Blouses
  - Long-sleeved
  - White or light colors
  - Solid or thin-striped
- Shoes
  - Black or navy blue
  - Closed toes and heels
  - Half-inch heel or plain flats
  - Well polished
- Hoisery
  - Neutral-toned nylons with skirts or dresses
  - Trouser socks with slacks
- Makeup
  - Lightly applied, natural look
- Nails
  - Short to medium length

- Manicured
- Fresh, light polish or no polish
  - Jewelry
    - One pair of small earrings
    - No other piercings with rings
    - One ring or one ring per hand
    - Thin bracelet or necklace (optional)

Business Casual

Dress slacks or khakis, less formal business dresses or skirts and blouses.

"Before even uttering a word your visual image will say a multitude about you as an individual and about the organization you represent."

Nina Jamal, AICI, Image Communications Consultant

Source: Retrieved November 14, 2013, from www. businessknowhow.com/growth/ dress-impression.htm.

Business Dress for Men

Business Professional

- Suits
  - Single-breasted jacket
  - Cuffed pants
  - Solid or thin pinstripe
  - Dark colors (black, navy blue, or gray)
- Dress shirts
  - Long-sleeved with an undershirt
  - White, light blue, or yellow
  - Solid or thin-striped
- Ties
  - Conservative, small pattern or striped
  - Silk
  - Belt length
  - Conservative colors
- Dress shoes
  - Black, cordovan, or brown
  - Laced style
  - Well polished
- Socks
  - Over the calf, trouser style
  - Dark color to match suit
- Belt
  - Leather belt to match shoe color
  - Small belt buckle
- Jewelry
  - One ring
  - Plain watch

Business Casual

Dress slacks or khakis with or without a blazer, button-down shirt or polo shirt, dress loafers with socks.

Use good judgment when dressing for company social events whether the event is formal or casual.

If you are invited to attend a sporting event or a cookout, choose nice casual clothing. Avoid jeans; wear casual slacks instead. Don't wear T-shirts that have writing or pictures on them; wear polo shirts or short-sleeved blouses instead. You want to portray a neat, yet stylish, image and avoid clothing that is sloppy or revealing.

Dress according to your personality and body type. Choose clothes because they complement your figure, not just because they are in style. Remember that dark (black, brown, gray) colors minimize size, while light colors (white, pink, peach) and warm colors (red, purple, yellow) maximize size.

Grooming and Dress on a Budget   Not everyone can spend a lot of money on expensive hair stylists or clothes when preparing for a job interview. You don't have to spend a lot to pull together a great look. Here are some tips:

- Buy discount clothing. There are great outlet stores in most locations or discount stores that sell clothing styles you need for your interviews at affordable prices.
- Check out reputable clothing resale shops.
- Buy one or two outfits. You need one for a first interview and a second one for a second interview. You can wear these outfits, if properly laundered, from interview to interview.

Some cosmetology schools invite the public in for free hair appointments from time to time. If you can take advantage of this kind of opportunity, just be sure to tell the stylist that you need a conservative look for a job interview.

ACTIVITY 4.8

Business Wardrobe Inventory

Complete the following wardrobe inventory to determine what pieces of business attire you have and what pieces you are missing or need to refresh. Indicate an approximate cost for what you need. This will help you plan to buy only what you need and budget properly for each purchase.

Women		Men	
Suits	$_____	Suits	$_____
Blazers	_____	Blazers	_____
Blouses	_____	Dress shirts	_____
Sweaters	_____	Sweaters	_____
Skirts	_____	Dress slacks	_____
Dresses	_____	Pants	_____
Slacks	_____	Coats	_____
Coats	_____	Shoes	_____
Shoes	_____	Boots	_____
Boots	_____	Hats	_____
Handbags	_____	Belts	_____
Belts	_____	Ties	_____
Scarves	_____	Scarves	_____
Gloves	_____	Gloves	_____
TOTAL:	$_____	TOTAL:	$_____

Regional Differences   In different parts of the country, professional dress may vary according to a region's culture or climate. The North and Northeast are generally the most conservative in business dress, reflecting the overall conservative attitude in these areas.

The colder climate also influences the selection of colors and fabrics. Colors tend to be darker and fabrics heavier (wool, gabardine, polyester blends). The South is not as conservative but is somewhat more formal in its attitude toward dress. In this warmer climate, colors and fabrics tend to be lighter (cotton, linen, silks).

The hotter climates of the West and Southwest tend to dictate less formal attire and, certainly, lighter fabrics and colors. However, it is important to note some things about this region. Even though the hot climate may be suitable for lighter-weight clothes, it does not give you license to wear low-cut, sheer, or see-through (voile, lace) clothing. These are simply not appropriate at any time in any business setting.

Accessories

Clothing accessories. Accessories that complement your business dress can complete, and help personalize, your professional look. When colorful clothing is the trend, you can use colorful accessories to express yourself. Scarves add color and soften dark-colored suits. A simple, understated lapel pin brightens a dark jacket, as long as the style is subdued.

In addition to clothing accessories, there are other items that you can carry at work or on an interview that are both useful and enhance your professional image.

iPads. You might consider bringing your iPad with you so that you can show examples of work in your online portfolio. Your iPad might also be useful for accessing your calendar should you need to check on dates during your meetings or interviews. If you do carry your iPad for business, buy an iPad case that is a solid, dark color. Save the neon and animal print versions for your personal use. If you bring your mobile phone, keep it off until you need to access the information you need and then turn it off again.

Leather-bound notebook. These can be used for holding notepads and documents you may need.

Briefcase: Regardless of the position you hold at work, using a briefcase is the best way to carry your paperwork, iPad, computer, or other items. Briefcases are not limited to use by executives; they are a useful and efficient way for almost everyone to keep important information and professional tools organized.

Dress can help you present a positive self-image if you choose clothing that is appropriate to your job, the area you live in, and your body type. Dress is a great form of self-expression and can reflect your individuality. How you dress can tell a lot about you and help you project confidence and pride in yourself.

◦• 4.4 PERSONAL FINANCES

Your ability to manage your personal finances tells a lot about your priorities, values, self-discipline, and overall ability to manage yourself. While good financial management skills are important to ensuring you have adequate personal financial resources for your lifestyle, they also impact your reputation and your ability to be hired by some companies.

SAVINGS

Having a plan to save money for your future is one of the most important habits you can develop. Establish an automatic deposit from each payroll check to a savings account.

Even small amounts are worth it because it will build over time. You should have a goal not to depend on your savings account for your monthly living expenses if you can.

BUDGETING

People make purchasing decisions they can't afford every day. Determining how much you can afford to spend once your monthly financial obligations are met is the first step to managing your money well. Include your monthly savings in the calculation as an obligation to yourself. You are probably familiar with the phrase "live within your means." Simply put, don't spend more than you earn and don't rely on credit as the extra money that you don't have. Make choices. Decide what things you can do without. If you really need or want something you can't afford right now, save for it as opposed to buying it on credit. When you learn these basic principles early and practice them regularly, you will become a good manager of your money. Everyone's actual budget dollars vary according to current income levels and the exact amount of take-home pay. Similarly, everyone's expense dollars are not exactly the same. So as you think about preparing your budget you can individualize it according to your situation.

The following sample budget worksheet is one example of how to approach your personal budgeting:

Type of Expense

- Housing: a mortgage, lease or rent, taxes, and insurance
- Transportation: car loans, gas, insurance, maintenance, parking or tolls, commuter passes, and rail cards
- Debt: credit cards, student loans, and other types of loans
- Food: grocery items including toiletries and other items used daily; restaurant or take-out food
- Household: energy, phone, and cable bills
- Savings: for something short term, like a vacation, or something long term, like retirement
- All others: clothing, charities, child or elder care, routine medical expenses, and miscellaneous monthly expenses

ACTIVITY 4.9

Your Budget Worksheet

To calculate the dollar amount of your expenses each pay period, enter the amount of your total take-home pay per pay period and multiply it by the recommended percentage allocated to each major expense item.

Your Total Take-Home Pay per Pay Period = $_____	% × Your Total Take-Home Pay per Pay Period	Total Dollars per Pay Period
Housing	30% × $_____ =	_____
Transportation	18% × $_____ =	_____
Debt	10% × $_____ =	_____
Food	14% × $_____ =	_____
Household	7% × $_____ =	_____
Savings	10% × $_____ =	_____
All other	11% × $_____ =	_____

Now, write in and calculate your approximate monthly and annual itemized expenses.

	Monthly Total	Annual Total
Housing		
Mortgage, lease, or rent		
Taxes		
Insurance		
Transportation		
Car loan		
Gas		
Car insurance		
Maintenance		
Parking/tolls		
Commuter pass		
Rail card		
Debt		
Credit card		
School loans		
Food and groceries		
Household		
Phone		
Cable		
Energy		
Savings		
Vacation		
Purchases		
Retirement		
Other		
Clothing		
Medical		
Charity		
Child or elder care		
Miscellaneous monthly expenses		

DEBT MANAGEMENT

Most debt can and should be avoided. There is such a thing as good and bad debt. For example, your student loans are an example of good debt because when you graduate there is a return on your investment. We saw in Chapter 1 the incremental increases in lifetime earnings related to degree attainment. Because your earning potential is significantly enhanced by earning your degree, your choice to borrow money to fund your education is a good, long-term investment. Credit card debt, if not managed properly, is an example of bad debt.

CREDIT SCORES

There is a double risk to you associated with credit card debt. The first is the financial threat posed to you if the debt is maintained over a long period of time. The second is your reputation. Your credit rating is a publicly held record that can be accessed by anyone who might be loaning you money. A poor credit rating can impact many aspects of your life. It can stop you from receiving education loans, a home mortgage, a cell phone account, or a car loan. More importantly, it damages your reputation for a long time. (Figure 4.5).[3]

Employers often conduct background checks, which include inquiries about a candidate's credit rating. Employers check credit scores for a variety of reasons. The way you manage your credit can be an indicator of your honesty and character. For example, banks and investment firms and other companies that require handling large sums of money view poor credit as a risk for theft. How you manage your personal finances tells what type of person you are. Because your credit profile also contains your employment history,

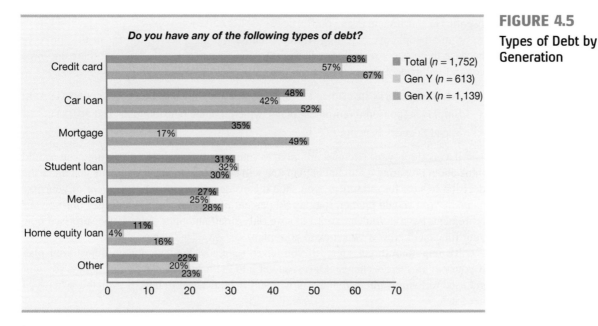

FIGURE 4.5

Types of Debt by Generation

[3] American Savings Education Council and AARP. (March 2008). "Preparing for Their Future: A Look at the Financial State of Gen X and Gen Y." Retrieved September 1, 2009, from www.choosetosave.org/pdf/preparing.pdf.

FIGURE 4.6

How Your FICO Credit Score Is Calculated

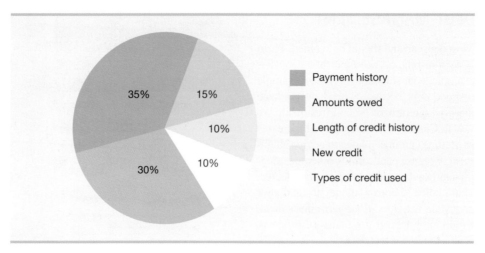

- Payment history
- Amounts owed
- Length of credit history
- New credit
- Types of credit used

employers may use it as a way to verify your previous employment. On the other hand, a good credit score can work in your favor.

There are simple steps you can take to manage your debt. Maintain a checking account, and try to pay everything you can from that account on a monthly basis. If you need to have a credit card, have only one. It is so easy to be tempted to apply for more cards because there are always great promotions to tempt you to open a new account. Better than a credit card is a debit card. The debit card enables you to draw money or to have the cost of a purchase charged directly to your bank account. It is used as an alternative method to paying cash. Using a debit card is the safest way to manage your spending as long as you are able to limit your spending to the amount available to you. Credit and debit cards and checking accounts are not a threat to your financial reputation if you use them properly.

> "It's still standard practice for many employers to look to your credit history as one indicator of future job performance."
>
> Jill Krasny, Credit.com

Source: Retrieved November 14, 2013, from http://blog.credit.com/" \t "_blank" Jill Krasny, Credit.com; http://money.msn.com/credit-rating/3-jobs-where-good-credit-counts.

Your Credit Score   Figure 4.6 shows what makes up your credit score. You need to be aware of the areas that can impact your score negatively or positively to be able to manage them. The myFICO.com website is a comprehensive site that provides useful information about credit scores and related credit management topics.[4]

Planning for Your Future   It is not a surprise that interest in retirement savings grows with your age. It's hard to think about yourself being in your sixties when you are in your twenties or thirties and even your forties.

Some people avoid getting started because the need seems too far in the future or because the process seems complicated. As you get started, be aware that there are three common sources of income for retirement.

- Private savings or investments, which include individual retirement accounts (IRAs).
- Employer-sponsored retirement plans, which include pension plans and 401(k)s.
- Social Security benefits.

If you are in your twenties and plan to retire in your mid- to late sixties, you should think about preparing a retirement plan that will cover at least 20 years. Once you make the decision to save for retirement, you should consider saving about 10 percent of your pay annually. You should plan on roughly 80 percent of your annual working pay during your retirement. Even if you can afford to save only small amounts, you will be surprised how your funds will grow if you stick to your plan.

It's important to get started if you haven't already. You can always adjust your plan if your circumstances change. Once you get into the habit of saving your money, you will get used to living without it and you will surely be pleased to have it available when you need it.

[4]MyFICO.com. (2009). Retrieved August 31, 2009, from www.myfico.com/Default.aspx.

Think about the preceding personal finance skills. List two things you think you currently do well.

EXAMPLE

Savings

Budgeting

_____

_____

Identify a personal financial goal.

EXAMPLE

Debt management

Retirement planning

_____

_____

_____

Goal: _____
Write how your goal is:
Specific _____
Measurable _____
Achievable _____
Realistic _____
Timely _____

ACTIVITY 4.10

Set a SMART goal for Improving Personal Finance Skills

Throughout your life and your career, you will continue to develop many important self-management skills. Some you may develop through further education in the classroom. You will also have the opportunity to improve self-management skills by participating in workshops or seminars. Perhaps the most effective way to ensure your continuous development of these important skills is by practicing them in your daily home, work, and social life. It takes repetition to form habits that can result in the behavioral changes you want to make.

This chapter focused on the importance of self-improvement in communication, time and stress management, presenting a professional image, and managing personal finances through the use of goal setting. By applying the goal-setting method you learned in Chapter 3, you gained practice in how to set self-improvement goals. You should now be aware of more aspects of verbal, nonverbal, professional online, and visual communication, and what particular skills in each area you think you need to work on. Managing time and stress is critical to success in your career and your life. Not enough people take the time to develop a plan that they can stick with to overcome problems with managing their time and their stress. Not having these two areas under your control can be damaging to your career and your health. Time and stress management are closely connected. When you are successfully managing your time, you will probably be less stressed. When you are stressed, it can interfere with your ability to stay focused on your time management plan. Keeping physically fit can help a great deal in both of these areas. Many of the same techniques for managing your time also apply to managing your stress.

Presenting a good image by practicing good grooming habits and dressing appropriately for job search and workplace situations will ensure you make a positive impression with employers and may help them see you as a serious job candidate.

While managing personal finances has always been a critical life and career skill, its importance has been made more prominent in recent years in light of an unstable economy that impacts personal finances. Knowing how to manage your personal finances is important to many aspects of your life. Being financially responsible for your personal money reflects positively on your reputation and sets the stage for you to better manage your future financial needs as you get older. A big key to managing

CHAPTER SUMMARY

your personal finances well is staying out of debt. Debt can burden you for a long time and negatively impact many aspects of your life and your well-being. The next key is to plan for the future. If you are young, you may think that planning for your retirement can wait. It can, but the longer you wait to start, the less chance you will have to catch up on those missed savings that could diminish your financial potential later in life.

You will probably find these areas to be a focus of some of your interview questions when you apply for a job. As employers told us in the Partnership for 21st Century Skills report, these are among the critical self-management skills necessary for career success. Taking control of these areas and managing them well should be your goal.

REFLECTION EXERCISE

PERSONAL DEVELOPMENT AND CAREER DECISION MAKING

Using the decision-making process you learned in Chapter 3, complete the following questions to better understand how communication skills, time and stress management skills, good grooming and dress skills, and personal finance skills might be connected to your career decisions.

1. What am I trying to decide?

Example: I am trying to decide how to better balance my time at work, home, and school.

Example: I am trying to decide whether or not I can afford a mortgage or if renting is a better option for me right now.

_____

_____

_____

2. What do I need to know?

Example: I need to know how I am currently spending my time, what amount of time I consider to be appropriate, and what distracts me from managing my time.

Example: I need to know what my monthly expenses are compared to my income.

_____

_____

_____

3. How will it help me make a more informed career decision?

Example: By better managing my time I can choose jobs that match the amount of time I can or want to dedicate to my career.

Example: I can consider whether the current salary I am earning now supports my decision or whether I need to consider a higher-paying job in the future.

_____

_____

_____

4. How can I obtain what I need to know?

People

Example: My teachers, the training coordinator at my company, a friend, a family member.

Example: My math or finance teacher, a customer service person at my bank, my parents or spouse, a financial advisor.

_____

_____

_____

Experience

> *Example:* A workshop on time management can help me improve my time
> management skills.
>
> *Example:* Calculating my current budget and the budget I need to afford a mortgage
> will tell me if I can meet all of my financial obligations if I am responsible for a
> mortgage.

_____

_____

_____

Research

> *Example:* I can explore online resources that provide useful advice on time
> management.
>
> *Example:* I can explore online resources that provide useful information on
> budgeting for and financing a mortgage.

_____

_____

_____

5. Who are my best resources for the information I need?
   Example: My teachers and my training coordinator at work.
   Example: The customer service person at my bank would be the best resource or one
   of my math or finance teachers.

_____

_____

_____

Now that you have practiced reflecting on what you learned in Chapter 4 and seeing how to apply it
in your career decision-making process, using examples, you will be able to repeat this process on
your own in future chapters. You are on your way to further developing how to apply career decision-
making skills, which are transferable skills that you will apply throughout your career.

"A career is no longer a race up the ladder, it's a collection of experiences."

Dan Schawbel, managing partner, Millennial Branding[1]

[1]Retrieved March 15, 2013, from www.personalbrandingblog.com/quotes/.

Career and Job Research Tools

After completing this chapter, you will:

1   **Explore** industry career trends

2   **Describe** types of career paths

3   **Conduct** industry and company research

4   **Conduct** job research

Exploring different types of careers, companies, and jobs helps you consider a wide range of career options. This is important because the career path you select now isn't necessarily one you will follow for a lifetime. You may discover new career interests and opportunities as you gain experience in a particular job or industry. A career path is a way of identifying both your ultimate career goal and the set of job experiences that might take you there. It is important to have realistic expectations about levels of jobs along the way. Some will advance your experience and knowledge, while others will advance your position and salary. What's important is to focus on how each job fits into the larger picture of your overall career plan.

In this chapter, you will learn how people, experiences, and other resources provide the information you need to explore industries, companies, and job opportunities.

CASE STUDY

Linda's Tool Kit—People and Technology

Linda completed her nursing degree and wanted to gain some work experience before applying for a full-time nursing position. She was working full time as an office manager for an insurance company, a position she held for the last 10 years while raising her daughter and attending nursing school part time. Linda was open to working in a variety of settings. She searched the Internet for job postings in her area to keep informed about the various types of nursing jobs available. She knew from fellow adult students, also making a career change, that it was sometimes difficult to find a job in a new field without some work experience. Even though the job market was very good for nurses in the state she lived in, Linda decided to work for a temporary services agency that specialized in placing nurses and obtained a weekend job as a visiting nurse.

Linda had her profile posted on Facebook and LinkedIn. On LinkedIn, she connected with others in the nursing field and sometimes learned of open positions. One weekend, Linda had lunch with a friend who connected her to a relative with a job lead for a nurse at the children's hospital where he worked. The children's hospital encouraged employees to refer qualified individuals to open positions through its employee referral program. Her contact explained that although Linda would still need to follow the company's policy to apply directly online, she would probably obtain an interview since she was referred directly through the employee referral program. The hospital preferred to hire qualified people referred by reputable employees. In the meantime, Linda also received an e-mail from another insurance agency about an available position. The company had several hundred employees working at the home office which was located a few miles from where Linda lived. The e-mail described a position for a corporate nurse to work Monday through Friday, providing basic on-site health services for employees. The company found Linda through a passive search online. The company regularly used the Internet to find people it might be interested in hiring, regardless of whether the candidate expressed interest in the company. It used an online service that made it possible to search resume databases and profiles on websites, such as LinkedIn. The company used this system to build a list of potential candidates to have available for key positions, even when there were no job openings. This time, the system found Linda as a perfect match. Linda accepted the position and now had firsthand experience with the importance of both people and technology in her career tool kit.

Discussion Questions

1. Can you identify direct and indirect sources of job information available to Linda?
2. What other resources could Linda have used to further explore the hidden job market?
3. What do think are some advantages to an employee referral program for a company?

5.1 INDUSTRY CAREER TRENDS

Researching industries and career trends helps you understand your career options. Reliable resources for industry information include the Bureau of Labor Statistics and professional associations such as the National Association of Colleges and Employers (NACE). Chapter 1 reviewed how the economy, trends, and events affect industry growth or decline and new job creation (Figure 5.1). As you conduct your own research you will learn more about how this applies to your areas of interest. You should include in your research a look at high-growth industries, emerging careers, and steady-growth careers.

HIGH-GROWTH CAREERS

High-growth careers are defined by both the rate of growth and the actual numbers of jobs. Rate of growth refers to the percentage change in jobs while actual number of jobs refers to the numeric change. Both are important to gaining a full perspective of high-growth careers. There are many ways to depict high-growth careers. Figure 5.2 considers rate of growth and the impact of degree attainment on numeric growth.

FIGURE 5.1

Trends and Events Affect Industries and Job Creation

Social media

Technology   Identity theft

Terror threats   Medicare

Hurricanes   Elder care

Presidential elections

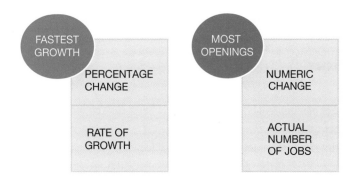

FIGURE 5.2

Evaluating Change in the Job Market

Source: Retrieved July 3, 2013, from www.bls.gov/ooh/About/Projections-Overview.htm.

Fast-Growing Industries by Percentage Change through 2020

Construction 33%
Health care 29%
Professional and technical services 29%
Personal care services 27%
Computer information technology 22%

Business and finance 17%
Educational services 14%
Media communications 13%
Food service 10%
Arts and design 10%

As you can see by comparing these two charts, you need to consider both the percentage change and the numeric change in new positions. In a smaller field, for example Software development, a jump in positions that is relatively small in number can look larger as a percentage. Be sure when you're looking into a "growing field," that it's growing in raw numbers of positions.

2010–2020

Openings Requiring a Bachelor's or Associate's Degree	Numeric Changes in Total Employment
Registered nurses	3,349,000
General and operations managers	1,849,000
Construction managers	610,000
Preschool teachers, except special education	571,000
Paralegal and legal assistants	303,000
Radiologic technologists and technicians	281,000
Dental hygienists	250,000
Elementary school teachers, except special education	248,000
Accountants and auditors	191,000
Management analysts	157,000
Respiratory therapists	144,000
Software developers, applications	144,000

Source: Retrieved July 3, 2013, from http://data.bls.gov/oep/noeted.

Biometrics: "the measurement and analysis of unique physical or behavioral characteristics (as fingerprint or voice patterns) especially as a means of verifying personal identity."

Merriam-Webster.com [2]

[2]Retrieved June 8, 2013, from www.merriam-webster.com/dictionary/biometrics.

New careers and career types are being created all the time, and it's a good idea to stay on top of the latest trends and titles.

Emerging Careers

Cybersecurity

- Brand protection analyst
- Internet fraud analyst
- Security penetration tester
- Application security specialist

Homeland Security

- Biometrics analyst
- Intelligence analyst
- Cryptanalyst
- Transportation security specialist

Social Media Marketing

- Social media security specialist
- Global search engine optimization (SEO) specialist

- Search marketing strategist
- Web marketing analyst

IT Development and Design

- iPhone game designer
- Infographics analyst
- Visual artist
- Graphic journalist

Health Care

- Nurse informatician
- Health information technician
- Chronic illness coach
- Speech pathologist

> "Take pride in what you do and don't be afraid to take risks."
>
> Deepti Sharma Kapur
> Founder, FoodToEat.com
>
> Source: www.forbes.com/sites/ deniserestauri/2013/11/04/ this-20-something-ditched-law-school-and-a-life-in-politics-for-a-new-york-cupcake/.

STEADY-GROWTH CAREERS

> "Think beyond traditional career opportunities . . . prepare for future careers."
>
> *Allen Tate*, American poet[3]

Accounting   Career opportunities in accounting usually remain high regardless of the state of the eceonomy. The advice that accountants provide is often the most important information for business decision making. Individuals also rely on the best financial advice to make well-informed decisions regarding their investments. The fastest-growing jobs in the accounting field include consultants and credit specialists. Public accountants, management accountants, government accountants, and internal auditors are always in demand.

Customer Service   The customer service representative's job can take on various functions, ranging from resolving customer complaints to generating new business through new sales to servicing existing customer accounts. Customer service representatives are key to providing important customer feedback that can help drive business planning. Some companies staff this role within their organization, while many outsource this function.

Entrepreneurship   As many large corporations continue to downsize and restructure, and more small to medium-sized firms emerge, the opportunities for entrepreneurs continue to multiply. Most entrepreneurs own businesses involved in delivering services or creating and manufacturing products. Entrepreneurs must be resourceful to bring the right combination of talent to their businesses.

Hospitality   Careers in hotel management continue to grow. A wider range of leisure industry careers spans opportunities in sports, entertainment, and event

[3]Retrieved March 28, 2013, from www.careerthoughtleaders.com/blog/8-emerging-careers-from-2012/.

management, recreation and travel, spa management, golf management, and careers in the gaming industry. Careers in management of life care facilities will continue to grow in response to changing lifestyle needs of the older population.

Marketing   Businesses depend on creative marketing strategies to differentiate themselves to customers. Advertising, marketing, promotions, public relations, and sales managers are needed to coordinate market research, marketing strategy, sales, advertising, promotion, pricing, product development, and public relations activities. Brand management has emerged as a leading sector in the marketing industry. It focuses on identifying the brand essence of a business, mapping out competitors in the brand's category, creating marketing strategies, and communicating the unique benefits of that product or service. Career growth in marketing is a result of domestic and global competition in products and services offered to consumers.

Offce and Administrative Support   The demand for administrative services managers, responsible for a broad range of duties in virtually every sector of the economy, will increase. Administrative services managers coordinate and direct support services to organizations as diverse as insurance companies, computer manufacturers, and government agencies.

Retail   The faster-growing segments of the retail career field include e-commerce, catalog sales, and the Internet. Consumer spending on retail goods accounts for a major portion of the nation's gross domestic product.

5.2 CAREER PATHS

Understanding career paths can play a significant role in your career decision making. For example, being well informed on the types of jobs that fit into a variety of career paths can help you better understand how roles compare across a company and where you fit in. Your knowledge of career paths and how they work in different companies makes it easier for you to explore and create diverse career options and develop realistic career goals. The information that follows will help you understand how career paths can be different from one another. You can apply what you learn by writing two sample types of career paths and defining your own career path inventory that can guide you once you begin your job search.

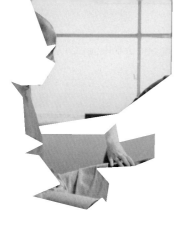

JOB VERSUS CAREER

Many people have difficulty understanding the difference between a job and a career. Since it is an important part of making good career decisions, you should take some time to review your own thoughts about the relationship between jobs and careers and what it means to you.

Generally, a job can be a distinct period of employment, not necessarily related to a previous or future job. A career is made up of a path of jobs that are usually related. For some, a career is a planned, logical progression of jobs within one or more professions that can span the majority of your working life. For others, a career is a group of related experiences, not necessarily on a straight path. Your jobs might either take you to a desired, long-term goal or help you build experiences that modify your original goal. In most cases, a career is a life-long process that can take you to planned or unexpected experiences that help you fulfill a passion, make a positive contribution to your community, and ensure a comfortable living.

While you are planning your job search, think about what is important to you. While it helps to have a clear goal established, you may still be unsure of the exact career path you would like to pursue. Your job choice can help you "test run" your career preferences and help you decide what is right for you. Whether you prefer to pursue a career or a job is a personal decision that you make. Your choice really depends on what your view of work is for yourself. One is not more valid than the other. Initially, you might accept a job to gain needed financial income or experience. Over the long term, you should maximize the value of your education by identifying a career path that will challenge you and help you grow over your years of work. For many, work and personal life become closely intertwined as shown in Figure 5.3.

"In September, we launched a multi-channel initiative, also referred to as omni-channel technology."

Kay Krill, CEO, ANN (Ann Taylor) Inc.

Source: www.forbes.com/sites/jennagoudreau/2012/12/05/ann-taylor-ceo-reveals-her-most-important-career-lesson/.

FIGURE 5.3

Work as Part of Life

Source: Copyright © 2007. Deloitte Development LLC, from Mass Career Customization: Aligning the Workplace with Today's Non-traditional Workforce. All rights reserved.

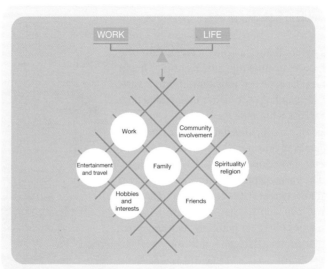

TYPES OF CAREER PATHS

One way to think about types of career paths is to visualize a ladder or steps moving in an upward direction. Another way is to visualize a web or the pattern of a chain-link fence where the design zigzags up, down, and across. There are many ways to get to different points, and no way is necessarily right or wrong. Career ladders are usually depicted as linear jobs that move from the bottom up, with increased responsibilities through each phase. While this traditional type of career path is still common today, many companies have developed more flexible and personalized career paths, which are frequently referred to as career lattices. Figure 5.4 summarizes some of the differences between laddered and latticed career paths.

Laddered Career Paths   In an organization that promotes career ladders, you might expect more predictable career moves from an entry level to senior role over a period of time. There are defined experiences that are spelled out that are critical steps to moving up the "corporate ladder." This type of environment works well for you if you have a clearly defined career goal in a specialized area and are fairly certain that you would like to advance upward to a top position in your field. In an entry-level phase of your career, you will probably be more of a generalist, being trained in and being exposed to a wide range of roles and responsibilities. The purpose is to acquaint you with an overall picture of your job and how it fits into the company. The first phase is meant to provide you with work experience that prepares you for the next job level over a period of time that may last anywhere from six months to a few years.

The second phase of your career will be characterized by jobs that are more specialized. You can expect to spend a few years in midmanagement and/or specialized jobs. Specialists play a significant role in the company because senior management relies so heavily on the expertise and specific knowledge of individuals in specialized roles. A rewarding career can result in maintaining jobs within this area because they are highly interesting, make use of your special skills, and have a tremendous impact on keeping the company current enough to maintain a competitive edge.

The third phase of your career would likely be management, which moves you back to a more generalist position with significant responsibility and authority. Each job prepares you for the next, more advanced, better-paying job. The example in Figure 5.5 represents a career path that is more laddered than latticed.

"A career is now a checkerboard."

Tom Peters, business consultant

Source: Retrieved November 14, 2013, from www.fastcompany. com/28905/brand-called-you.

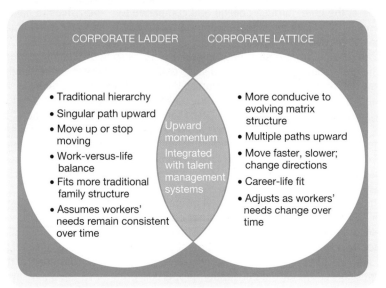

CORPORATE LADDER   CORPORATE LATTICE

- Traditional hierarchy
- Singular path upward
- Move up or stop moving
- Work-versus-life balance
- Fits more traditional family structure
- Assumes workers' needs remain consistent over time

Upward momentum

Integrated with talent management systems

- More conducive to evolving matrix structure
- Multiple paths upward
- Move faster, slower; change directions
- Career-life fit
- Adjusts as workers' needs change over time

FIGURE 5.4

Ladder versus Lattice

Source: Copyright © 2007. Deloitte Development LLC, from Mass Career Customization: Aligning the Workplace with Today's Non-traditional Workforce. All rights reserved.

FIGURE 5.5

Sample Laddered
Hospitality Career Path

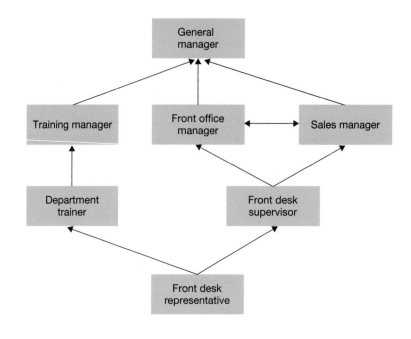

Real Life Stories

Hospitality Career Ladder

In high school, Juan worked at a local hotel during his summer vacations. He worked in a number of seasonal positions to earn some extra money to help pay for his tuition. He liked working with people and enjoyed the energy and fast pace of the hotel environment. He spent most of his time near the reception area since he rotated between working as a bellman and parking attendant. He observed the day-to-day interaction that the front desk staff had with the guests and began to realize what an important role they played with ensuring that the guests were satisfied with their stay. Juan enrolled in a Hospitality Management program at the college where many of the hotel staff had graduated from. He continued to work part time at the hotel through college and completed two internships to have some meaningful work experience when he was ready to apply for a full-time position at graduation.

He completed a front desk internship and an internship in the rooms division. When he graduated, he was hired as a sales assistant. He really liked the hotel company, which had hundreds of properties throughout the United States. To Juan, this meant that there would likely be many career experiences at different types of hotels within the same company. His next job was sales manager at one of the smaller economy hotels. He wanted to vary his experience and applied for a sales manager's position at a larger convention hotel that did three times the amount of annual sales as the smaller property he started at. He was hired and soon became responsible for event booking at 15 hotel properties. Juan wanted to add one more experience to his resume.

He moved on to a small luxury hotel property as a senior sales manager. By now, Juan had created a variety of career options for himself. He could continue in a sales role at any one of the hotels within the company. He could also plan a next step to a general manager's position at any of the three types of hotel properties. Juan decided to take that next step and was promoted to a general manager's position at one of the convention properties, an area where Juan saw a lot of challenge, a work environment that he favored, and much room for further career growth.

Latticed Career Paths   Companies are now moving toward more flexible models of career advancement to be more responsive to the changing needs of both the company and individuals over time. This has become a key strategy to attracting and retaining Generation Y talent who look for more career customization or opportunities to build individual career plans. In latticed career paths, the employer and the employee work together in partnership to develop an individualized career plan. As a result, more career-long options can be developed for individuals creating a stronger connection to the employer. This helps build more company loyalty and the tendency for individuals to stay longer with their employer. The new latticed model is flexible and involves career-long learning and relearning in the workplace. The TJX Companies, Inc.; Deloitte USA, LLP; and Ogilvy and Mather, one of the world's largest marketing communications organization, are examples of companies committed to building latticed career pathing for their employees. The latticed model also works very well in smaller businesses. The nursing and teaching professions use the career latticed approach to career development to provide accomplished teachers and nurses with opportunities for career growth where they do not have to move out of a classroom or nursing practice.

The flexibility in latticed career paths makes it easier to adjust career decisions to better match your personal priorities as they change throughout different phases of your life. The example in Figure 5.6 represents a career path that is more latticed than laddered.

"The corporate lattice metaphor signals a shift in mindset. It's better reflective of today's employees, who want variety and flexibility and reject a one-size-fits-all approach."

Barry Salzberg, CEO, Deloitte USA, LLP

Source: Retrieved November 12, 2013, from http://knowledge. wharton.upenn.edu/article/ deloitte-ceo-barry-salzberg-on-leadership-as-the-norm-not-the-exception/.

Real Life Stories

Information Technology Career Lattice

Sarosh was enrolled in a technology program but was not yet sure what he wanted to do. He liked his part-time jobs as a repair technician in a computer store and at the computer lab help desk at school. He always had a curious mind and enjoyed troubleshooting to resolve problems with systems or processes. When Sarosh was an information technology (IT) intern at a bank, part of his assignment was to interview two people to learn about their IT career paths. He decided to interview Adam, the IT manager, and Shabri, the database administrator. He asked them to describe their career paths.

Adam started as a computer support specialist and soon moved on to become a computer programmer. His next jobs were in network systems starting as an analyst and then moving into an administrator role, which he enjoyed and found challenging. It allowed him to use many transferable skills, in addition to his technical skills. He enjoyed mentoring team members and leading the annual planning and budgeting process with the team. He became known as a leader with excellent communication and decision-making skills. His next role was IT consultant, which led him to his current position as the IT manager.

Shabri's career path was very different. She also started as a computer support specialist and, like Adam, moved on to a computer programmer's position. She really enjoyed the detail of her project work and wanted to further develop her technical skills. She spent time as a network systems and data communications analyst, until she assumed the role of database administrator. Shabri preferred her lead role in a specialized area to the management track that Adam took. She was easily frustrated with difficult to manage staff members and did not have the patience to work with the staff through planning and budgeting exercises. As database manager, she had a small staff and her interaction with them was mostly helping them resolve technical issues and find new ways to upgrade systems and processes. Both Adam and Shabri were satisfied with the different paths they chose. The contrast in interests and their experiences demonstrated to Sarosh that successful career progression did not always mean working up the corporate ladder but that lateral moves can be just as satisfying.

FIGURE 5.6

Sample Latticed
Information Technology
Career Path

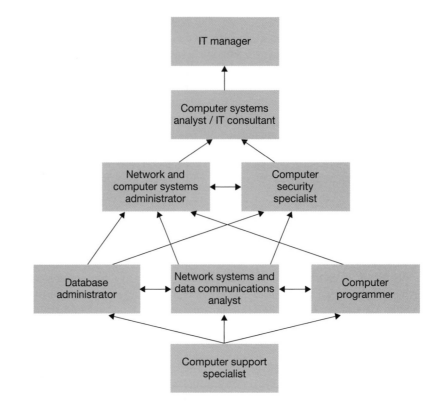

ACTIVITY 5.1

**Identifying Types of
Career Paths**

Write an example of a career ladder and lattice for long-term health care either
using the diagram (Figure 5.7) or researching more long-term health care career
paths in the *Career Directions Handbook* or the Internet.

Refer to the health care career paths in the *Career Directions Handbook* and on the
Internet. To identify a career ladder in this field, choose one career area within the
health care career paths and write down a list of jobs that move from bottom to top
to represent a career ladder within that single career area. To identify a career lattice
in this field, choose one or more career areas within the health care career paths
and write down a list of two or more jobs across these health care career areas that
might represent a latticed career path within a few different areas.

HEALTH CARE

Sample Career Ladder	**Sample Career Lattice**
(Jobs move from bottom to top in one career area)	(Jobs move across from one career area to another)

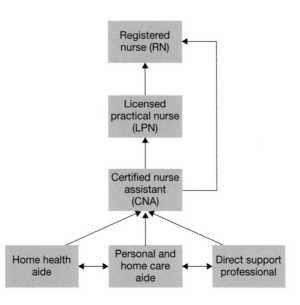

FIGURE 5.7

Sample Career Path: Long-Term Health Care

5.3 INDUSTRY, COMPANY, AND JOB RESEARCH

Making use of a variety of research tools can help provide a more complete picture of the industries, companies, and jobs you explore. Often, the first thing we associate with research is going online or reading printed materials. We sometimes overlook people and experiences that can help complete the picture. To simplify your research, the *Career Directions Handbook* contains career information on a wide variety of industries including over 1,000 job descriptions. All of these resources become part of your research tool kit.

"The only way to do great work is to love what you do."

Steve Jobs, former co-founder and CEO, Apple Inc.[4]

YOUR RESEARCH TOOL KIT

People   Word of mouth, face-to-face exchanges, and speaking firsthand with people in the know are effective ways to conduct career research. People in the know might include industry experts, alumni and classmates, current and past employers, mentors, teachers, counselors, community leaders, friends, neighbors, relatives, or coworkers.

Experiences   Work experiences—including co-op or internship programs; study abroad programs; home management experience; or club, organization, or volunteer experiences may link you to people or information helpful to your research.

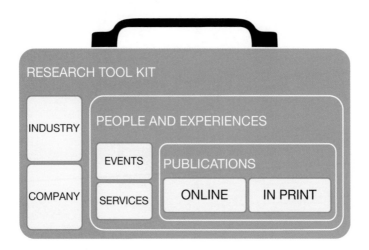

Events Career fairs, industry and professional association events, campus interviews, informational interviews, sporting and community events, and other social events are opportunities to conduct research with individuals who may be knowledgeable about industry and company trends and able to connect you to job leads.

Services Career services, employment agencies, government employment offices, state and local employment agencies, and employee referral programs are other reliable sources.

Printed Resources and Online Resources Business directories, the Encyclopedia of Associations, professional and trade association websites, magazines and trade journals, lists of new firms with 100 employees or fewer, and company literature and annual reports, available in print or online, provide current and accurate research information.

EXAMPLES OF RESEARCH TOOLS ONLINE
Bureau of Labor Statistics
Career Voyages
O*NET OnLine
Yahoo! Business and Economy
Career OneStop
Hoover's Online Vault

For more information on online resources visit **www.mhhe.com/yena6e.**

Not familiar with an industry? Want to explore potential companies to work for? Want to clarify some unfamiliar job terms? Use a variety of resources to conduct your own research. Go ahead and dive in!

INDUSTRY RESEARCH

First, determine what you need to know, and then consider the resources you need. The following topics should be components of your industry research.

TRENDS	FORECAST
Fastest-growing industries	Where is the industry now?
Job growth by number of openings	Where will it be in 6 months? 1–5 years?
CURRENT ISSUES	**CAREER PATHS**
Legal	Are career paths easy to identify?
Financial	What type of experience do you need?
Social	What type of experience will you gain?
SALARY	**PROFESSIONAL ASSOCIATIONS**
Entry	What are the major associations?
Mid-level	Are there trade shows or key events?
Advanced	Are student associations available?

ACTIVITY 5.2

Industry Research

Select an industry you might want to work in. Decide which resources will be most helpful, and research as much as you can about that industry. The Career Directions Handbook contains some of the information you need on career paths, salary ranges and professional associations. Make notes on what you find.

INDUSTRY _____

Trends _____

_____

Forecast _____

_____

Current issues _____

_____

Career paths _____

_____

Salary ranges _____

_____

Professional associations _____

_____

Progress Check Questions

1. What do you think? Could this industry be a fit for you? Why or why not?
2. Is there another industry that you think would be better for you? Why or why not?

As you explore other industries, keep your research current by following them online.

COMPANY RESEARCH

First, determine what you need to know, and then consider the resources you need. The following topics should be components of your company research.

MISSION	GOALS
Philosophy	Market share
Primary customer	Future direction
Products and services	Technology
Market distinction	Geography
REPUTATION	**CORPORATE CULTURE**
Financial	Community engagement
Quality	Diversity programs
Fair treatment of employees	Work–life balance
Industry ranking, awards, and recognitions	Informal or formal
EMPLOYEE DEVELOPMENT	**TYPES OF JOBS**
Training programs	Match with your education or experience
Support for continuing education	Salary ranges
Mentoring programs	Travel requirements
Evaluation process	Evaluation process
HOW DO YOU APPLY?	**LOCATIONS**
Print application or online	National, global
Print resume or online	
Person to person	

Select a company you might want to work for. Decide which resources will be most helpful, and research as much as you can about that company. Make notes on what you find.

COMPANY _____

Mission _____

Goals _____

Reputation _____

Corporate culture _____

Employee development _____

Location(s) _____

Types of jobs _____

How do I apply? _____

ACTIVITY 5.3
Company Research

"The goal of an informational interview is to build knowledge, get advice, and maybe even get leads to people or opportunities that can help your job search."

Ron Thomas, Human Resources Professional

Source: Retrieved November 16, 2013, from www.pongoresume. com/blogPosts/705/what-is-an-informational-interview-&-how-do-i-get-one-.cfm.

Progress Check Questions

1. What do you think? Could this company be a fit for you? Why or why not?
2. Is there another company that you think would work better for you? Why or why not?

As you explore other companies, keep your research current by following them online.

INFORMATIONAL INTERVIEWS

Two commonly used types of informational interviews are interviews with a company and interviews with a person who holds the type of position you are interested in. Informational interviews are a great resource for gaining firsthand knowledge needed for your research.

ACTIVITY 5.4

Conducting Informational Interviews

QUESTIONS TO ASK

Name of the person to be interviewed _____

Job title _____

What do you like about your career and why? _____

What do you dislike? _____

How competitive is entry into the field? _____

What future changes do you anticipate in the field? _____

What is a typical career path? _____

What skills are most important to perform your job? _____

_____

What personal qualities do employers look for? _____

_____

What certifications and education does your career or job require? _____

_____

Can you recommend companies I might fit with or best resources for researching companies in the field? _____

_____

Can you recommend the names of other people I can connect with to learn more?

_____

What is the application process at your company? _____

_____

5.4 JOB RESEARCH

The two main reasons for conducting job research are to obtain information about jobs in different fields and to source job leads to actually obtain a job.

JOB INFORMATION

Job functions, qualifications, and salary ranges are the basic areas of focus for obtaining information about jobs.

- Titles
- Basic functions
- Education requirements
- Experience needed
- Salaries

Use a variety of resources both online and offline to explore job information. You can simplify this part of your job research using the information on salary ranges and over 1,000 job descriptions contained in the Career Directions Handbook.

JOB LEADS

A job lead is information about a job opening. In general, people are the greatest source of job leads. More job leads are developed through networking than any other method. As discovered in your research tool kit, experiences, events, and services are other sources. In addition, publications online and in print uncover many leads.

One key method of sourcing job leads is maximizing the best use of job search engines, websites, and social media tools.

> **NOTES** | Sources of Job Leads
>
> Job search engines
> Advanced search feature
> Company websites
> Social media
> Job alerts
>
> Networking
> Word of mouth
> Classified ads
> Trade journals
> Employment agencies

JOB SEARCH ENGINES, WEBSITES, AND SOCIAL MEDIA TOOLS

Job Search Engines Job search engines centralize jobs from multiple sources on one site. Multiple sources might include job boards, newspapers, and company or association websites. Using job search engines saves time spent searching individual sites. A disadvantage is depersonalization which results in getting lost in a large pool of applicants with potentially little or no results. You can improve your results using customized job search engines. The following are examples of specific job search sites that help you customize your search.

Specific Job Search Sites Specific job search sites may include:

- Industry-specific job sites
- Job-specific sites
- Geography-specific
- Company-specific job sites
- Professional association–specific job sites

Advanced Search Feature Advanced search features on job search sites help you target jobs that fit your specific criteria such as type of job, type of company, skills, location, or salary. Keywords are the single words or phrases used to describe these criteria.

> Keywords: Specific words or phrases that narrow online searches to result in best matches.

Keywords in Job Descriptions In job decriptions basic keywords or phrases might include job title, industry skills, technical and general skills, education, experience, and location. The example below highlights keywords in a job description.

EXAMPLE

Software Technical Writer

Core Responsibilities

- Write, edit, and maintain all **technical documentation,** including **instructional materials,** training documents, specifications, processes, standards, forms, work flows, quick reference cards, in print and online.

- Work closely with **developers** to determine content for technical documentation.
- Gather information and requirements.

Qualifications and Personal Attributes

- **Bachelor's degree** or certificate in technical or professional writing, communications.
- Excellent command of English, with a working knowledge of French.
- Broad technical knowledge on a variety of topics including hardware, software, database systems, Web interfaces, and motivated to learn new technical concepts.
- Meticulous attention to detail, organized, and structured with excellent analytical skills.
- Excellent knowledge of **Microsoft Word** and Excel, Adobe Acrobat, and graphics programs like **Adobe Photoshop** and Fireworks.
- Knowledge of Microsoft Visio and Access, **Dreamweaver,** and FrameMaker are assets.
- An understanding of **pharmacy** is an asset.

Keywords will be discussed in greater detail in Chapter 6.

Company Websites   Job postings are directly available on many company websites. There are a few ways to find them. You can google the company name plus "jobs" or try entering the company name plus ".com." The job search engine LinkUp searches for jobs on company websites. You can also search the careers section usually accessed on the About Us section of the company website.

Social Media Job Sites   Facebook, LinkedIn and Twitter are the more frequently used social media sites for sourcing job leads. Below are examples of these social media job sites.

Facebook Marketplace Jobs

LinkedIn Jobs

TweetMyJobs

As social media sites continue to evolve at a rapid pace, these specific resources may change, but access to job leads on social media sites will likely be a constant in various forms.

Job Alerts   Job alerts are automatic notifications of new job postings that meet criteria and are listed as soon as they are available. E-mail job alerts enable job notifications to be sent directly to your inbox. Mobile job alerts enable you to receive text messages about

---

Job Leads Online

GENERAL JOB SITES

CollegeRecruiter.com	Job Central.com
Facebook Marketplace Jobs	Net Temps
Indeed.com	Saludos.com
Career Builder.com	TweetMyJobs
SimplyHired.com	The Black Collegian Online
Job.com	Salary.com
LinkedIn Jobs	INDUSTRY-SPECIFIC JOB SITES
Monster.com	GEOGRAPHY-SPECIFIC JOB SITES
USA.gov	COMPANY AND PROFESSIONAL ASSO-CIATION JOB BOARDS
Yahoo Hot Jobs	

new job notifications. When you set up your job alerts, be sure to identify criteria that match your targeted jobs. Job alerts can be sent from many types of sites including company and professional association websites, job search engines, and social media job sites.

Knowing how to use job search engine, website, and social media job tools can save you time and help you better target job leads that match you career interests.

ACTIVITY 5.5

Job Research The Career Handbook is a ready reference tool for researching over 1,000 job descriptions.

JOB INFORMATION AND LEADS

SELECT A JOB TO RESEARCH _____

OBTAIN INFORMATION ABOUT THE JOB

Identify people and online resources to obtain information and write down key points _____
_____

Basic function _____

Education requirements _____

Experience needed _____

Salary _____

TARGET JOB LEADS by identifying one of each of the following specific sites:

Industry- or job-specific site _____

Geography-specific job site _____

Company job site _____

Professional association job site _____

TARGET JOB LEADS using online tools:

Advanced search feature _____

Keywords _____

Job alerts _____

For more information on online resources visit **www.mhhe.com/yena6e.**

By exploring the career paths overview in this chapter, you have had the opportunity to build a strong career planning foundation and establish direction for your job search.

Beginning with knowing the difference between a job and a career is important in two ways. First, it helps you decide which of the two is a better choice for you and why. And second, while you can change your course at any time in the future, it is best to have a direction so that you don't lose time with a series of unrelated jobs if you later decide you want to pursue a career.

Understanding how jobs relate to different career paths is key to successfully managing your career moves as you work your way along your career path. The number and types of career paths available to you will always be changing along with periods of growth and decline in the economy and the rate at which companies are able to create more or new job opportunities in response to changes in the market. Being knowledgeable about current trends in job growth or emerging career areas is important. It will ensure you know whether you have a strong future in your career field or need to think about a change moving forward. You might learn that some new jobs require different education or training than you currently have. Then you will need to decide whether to further your education or training or choose different jobs or a new career path. The more familiar you are with a wide variety of career paths, the more comfortable you may be with being open to new career opportunities.

CHAPTER SUMMARY

Being flexible in considering different career options can help you advance your career more quickly and ensure that you have options during periods of recession and high unemployment. Another way to building career options for yourself is to think about what other industry sectors have jobs that you qualify for. For example, when there may be a decline in hiring training staff in private industries when unemployment is high, there may be opportunities with the federal government or in education to apply your training skills.

Your career path inventory will be a reminder of what you need to know to stay current on career trends. By having this tool and updating it regularly, you can evaluate whether you are moving along a career path with high-growth potential. Having a good understanding of different career paths can help you remain flexible and better deal with changes in the job market.

REFLECTION EXERCISE

CAREER PATHS AND CAREER DECISION MAKING

Based on what you have learned about career paths in this chapter, identify two potential career paths you think you would like to pursue:

_____

_____

To try to decide which career path might best suit you, answer the following questions.

1. What am I trying to decide between my two options?

_____

_____

2. What do I need to know?

_____

_____

3. Why do I need to know it?

_____

_____

4. How will it help me make a more informed decision?

_____

_____

5. How can I obtain what I need to know?

People _____

Experience _____

Research _____

6. Who are my best resources for the information I need?

_____

_____

_____

_____

part **two**

Brand Your Potential

"Well done is better than well said."
Ben Franklin[1]

[1]www.brainyquote.com/quotes/quotes/b/benjaminfr103731.html.

Your Career Portfolio

After completing this chapter, you will:

1 **Learn** how to build your Career Portfolio

2 **Plan** your Career Portfolio

3 **Collect** Career Portfolio materials

4 **Organize** and assemble your Career Portfolio

5 **Practice** and present your Career Portfolio

6 **Reflect,** refine, and edit your Career Portfolio

7 **Create** a Career Portfolio entry

Your Career Portfolio is a tool you can use to present your unique employment skills to a potential employer on a job interview. Your Career Portfolio should contain samples of work and other documentation of your skills and credentials that employers in your career field are interested in. This will be an enhancement to using only a resume to present yourself professionally. While certain fields, such as advertising and public relations, have traditionally required job candidates to have portfolios, the use of portfolios is now more widespread as employers focus on finding job candidates with specific workplace skills.

Because usually you do not assemble your actual portfolio until just before a job interview, you might make the common mistake of not starting early enough to focus on developing and collecting evidence of your skills for a portfolio presentation. If so, your portfolio will be incomplete and a less effective tool for promoting yourself.

At the very beginning of your career education, you should develop your plan to build the skills employers value and collect evidence of those skills on an ongoing basis. Together, your plan and your collection of accomplishments and skills will help you demonstrate your unique qualifications to potential employers.

CASE STUDY

Kim Shines and Leila Moves Fast Forward with Her Career Portfolio

Kim started attending resume workshops in January to prepare for her job interviews in the spring. Kim frequently went to her school's online career center and used the tutorials to practice writing resumes and job search letters.

At one of the workshops she learned that many graduates were also preparing portfolios for their interviews. Kim had saved some samples of her accomplishments from time to time, but never had a plan for developing and organizing a portfolio. She had many experiences listed on her resume that she thought would help her stand out during her interviews. She had completed two internships, traveled to Germany for a study abroad experience, and had three months of community service experience. Kim was an honors student and had several merit certificates to prove it. She felt well prepared after practicing talking about her resume in mock interviews with her career advisor.

Leila remembered her high school guidance counselor stressing the importance of documenting skills for prospective employers. Leila developed her first portfolio in her high school communications class. She used it when she interviewed for admissions to her college and found that it really gave her a lot of confidence knowing she was able to show her skills and accomplishments through some original work. In her first year in college, she started planning her Career Portfolio. As she started to prepare for her interviews, Leila reviewed those portfolio entries that she felt best demonstrated skills that matched the jobs she was interviewing for. Leila had performance evaluations from the same two internships she did with Kim. She had a few writing samples from her communications classes, letters of recommendation, and a copy of the case study she completed with her team during her community service experience. Her grades were average, but she felt prepared for her interviews. Kim and Leila both received several different job offers. Kim was very excited to obtain an offer to join the management training program at her company of choice. Leila received an offer from the same company but was placed directly into a higher-level position than Kim based on her proof that she had already developed many skills that would normally be learned in the company's training program. For both Kim and Leila, their hard work paid off. Leila's portfolio was a tool that helped her show that she had the skills needed for the job and gave her a competitive edge in her job search.

Discussion Questions

1. Do you think that Leila actually had better experience than Kim or was she just able to market herself better with her portfolio?
2. Based on her experiences, what type of documentation would have made Kim more competitive during her job interviews?
3. What are some of the specific things that Leila did in preparing and presenting her portfolio that really helped her stand out?

6.1 YOUR CAREER PORTFOLIO

Your Career Portfolio is a powerful tool for showcasing your best works and outstanding achievements to prospective employers. The two main parts of your Career Portfolio are your job search documents and your work samples and accomplishments. Throughout this textbook you will be completing activities to build entries for your Career Portfolio. In this chapter, you will also see examples of other work samples and accomplishments that can be included in a portfolio.

BUILDING YOUR CAREER PORTFOLIO ENTRIES

Career Portfolio Entry Activities by Chapter

Communication Skills	Career Portfolio 4.1: Demonstrate Communication Skills, Chapter 4
Career Portfolio Inventory/Index	Career Portfolio 6.1: Career Portfolio Inventory/Index, Chapter 6
Career Networking Card	Career Portfolio 8.1: Create Your Mini-Message and Career Networking Card, Chapter 8
Internship Work Samples/Accomplishments	Career Portfolio 9.1: Internship and Co-op Work Samples and Accomplishments, Chapter 9
Resume	Career Portfolio 10.1: Write Your Resume, Chapter 10
Cover Letter	Career Portfolio 11.1: Write a Cover Letter, Chapter 11
Interview	Career Portfolio 12.1: Questions to Ask on an Interview, Chapter 12

TYPES OF CAREER PORTFOLIO ITEMS

Examples of Types of Career Portfolio Items by Chapter

Photo: Sample Chef's Plate	Chapter 3
Class Project Video: *"Publishing a Video"* Class Project Writing Sample: *"Publishing a Video: Presentation Guide"* Class Project Video: Community Service, *"Growing Team Spirit"*	Chapter 4
Community Service Award Certificate Events Programs Facilities Blueprint Career Portfolio Inventory/Index	Chapter 6
Career Networking Cards	Chapter 8
Internship Project Sample: *"Community Hospital Orientation Manual"*	Chapter 9
Print Resume Infographic Resume Social Resume	Chapter 10
Cover Letter	Chapter 11
Questions to Ask on an Interview	Chapter 12
Digital Portfolios Can Also Include:	
Hyperlinks to work samples and professional social media sites	Chapter 7
Infographic Resume Social Resume Video Resume Web Resume	Chapter 10

"Your portfolio is a physical representation of your professionalism and potential."

Chris Oatley, Disney Character Designer

Source: Retrieved November 16, 2013, from http://chrisoatley.com/illustration-portfolio-pitfalls/.

(The digital items listed as part of a digital portfolio can also exist as independent URLs. When you have just a few portfolio items online, but not enough to build a digital portfolio, you can list the URL hyperlinks on your print resume. Employers will need to copy the URL into the address bar of a browser.

Using the above examples of types of Career Portfolio items, you will see how portfolio items validate claims about experiences and accomplishments in cover letters and resumes in Chapters 10 and 11.

Real Life Stories

Amanda and Derek

Amanda's Career Portfolio

Amanda chose to use a hard-copy version for her Career Portfolio. This is appropriate for the type of job she is applying for and the type of experience she has so far. Amanda has a class project video and link to an online sample of her project with the American Cancer Society. She could start a digital Career Portfolio using these items, but she feels it would be better to wait until she has more developed digital content. In the meantime, Amanda can include a list of URL's to her work on her print resume and provide a sampling of her online work in print form in her Career Portfolio. The only disadvantage to her approach is that an employer will need to copy the URL's into the address bar of a browser. The advantage is that she will not prematurely develop her digital version of her Career Portfolio.

Derek's Digital Career Portfolio

Derek started early building samples of his skills in some classes. Because his career path is in the technology field, Derek wants to build a strong digital Career Portfolio. Derek does not have a lot of work experience yet, but he has enough examples of his technical skills to support a digital Career Portfolio. His Web resume and personal website are examples. He will use his digital portfolio as the place to access these along with other items. As he gains more work experience, his portfolio items will develop more fully and he will begin to update and replace some items. He will use his Career Portfolio Inventory to monitor his entries and keep his index updated as needed. Derek has the technical skills to add an infographic resume or social resume, but they are not essential starting out. Eventually adding them would build out his Career Portfolio and may draw interest from a wider pool of potential employers. But for now he is off to a good start.

FOLLOW AMANDA AND DEREK AS THEY BUILD THEIR CAREER PORTFOLIOS

In Chapter 4, you saw the beginnings of Amanda's and Derek's Career Portfolios. Both of them began the process early using some quality classroom projects to get started. In this chapter, you will see how their Career Portfolios develop to include the items below.

Amanda's Career Portfolio	Derek's Digital Career Portfolio
Class Project Video: Community Service, "Growing Team Spirit" Community Service Award Certificate American Cancer Society Online Giving Link	Class Project Video: "Publishing a Video" Class Project Writing Sample: "Publishing a Video" Career Networking Card

Amanda's Career Portfolio	Derek's Digital Career Portfolio
Career Networking Card	Cover Letter
Print Chronological Resume listing URL's	Print Functional or Chronological Resume listing URL's
Plain-Text Resume (with Links Removed)	Plain-Text Resume
Cover Letter	Web Resume
Hard-Copy Career Portfolio	Personal Website
	Digital Career Portfolio
	All Other Work Samples and Acccomplishments

Progress Check Questions

1. At this time, will your Career Portfolio be based more on work-related experiences or class-related experiences?

2. What online tutorials can you identify to help you learn more about building a Career Portfolio?

6.2 PLAN FOR YOUR CAREER PORTFOLIO

As you move through each experience of your education, you will acquire new workplace skills and obtain documentation that provides evidence of your skills. This documentation will help you create a personal Career Portfolio that can be used on your job interviews to prove your qualifications to a potential employer.

IDENTIFY OPPORTUNITIES TO BUILD SKILLS

The more employment skills you build in school, the more career opportunities you will have and the higher your earnings can be over your lifetime. We saw in Chapter 1 that earnings increase with increased levels of education and that unemployment rates are usually lower for college graduates than for the general population. Take advantage of every opportunity your education affords you to build employment skills. The following sections show you how to develop a plan to do just that.

Opportunities in the Classroom   Each course you complete as part of your progress of study is designed to help you develop employment skills. While some courses teach you technical skills, such as cost accounting, ice carving, or computer repair, others teach you life skills that are transferable from job to job, such as leadership, time management, or critical thinking. At the beginning of each course you take, identify, with your instructor, the employment skills you can develop throughout the course. When you complete the course, review and record the skills you have developed.

ACTIVITY 6.1

Applied/Transferable Skills Developed through Course Work

For each course you complete, begin to record the employment skills you have developed.

Course Name	Skill Developed
1. English Composition	1. Research paper writing
2. Communications	2. Meeting presentation

"Community Service—
is a great way to
create new work
samples."

Learnovation

Source: Retrieved November 14,
2013, from www.learnovation.
com/careerportfolios/cptips.htm.

Course Name	Skill Developed
3. Intermediate Information Technology Application	3. Information technology application
4. Leadership for Business	4. Leadership
5. Business Ethics	5. Ethics
Course Name	Skill Developed

FIGURE 6.1

Amanda Soto's
Community Service
Award Certificate and
Career Networking
Card

You will use this list to help you organize your resume, prepare for a job interview, and work with your career advisor to assemble your Career Portfolio. (You may need to develop your own or additional lists to record all the courses in your program of study.)

Opportunities outside the Classroom

Opportunities to develop employment skills outside the classroom include, but are not limited to, part-time and summer jobs and internships, externships, and cooperative education experiences. Beyond work experience, opportunities outside the classroom include volunteer work, involvement in clubs or professional associations, and sports activities (Figure 6.1). To take full advantage of the opportunities outside the classroom you need to know what they are. Complete Activity 6.2 to help you identify these opportunities and Activity 6.3 to help you choose those you wish to take advantage of.

Employment skills can be developed through your accomplishments in any of these areas. For example, if you are an accounting major, you may learn how to complete an income tax return in your tax accounting class, prepare computerized monthly budget reports on your part-time job, and teach high school students how to balance a checkbook through your volunteer work in the community. Developing a plan to select experiences that will build your career skills is the first step to developing your Career Portfolio. The more experiences you have, the more entries you can make in your portfolio (Figure 6.2).

While it is natural to refine your job target from time to time, it is important also to refine your plan for building proper credentials for your job if necessary.

FIGURE 6.2

Brittany Smith and Derek T. Thompsen Project Samples

Opportunities to Develop Skills outside the Classroom

Working with your instructor or a student service professional at your school, list all the opportunities available outside the classroom to help you build employment skills.

Opportunities outside the Classroom	Possible Skill Development
1. National student organizations	1. Leadership
2. Community service	2. Social responsibility
3. Sports teams	3. Teamwork
4. Cross-cultural workshops and seminars	4. Diversity
5. Spanish lessons	5. Important non-English (Spanish) language skills

Opportunities outside the Classroom	Possible Skill Development
_____	_____
_____	_____
_____	_____

(You may need to develop your own or additional lists to record all the opportunities available to you.)

ACTIVITY 6.3

Choose Your Opportunities

Review the list of opportunities available to you outside the classroom and the skills they can help you develop (Activity 6.2). On the basis of your knowledge of the job you want and the skills you need to qualify for the job, prepare a list of the opportunities outside the classroom you will choose to become involved with. For each opportunity you choose, indicate the skills you plan on developing.

EXAMPLE

Opportunities outside the Classroom	Skill to Develop
Volunteer work	Teamwork
Opportunities outside the Classroom	Skill to Develop
_____	_____
_____	_____
_____	_____

You will use this to help you organize your resume, prepare for a job interview, and work with your career advisor to assemble your Career Portfolio. (You may need to develop your own or additional lists to record all the opportunities you choose.)

6.3 SAVE AND COLLECT CAREER PORTFOLIO MATERIALS

Begin with the end in mind. As you plan to start saving materials to include in your portfolio, try to visualize what forms of evidence you think will be most important to your career field. For example, if you are an art major, it is obvious that your prime portfolio entries will be the best of your personal artwork. If you are a marketing major, writing samples or business plans you might have written for a class or an internship might be important. A hospitality

NOTES | Portfolio Time Line

Planning Phases	Months/Weeks Prior to Interviews	
	Hard-Copy Portfolios	**Digital Portfolios**
Phase 1: Plan your portfolio	6+ months	6+ months
Phase 2: Assess your inventory	6+ months	6+ months
Start saving materials	6+ months	6+ months
Phase 3: Save materials	2–4 months	2–4 months
Organize and assemble	2–4 months	2–4 months
Publish digital portfolio online		2 months
Phase 4: Practice presenting	1 month	2 months
Final edits	2 weeks	1 month
Phase 5: Present your portfolio	Interview time	Interview time
Phase 6: Reflect, refine, edit	After interviews	After interviews
	Before next interviews	Before next interviews
	After interviews	After interviews
	Before next interviews	Before next interviews
Target dates:	Interview dates: _____	
Target date:	Graduation: _____	

major may keep a customer service award earned at a part-time job or internship or a facilities plan completed for a facilities management class. Graduates from almost every major will benefit from keeping good writing samples or evidence of awards and recognition and copies of special licenses or certifications important to the industry you are about to enter (Figure 6.3).

TYPES OF CAREER PORTFOLIO ITEMS

Many forms of evidence can document your skills. Even though you may not use all the documentation you collect for every job search, you should still be sure to collect as much evidence as you can to demonstrate and verify your skills. The following are some examples of evidence you can collect and explanations of how each one can help you.

Resume   A well-prepared resume is evidence of good career planning and job search skills. In particular, it demonstrates your ability to set and communicate your career goal. A good resume can convince an employer you have the best background for the job.

FIGURE 6.3

Louis Ricci and Elizabeth Cole Events Program Samples

Photographs   Photographs may include those of your work, of you receiving an award or recognition, of you in a professional publication, or of an event you planned. Try to collect photographs that are processed well and that portray your message professionally. As you collect your photographs, keep them stored in a plastic sleeve, album, or photo box to avoid damage or store your digital photos electronically.

Thumb Drives and CDs   Some employers may prefer your portfolio items stored on a thumb drive or CD for easy upload into their computer. If you use a CD, be sure to create a nicely done professional cover.

Writing Samples   Writing samples may include class or work-related projects you have written. An ad campaign written for your advertising class or as part of your accomplishments at work is an example. If you have written a published article, include it as long as the topic is not controversial.

Your job search documents are writing samples as well, along with business letters you may create in a business communications class. Be sure any writing sample is your original writing.

Use only writing samples that demonstrate good grammar, proper spelling and punctuation, and clearly organized thoughts throughout. Seek the advice of a faculty member when deciding what your best writing sample may be.

Letters of Reference   Your current and past employers are your best resource for reference letters. Most employers will be willing to write a reference letter for you if your employment with them has been a positive experience for the company as well as for you. Letters from past or current employers to prospective employers should prove your ability to perform in the workplace. Other sources of reference letters are professional associations, teachers, and in some cases, personal contacts.

Letters of Commendation   Any congratulatory letters you receive for winning an award or competition, receiving academic honors, or performing well on the job should be saved as evidence of your outstanding accomplishment. If you have customer contact, you

"No matter what your personal style of communication, your work samples speak for you. Look for your work samples in certificates, projects, reports, letters of support and community service activities."

Learnovation

Source: Retrieved November 14, 2013, from www.learnovation. com/careerportfolios/cptips.htm.

should focus on letters received from customers praising the level of service you provided them. These can be used to demonstrate that you have good customer service skills, one of the skills most widely sought after by employers.

Employer Evaluations   When you successfully complete an internship, externship, or cooperative education assignment, you will probably have at least one written employer evaluation of your work performance. Employer evaluations from part-time, full-time, summer, or volunteer work are also worth keeping if they are good.

Performance Reviews   Like employer evaluations of your work, your performance reviews are worth keeping. Most often, employers share with an employee written copies of his or her review both as documentation of what occurred during the review and as a guide to help the employee target the areas of performance that need improvement.

News Articles   If a newspaper has published an article about one of your jobs, awards, honors, or other accomplishments, be sure to save a copy.

Blueprints   A sample set of blueprints you have designed is a great example of your computer-aided drafting and design (CADD) skills.

Menus   If you are in the food service profession and have designed some menus of your own or helped someone else design menus, copies of those menus should be kept to show to a prospective food service employer. Menus that illustrate meals you have actually prepared, even if someone else created the menu, are also great samples of the types of cuisine you can prepare.

Facilities Designs   If you have learned how to lay out the design for new office space, a new restaurant or hotel, or a new retail store, you have a skill a prospective employer should know about. If you have designed one or more spaces, keep copies of your work to show the variety of designs you have worked with.

Business Plans   Writing a business plan utilizes many skills employers will be interested in. In addition to demonstrating your business writing techniques, your business plan communicates your ability to conceptualize, plan, promote, and potentially operate a business.

Certificates of Completion   Certificates of completion are often given to you when you attend a professional workshop, conference, or seminar. Keeping these types of certificates is important because they confirm your participation in a program that has contributed to your professional growth and shows your commitment to continued education and lifelong learning.

Grades and Transcripts   It may be worthwhile to show employers that you have done well in the courses aimed at developing the particular skills they are looking for. If all your grades are good, then it can be a help to show your transcripts to an employer. If some of your grades are below average but you have done well in the courses that specifically trained you to do the job you are applying for, then it isn't a problem to show an employer your transcripts. If your academic performance is consistently below average, then you may want to focus more on skills gained from your volunteer work, work experience, or involvement in sports or clubs and organizations.

Attendance Record   Many college students do not think of attendance in school as a factor that can affect their employment prospects, but employers say good attendance in school is a potential indicator of good attendance on the job. Good attendance is evidence to an employer of your reliability, dependability, and work ethic—all of which are important to success on the job. Keep your record of attendance to demonstrate both your commitment to your education and your professionalism.

Manuals and Procedures Developed   A procedural manual you helped develop through one of your jobs, for a club or organization, or through your volunteer work is a great sample of the work you are capable of doing.

Honors and Certificates   The reason you are working toward developing a Career Portfolio is to show employers your special distinctions. Any honor or award you receive usually recognizes some type of accomplishment that gives you special distinction. Keep copies of letters or certificates you receive for doing something special. For example, a certificate of

> "Choose your finest work, which may not necessarily be your most recent, but represents you professionally."
>
> Avishai Abrahami, chief executive, Wix.com

Source: Retrieved November 15, 2013, from www.nytimes.com/2012/07/01/jobs/an-online-portfolio-can-showcase-your-work-career-couch.html?_r=0.

achievement for completing a leadership course or a certificate verifying you were the employee of the month at your part-time job would be good evidence of your special achievements.

Licenses   Certain professions require job candidates to have licenses for work in the field. Whether it is required or not, if you have a special license that attests that you can perform certain skills, keep it ready to show to an employer.

Now that you know the types of documentation that can be presented in your portfolio, you can set goals toward accomplishments that will help you collect evidence of your employment skills. In this process, it is very important to remember that although the items listed are only a few of the many possible items you can accumulate, you do not need all of them to prepare an effective portfolio. Also keep in mind that you should collect evidence mainly of your best work. If you have any of the listed items that do represent some of your best work, then be sure to save them. On the other hand, you may have improved significantly in a skill area and want to show an employer the progress you made because of your persistence and hard work. In this case, it may be helpful to keep samples of both your average work and your excellent work to show how much improvement you have made over time.

In any case, do not feel compelled to keep work that is not your best. Everyone is better at some things than at others. You should end up with a portfolio that focuses on your strengths, not your weaknesses. Remember, the purpose of creating your Career Portfolio is to promote your unique talents and skills.

· ·

Progress Check Questions

1. What kinds of evidence do you need to build for your Career Portfolio?
2. What are the most important forms of evidence you have to date?

· ·

CAREER PORTFOLIO 6.1

●● CAREER PORTFOLIO ENTRY:
●● CAREER PORTFOLIO INVENTORY/INDEX

As you collect evidence of some skills, keep a list of the documentation you have and the skill(s) you think it helps you demonstrate to a prospective employer. By maintaining this record, you will readily know the possible Career Portfolio items available to you when you prepare for your job interviews.

Record of Evidence and Documentation	What It Demonstrates
Attendance record	Professionalism, reliability, work ethic
Letter of recommendation	Validation of proven success
Writing sample	Writing skills
Team project	Teamwork

6.4 ORGANIZE AND ASSEMBLE YOUR CAREER PORTFOLIO

At this point you have already collected much of the evidence to show you have industry credentials. When you are about to interview with potential employers, select the evidence that is most valued by each employer and plan to present that evidence effectively. You can organize and assemble your Career Portfolio in either a hard-copy or electronic format. Whichever you choose really depends on what you are comfortable with using as your presentation to employers. How comfortable you are with your computer skills also makes a difference, since creating a digital portfolio requires application of different types of computer files and software products.

TYPES OF PORTFOLIOS

As you think about preparing a portfolio to showcase your employment credentials, you will need to choose between preparing a hard-copy and a digital portfolio. Digital portfolios are more commonly used than hard-copy portfolios in almost all industries. In some industries a hard-copy portfolio may be more effective, but in today's digital recruitment environment, you will be expected to be able to share your documents and other portfolio entries online. While the following information provides some of the basic information you need about these two types of portfolios, you should make use of the websites listed in the online learning center.

Hard-Copy Portfolios   There are many types of portfolio products. The product you choose will depend largely on the career field you are interested in and the types of samples (photos, written material, etc.) you are likely to present.

Three-ring binders ($8\frac{1}{2}'' \times 11''$) that hold acetate-covered pages or plastic sleeves are commonly used for portfolios. These are practical because the pages or sleeves can hold all types of written evidence as well as photographs. Special vinyl slide sheets, three-hole punched, can be added to hold slide samples if appropriate.

Large portfolio cases ($17'' \times 22''$) are available in most art supply stores and are usually needed by writers, journalists, artists, photographers, or advertising majors. They provide enough space to display full-page ads and printed articles from all sizes of newspapers and magazines. Both types of hard-copy portfolios are excellent vehicles for saving and displaying your work samples and other credentials. Be sure to make copies of whatever you put into your portfolio in case an employer asks you to leave your portfolio behind. You should try not to leave any original pieces of your work. To respond to an employer's request to keep the content of your portfolio a little longer for others in the company to see, have copies of as many things as you can. Art supply stores and bookstores at colleges that offer a degree in art are two great places to purchase some of the materials necessary to assemble your portfolio.

Digital Portfolios   Kelly Driscoll, president and founder of Digitation, a digital portfolio service, describes what digital portfolios are and how they can be an advantage to you in your job search. Driscoll explains, "An e-portfolio is a collection of work, published online to document achievements, ideas, progress, performance, and activities. It can also showcase, publish, and compile your work to expand on a personal vision or life goal and create an archive of experiences"[2]

Digital portfolios have several advantages. An electronic version of your credentials makes it possible to share them with a wider audience, regardless of location. They are more practical than the hard-copy versions, usually binders, because your work can be better protected online and there is no need to transport the materials with you to interviews.

When you develop a digital portfolio, you are applying your technology skills. You may prepare media presentations or use different software programs. Your digital portfolio

[2]R. Zupek. (February 29, 2008). Stand Out with an E-Portfolio. Retrieved September 3, 2009, from http://msn .careerbuilder.com/Article/MSN-1486-Cover-Letters-Resumes-Stand-Out-With-an-E-portfolio/.

can contain digital versions of your resume, references, work samples, program sheets, letters of recommendation, evidence of community service work, a performance review, or certificates, awards, and scholarship award letters. The specific materials you use for interviews will depend on the type of job you are applying for. In one survey about the use of digital portfolios in the hiring process, employers expressed their preferences for types of portfolio materials.

Digital Portfolios

Top Five Types of Information Employers Say Are Valuable

Information	Employer Rating (%)
Resumes/references	93%
Written work	39
Projects	37
Presentations	33
Lesson plans	23

Source: www.educause.edu/EDUCAUSE+Quarterly/EDUCAUSEQuarterlyMagazineVolum/EPortfoliosasaHiringToolDoEmpl/163439.

"Having a consistent, online record of your accomplishments will make you visible on the Web and stand out to recruiters."

Angela Hills, executive vice president, Pinstripe

Source: Retrieved November 13, 2013, from www.nytimes.com/2012/07/01/jobs/an-online-portfolio-can-showcase-your-work-career-couch.html?_r=0.

Digital Portfolios

Examples of Electronic Files

Text	Presentations
Images	Hyperlinks
Audio files	JPG files
Video files	Tiff files

Of the employers surveyed, 95 percent said they preferred to access digital portfolios via a Web-based link.[3]

To collect and organize your work in a digital portfolio, you should think about using multiple file types and decide on a type of software that will be easy for you to manage. File types may include word documents, spreadsheets, and photographs. In some cases you might enhance your presentation with a sound recording or video clip. The use of various file types demonstrates the diversity of your technology skills as well as different forms of learning you have experienced. Most important, they provide vivid examples of what you can do for a prospective employer.

There are many software options for developing your digital portfolio. The following are examples that range from easy-to-use to more advanced options.

Digital Portfolios

Examples of Types of Software
Google Drive Application
Mozilla Composer
Blackboard 6 ePortfolio environment
Adobe Dreamweaver, Fireworks, and Flash (photo gallery and video clips)

---

[3]C. Ward and C. Moser. (October–December 2008). E-Portfolios as a Hiring Tool. Retrieved September 3, 2009, from www.educause.edu/EDUCAUSE+Quarterly/EDUCAUSEQuarterlyMagazineVolum/EPortfoliosasaHiringToolDoEmpl/163439.

Using the Google Drive Application on the iPad, you can create your entire portfolio on your iPad. Mozilla Composer enables you to create and edit web pages, e-mail, and text documents easily. Blackboard 6 ePortfolio environment is a more intermediate application of digital portfolio software but still very versatile and an effective tool for creating a portfolio.

Adobe Dreamweaver, Fireworks, and Flash are advanced software applications that provide a wider range of features such as audio and visual capabilities for websites.

These are only a few examples of file types and software that can be used to develop your digital portfolio. There are many more, and with continuous advances in technology, new tools are constantly becoming available. The Internet is the best source for keeping informed on the most current file and software options for digital portfolios.

Tips for Digital Portfolio Users   There are some things you should consider when using a digital portfolio.

Protect Your Privacy Manage the access to your information online. Be selective about who you give your password to. You can password protect your documents to ensure that only those you grant permission to can access your documents. This will reduce your risk of identity theft and ensure that only appropriate individuals can view it.

Manage a Variety of Content Being able to use multiple file types will help you demonstrate your accomplishments in a variety of ways. For example, the sample portfolio shown in Figure 6.4 contains a wide range of content ranging from word documents (resume, transcript) to work samples that might take a variety of forms (artifacts). Using different methods to tell your story will help you stand out from others and will better engage those you are presenting your accomplishments to. If you need to learn different file types, ask a teacher for some help. You might also find some online resources easy to understand.

Prepare Off-Line Access to Your Digital Portfolio Although you will probably create your digital portfolio as a Web-based link, you should know how to download it onto a jump drive, a CD, or other devices. There may be times when you will want to present your portfolio off-line, and you will want to be prepared to do so in advance.

Make Your Digital Portfolio Searchable Online In Chapter 1 you learned that employers frequently use online social and professional networks to screen job candidates. When employers are screening online, digital portfolios are also accessible to them. You can stand out as someone who is professional and serious about your job search with your digital portfolio. Use keywords throughout to be sure employers can find you online. Examples of keywords for applied and transferable skills and keywords that are used in particular industries can be researched on the Internet.

> "It's very impressive to employers when someone who wouldn't necessarily have an online portfolio has one,"
>
> Alexandra Levit, Career-trend consultant and author.
>
> Source: www.marketwatch.com/story/boomer-job-seekers-consider-an-online-portfolio-2013-03-25?pagenumber=2.

FIGURE 6.4

Digital Portfolio

Source: © Florida State University Career Center.

FLORIDA STATE UNIVERSITY

Career Center | Portfolio Home

Printer Friendly Format

| Profile | Resume | Skills | Transcript | Artifacts | References |

Lee Haines
Career Portfolio
Profile

Education:
- Junior at Florida State University.
- Major: Communications   Minor: Business
- Active Board member of Student Government.

Goals:
- Work for a marketing or public relations firm.
- Expand my technical and business-related abilities.

Qualifications:
- Creative, hardworking and highly-motivated.
- Computer skills - Microsoft Office and Adobe Photoshop.
- Bilingual in Spanish and English.

© 2000 Florida State University
ALL RIGHTS RESERVED

100 South Woodward Avenue, Tallahassee, Fl
32306-4162
Phone: (850) 644-6431 - Contact Us

FLORIDA STATE
UNIVERSITY

Promote Your Digital Portfolio Web Address It should be listed on your resume and the footer of your e-mail address for e-mails you send related to your job search.

Never include original work if you are leaving an off-line version of your digital portfolio with someone.

"Where it adds value is it makes you easier to find."

Angela Hills. executive vice president, Pinstripe

Source: www.marketwatch. com/story/boomer-job-seekers- consider-an-online-portfolio- 2013-03-25?pagenumber=2.

Progress Check Questions

1. Do you think a hard-copy portfolio or a digital portfolio is best for you? Why?
2. What types of computer files and software would you use to build your digital portfolio?

DECIDING ON CONTENT

Before you assemble your portfolio for presentation, determine how you will select the items to go into it. Until now, you have collected as much evidence as possible to show an employer. When you are about to interview with a potential employer, you must select the evidence that is most valued by that employer. Do not show your entire collection to every employer. Not only will there be too much material for an employer to review, but much of it will not even be targeted to the specific job you are interviewing for.

Plan your selection of portfolio items by focusing on evidence of skills that are industry specific, employer specific, and job specific as shown in Figure 6.5. For example, in the hospitality industry, excellent customer service is an industry-specific skill. A particular hotel chain may require candidates to have an international experience because new hotel construction in the Pacific Rim is producing more jobs there than in the United States; in this case, international experience is an employer-specific skill. A job-specific skill then might be the ability to speak Japanese for a reservationist's position in the hotel's Tokyo location. While evidence of good customer service skills is extremely important, this job probably cannot be filled by someone who does not speak Japanese. In this case, it is critical to build a portfolio around international experience including any evidence of experience with cultures in the Pacific Rim, in particular, Japanese culture.

For example, a nationally recognized food service employer in Rhode Island identifies work experience as the most valued credential an applicant can present. A worldwide beverage distributor, however, asks for prescreening of candidates by grade point average first. Although both these employers basically value candidates with appropriate industry training, each employer goes one step further in identifying a specific credential as being most important.

FIGURE 6.5

Your Portfolio Materials Represent Your Specific Skills

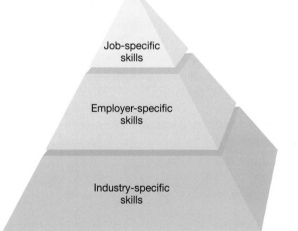

A candidate applying to both these companies for a job may, in fact, meet both these criteria for employment but should concentrate primarily on emphasizing the credential each employer is most interested in. As a result, the candidate may not show transcripts to the first employer but would be sure to highlight good transcripts to the other.

The real key to making your portfolio effective is knowing how to move it from being industry specific to being employer specific for a job interview. The more time you spend getting to know how employers may evaluate you, the more effective your portfolio can be during the interviewing process.

ARRANGING PORTFOLIO MATERIALS

You should give some thought to the order in which you will present the materials in your portfolio to maximize the effect of your presentation to a prospective employer. To arrange a winning portfolio, go through all the materials you initially decided to include. Choose two pieces that are evidence of your best work as well as different from what you think other candidates will have. Place one of these pieces on the opening page of your portfolio and one on the last

"Design the layout of each page of your portfolio just as carefully as you designed the work on the pages."

Chris Oatley, Disney Character Designer

Source: Retrieved November 16, 2013, from http://chrisoatley.com/ illustration-portfolio-pitfalls/.

page. The first should pique the employer's interest to go on to see more of your credentials. The last should leave the employer with a positive impression of you and your abilities.

One way to think about arranging the pieces in the middle of your portfolio is by theme, for example, international experience or community service and volunteerism. Your theme should be chosen keeping in mind the experience the employer is looking for and your own strengths. In each case, focus most of the entries in your portfolio on evidence demonstrating one of the preceding (international or community service work experience) as your strength or specialty area. This approach gives you the opportunity to focus your presentation on promoting a strength you know the employer is looking for. If you do not have enough experience in one specialty area but do have lots of experience in many different areas, then show the diversity of your experiences as your strength. Think carefully about how you arrange your portfolio so that it can make a maximum impact on a prospective employer.

6.5 PRACTICE AND PRESENT YOUR CAREER PORTFOLIO

Your time with an employer on an interview is limited, so manage your portfolio presentation well. You may have to narrate to provide both flow to the presentation and a coherent picture of your credentials to the employer, but be prepared to have only one or two succinct comments about each page you show. Plan what you will say to complement your interview, not monopolize it.

It is important for you to tell the employer at the beginning of the interview that you have your portfolio with you and will speak about it later in the interview. This alerts the interviewer that you are well prepared. The initial stage of the interview is the time for general discussion about the company, your career interests, and the type of position available. Once these topics have been covered, the interviewer will get into more specific questions about your experience and your qualifications for the job. This is the time to bring your portfolio forward. Use it to illustrate how you have already applied the skills you say you have. For example, when you are asked about your experience and skills, answer by first describing your skills and experience and saying that you have some examples that demonstrate your accomplishments and abilities (see Activity 6.4).

Finally, make sure you have created a memorable impression of yourself. Take a "leave-behind" piece from your portfolio on your interview (see Figures 6.6 and 6.7). Remember

FIGURE 6.6

Career Networking Card

DEREK T. THOMPSEN
Supports Web innovation and strategy to increase productivity of IT functions

WEB RESUME: www.dtthompsen2490.com/webres.html
EMAIL: dtthompson@xyz.com   PHONE: (412)483-9730
PERSONAL WEBSITE: www.derektthompsen2490.com
CAREER PORTFOLIO: www.derektthompsendrktportfolio2490.com

DEREK T. THOMPSEN

CARDON COMMUNITY COLLEGE
B.S., Information Systems A.S., Web Development
- Web and Video Innovation in Design, Student Award 2012
- Web development and Web page design
- HTML, XHTML, JavaScript
- SQL, SQL/PL, Oracle, Access
- Unix and Windows XP
- Self-monitored projects generated new contracts totaling $200,000

CAPSTONE COURSE PROJECT:
"Publishing a Video" www.dtthompsenclassvideo.com

to make a copy of something you can actually give to the employer with your resume. And then, when you write a thank-you letter for the job interview, mail one more short sample of your work to continue to remind the employer of how qualified you are for the job.

FIGURE 6.7

A Report Can Make a Good Career Portfolio Entry

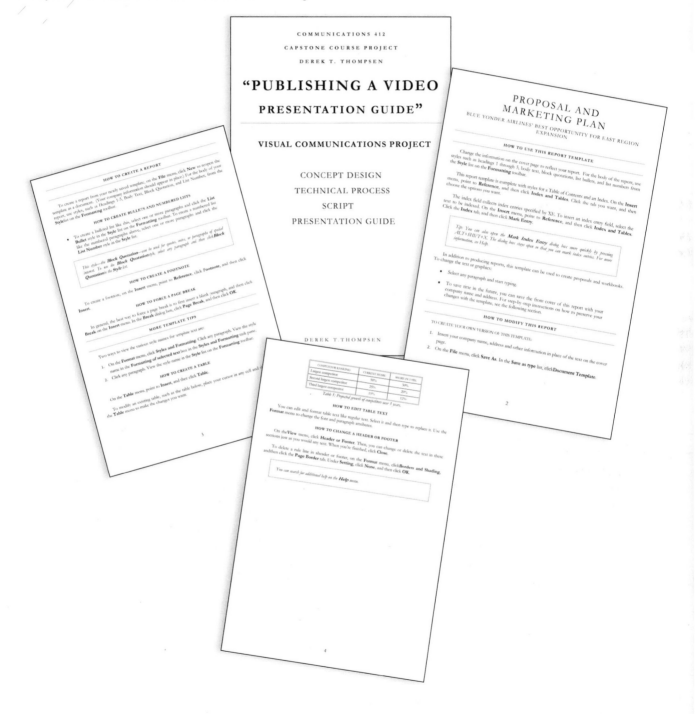

ACTIVITY 6.4

Summarize Your Skills and Role-Play

Work with another person, who will play the role of an interviewer. Summarize the skills and accomplishments you want to highlight to an employer, and select the evidence you have to demonstrate. Have the "interviewer" ask you about your skills, and role-play your response to each question and the presentation of your portfolio.

It may take a few practice sessions to become familiar with promoting yourself this way, but it will be worth it when you convince a prospective employer you are a highly qualified candidate for the job.

EXAMPLE

Interviewer Asks: Can you give me an example of a situation in which you displayed leadership skills?

Sample Response 1: Yes. As an offcer of Future Business Leaders of America, I was responsible for motivating the membership to initiate an annual fund-raiser for the homeless in our community. Let me show you some letters of appreciation from the mayor and the homeless shelter we worked with.

Sample Response 2: Yes. In my research and design class, I led our work group in presenting our marketing proposal to a local business firm. Here is a copy of our proposal, which was accepted and implemented.

Progress Check Questions

1. What parts of your Career Portfolio do you find easier to talk about?
2. What can you do to become more comfortable talking about the other areas?

6.6 REFLECT, REFINE, AND EDIT

Your portfolio will evolve over time with each new professional experience you build. It is helpful to have your portfolio assessed from time to time to help you determine whether or not you are building the best credentials for your career goal. The best evaluators of a portfolio are employers. Arrange to have an employer in your career field critique your portfolio at least twice during your academic experience. Career counselors and faculty members are also good resources for helping you assess your portfolio. When you have your portfolio assessed, focus on finding out what additional experiences you need to become better qualified to attain your career goal. You may show a lot of work experience but little evidence of community involvement. An employer may recommend more community involvement for you to help you demonstrate more of a balance in your life. Or all your work experience may be in one industry segment, and an employer may recommend more work experience but in different aspects of your industry.

Another area of major importance to your portfolio assessment is consideration of what further training you need to become better qualified for a particular job. If you need further training, you will need to decide whether to obtain that training directly with an employer, on the job, or in school. An employer, career counselor, or faculty member can help you with this decision. Before you conduct any employment interviews, be able to tell an employer what further training you think you need to be effective and the plan you have for obtaining that further training.

Progress Check Questions

1. Can you identify the next major accomplishment that will prompt you to update your portfolio?

2. What is your plan for regularly assessing your portfolio?

The information studied in this chapter is your guide to planning, developing, and presenting your Career Portfolio. A portfolio is an important tool for demonstrating your distinct qualifications to employers. Planning for your portfolio should start early. The more time you plan for experiences that build your workplace skills, the more evidence you can build in your portfolio. A strong portfolio should make your resume come alive with vivid examples of what you can do.

You need to make several decisions about your Career Portfolio. For example, you need to determine whether a hard-copy or digital version is best for you. Digital portfolios can be an advantage because when they are Web-based, employers can search for profiles online that match certain skills required for jobs at their company. Having a searchable digital portfolio can be helpful to your job search.

Whether you choose a hard-copy portfolio or a digital portfolio, you should be sure to update it often so that it reflects your most current qualifications. Employers will expect you to convince them that you are better qualified for a position based on evidence in your Career Portfolio.

Having experience talking confidently about your qualifications will also prepare you for career networking opportunities during your job search and during different phases of your career. In Chapter 8 you will learn more about career networking and the important role it can play in your career if done well.

CAREER PORTFOLIOS AND CAREER DECISION MAKING

Based on what you learned about portfolios in this chapter, think about what decisions you need to make about developing your Career Portfolio.

1. What am I trying to decide?

_____

_____

2. What do I need to know?

_____

_____

3. How will it help me make a more informed decision?

_____

_____

4. How can I obtain the information I need?

People _____

Experience _____

Research _____

5. Who are the best resources for the information I need?

_____

_____

"Social Media is now viewed as a 'must-check' piece in the hiring process."

Stacey Engle, Director of Marketing, Fierce, Inc.[1]

[1] Retrieved November 6, 2013, from http://finance.yahoo.com/news/tool-lets-job-seekers-clean-120000589.html

Social Media Profiles

After completing this chapter, you will:

1 **Understand** the importance of your professional brand and online identity

2 **Understand** the professional use of social media profiles

3 **Know** the importance of keywords in your job search

4 **Plan** how to grow your social media profile and measure your progress

As more employers use social media to screen and connect with potential job candidates, the more important it is for you to manage your social media content. During your job search, preparing your social media profiles for professional use will greatly enhance your professional image with employers. Your social media content should coordinate well with your other online information which might include a digital resume, Career Portfolio, or personal website. An important part of building a strong social media profile is using appropriate keywords. In this chapter, you will review key areas to focus on to build a strong professional profile. You will also use some tools to evaluate the readiness of your social media profiles to support your current job search and learn how to keep strengthening them over time.

CASE STUDY

Michaela's Success: Reputation Matters

Michaela was well on her way with her job search and was successful using her social media profiles and other online tools to attract interest from potential employers. Even though she was still building her work experience, Michaela found ways to build strong social media profiles to support her job search.

The first thing Michaela did was to make small changes that made a big difference. She always knew that LinkedIn was widely used by employers to screen and connect with potential candidates. But she recently noticed that many employers also consider candidates' Facebook profiles. She began to refine her Facebook profile to become another professional tool in her job search. She substituted her group of friends' profile photo on her Facebook page to match the headshot she used for her LinkedIn profile photo. Michaela also used her privacy settings more effectively to keep her personal connections with family and friends private. This would eliminate the risk of the casual posts jeopardizing her professional image. A friend of Michaela's lost out on a potential interview because information on her Facebook profile conflicted with information in her resume, and some content portrayed an unprofessional image of her. Michaela wanted to be sure that there was nothing in her online background information that would detract a potential employer. Gradually, her Facebook site moved from being primarily a social site to becoming a strong online job search tool.

Michaela next focused on strengthening sections in her social media profiles. She used her previous company research to learn what areas in her background mattered most to the employers she was interested in. She applied what she learned using keywords to update descriptions in her profiles. She developed more confidence in asking industry professionals who knew her to endorse some of her specific skills. She was pleased with how much just a few, selective professional endorsements strengthened her profiles.

Finally, Michaela periodically looked at the entire package of online tools she developed for her job search. She checked to ensure that information in her resume, social media profiles, and digital portfolio matched. Taking her job search seriously helped Michaela build a solid reputation that led to several interviews with her top-pick employers.

Discussion Questions

1. What types of college experiences could Michaela include in her profiles to compensate for her short work history?
2. Are there times when it is appropriate for a family member or friend to connect on a professional social media site being used during a job search?

"Are you displaying the same impression and individual personal brand in each of the places you choose to be online?"

Angela Hills, an executive vice president, Pinstripe

Source: Retrieved November 8, 2013, from www.marketwatch.com/story/boomer-job-seekers-consider-an-online-portfolio-2013-03-25.

7.1 PROFESSIONAL ONLINE IDENTITY AND BRAND

A brand promotes value to attract and persuade a targeted audience. Your professional online identity reflects your professional brand. Your professional online identity is the entire package you use to promote yourself online. This may include your traditional resume and cover letter, Career Portfolio, and social media sites. For some, it may also include other digital resume versions or a personal website. It is important to coordinate all versions of your professional online identity to ensure they convey quality, relevance, and consistency across the board. Using good judgment about what you make public online is important to your reputation. For many employers, your online identity is the "new background check" in your job search (see Figure 7.1).

FIGURE 7.1

Your Professional Online Identity

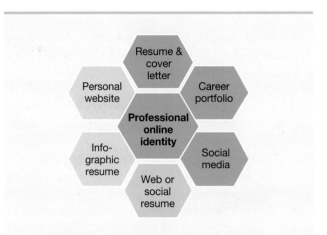

Begin with the end in mind. Think about how you want prospective employers to see you when they view components of your professional online identity. The following table illustrates how various brands convey value and how employers view those brands.

Your professional online identity is the whole package of online tools you use to promote yourself professionally. The quality and consistency of each component impacts your professional brand.

How a Brand Conveys Value	How Employers View Your Brand
Is unique, distinguished from others	"How is this person different?"
Is highly visible	"This person keeps coming up whenever we talk about . . ."
Communicates worth and potential	"It looks like this person can do the job—and more."
Targets a specific audience	"This person looks like a good fit for our company."
Attracts and engages a specific audience	"Let's go back and look at more details about this person."
Is consist	"Everything seems to match up!"
Builds a solid reputation	"Everyone feels the same way about this person; let's schedule an interview."

These are the types of responses you want from prospective employers. What's the best way to use your social media profiles to accomplish this?

7.2 PROFESSIONAL USE OF SOCIAL MEDIA PROFILES

LinkedIn, Facebook, Twitter, and Google+ are used in various ways by employers to screen and connect with potential job candidates. You can learn how to set up and use special features for different sites online, but you also need to know how to manage your social media profiles for professional use. A professional social media profile shows employers you think like a professional and take your job search seriously. To ensure your professional online identity measures up for your job search, you need to focus on its quality, relevance, and consistency.

QUALITY, RELEVANT, AND CONSISTENT CONTENT

Quality Content   What information you include and how you include it impact the quality of your social media profiles. The order you use and the words you choose help highlight your strengths in your profile. The following are key areas to focus on to build quality content:

- *Accomplishments and results.* Distinguish yourself by your accomplishments and results. They tell an employer some unique things about you. Be sure they take a lead position in your profile.

- *Skills and expertise.* Your skills and expertise communicate your worth and potential. They tell an employer whether you can do the job and more. Start by creating a complete list of your skills and expertise, and then narrow down the list to those you will include in your profile. In this case, more is not necessarily better. Select those that relate to the position and companies you are targeting in your job search. Keeping your list focused and short to moderate in length better emphasizes your main skills and expertise.

- *Keywords.* Using the right keywords will result in your profiles being more searchable and therefore make you more visible to prospective employers. Later in this chapter, you can review different categories of keywords to reference as you build your own list.
- *Correct grammar, spelling, and punctuation.* Make sure your profile is 100 percent error-free.
- *Accurate information.* The information in your profiles should reflect accurate dates, job titles, and responsibilities. There are many ways employers can verify this information online and through their professional networks. Inflating your job title or responsibilities to sound more important than they were is untruthful and in the end could permanently harm your reputation.
- *Images.* Include a professional profile photo. Be sure it is a good-quality headshot. Be well groomed and in business professional or business casual dress. The personal care and appearance tips in Chapter 4 are good guidelines to follow. Other images to include might be a few sample photos of best works from your digital portfolio. This not only helps support your profile but also tells employers you have a Career Portfolio that shows your work. You can provide the link to your Career Portfolio in your social media profile.

Relevant Content   Content is relevant if it relates to the job and employers you are targeting. You have limited space to build your profile, so take care to prioritize what matters most.

- *Job-related content:* Deciding what information to include in your profile is made easier if you know what matters most to the jobs and employers you are targeting. This is where the company and job research you did in Chapter 5 will help. Job-related content helps communicate experience and the value you bring to an employer.
- *Friends, endorsements, and connections:* Friend, endorse, and connect with reputable individuals. Be sure that they provide feedback about you that supports you professionally and that they are credible individuals. Invite a few individuals who really know you to make some comments specific to the skills and expertise you list.
- *Current information:* Make sure all of the information reflects your current status.

Consistent Content   If you have more than one social media site, be consistent with the written content, including keywords and images that you use. In all versions of your online identity, be consistent with the URLs (uniform resource locators, or addresses of resources on the Internet) you use. Use the same version of your name for each one. Like keywords, consistent URLs help make you more searchable and visible online during your job search.

A professional social media profile shows employers you think like a professional and take your job search seriously.

"When third parties validate your skills, your profile ranks higher in LinkedIn's search results."

Miriam Salpeter, owner, Keppie Careers

Source: Retrieved November 14, 2013, from www.realsimple.com/work-life/life-strategies/job-career/social-media-job-search-job-hunt-00100000107873/.

Consistent Use of URLs and E-mail

Site	Username	URL or E-mail
Facebook	maria.rodrigues	https://www.facebook.com/maria.rodrigues
LinkedIn	MariaRodrigues	https://www.linkedin.com/in/MariaRodrigues
Twitter	@MariaRodrigues	https://www.twitter.com/MariaRodrigues

Site	Username	URL or E-mail
Google+		https://www.profiles.google.com/Rodrigues
Digital portfolio		https://www.mariarodrigues.com
Personal website		http://www.mariarodrigues.com
Digital resume		https://www.mariarodrigues.com
E-mail		maria.rodrigues@mariarodrigues.com

You can research how to create shorter versions of URLs for use on a resume or other job search documents.

SOCIAL MEDIA METRICS

There are different ways to measure social media profiles. Complete content and quality content are the two most important measures to focus on.

Profile Completeness   Most social media sites have a tool prompting you to complete your profile. The LinkedIn Profile Strength indicator is an example. An advantage of a complete LinkedIn profile is that you can achieve an "All-Star" rating which allows you to share your profile on Facebook and Twitter. You don't move to an All-Star rating all at once, however. The Profile Strength indicator acknowledges the progress you make completing your profile with five ratings that follow you from Just Beginning through All-Star level. If you are a beginner, it is fine to take your time completing your profile. Set goals to gradually complete sections and post your content only when it is ready for public viewing by prospective employers.

Profile Quality   There are tools you can use to measure how effective your social media sites are in helping your job search. Klout and Kred scores and Tweet Grader are examples. A Klout score tells you the number of people who follow you and how interested they are in you. If they stay connected by sharing or commenting on your Facebook and LinkedIn status updates, you've created interest. Google Analytics is another tool for measuring the quality and relevance of your content. It shows a viewer's level of interest in you by the time spent on a page and the total number of pages viewed. During your job search, these tools can help you evaluate employer activity with your social media sites (Figure 7.2).

If you are a beginner, focus on the completeness of your profile first. If you have a lot of experience and if your sites have been public for a long time, you should still set goals to improve your sites. You may have great content that could be packaged in a better way. Metrics can be a helpful way to know if you are focusing on the right areas.

While it is important to know about these ratings, your focus should always be on building a social media profile that best represents you. The ratings will come in time.

> "If I go to your page and the link is broken or it's out of date, that speak volumes to me that you're . . . not managing your own personal brand the way I would want you to manage my client's brand."
>
> Camille Weas, a hiring manager, RBA consulting firm
>
> Source: Retrieved November 17, 2013, from www.marketwatch.com/story/boomer-job-seekers-consider-an-online-portfolio-2013-03-25.

ACTIVITY 7.1

Learn about Social Media Metrics

To learn more about social media profile metrics, go online and research the following keywords: *LinkedIn Profile Strength, Klout score, Kred score,* or *Tweet Grader.* Write down a few notes about what you learned, and indicate one or two things you could do differently to improve your current social media profile.

Social Media Metrics:

_____   _____

_____

_____

FIGURE 7.2

Who's Viewed Your
Profile

Who's Viewed Your Profile

7 Your profile has been viewed by 7
people in the past 30 days.

19 You have shown up in search results 19
times in the past 7 days.

Profile Strength

All-Star

"A careless public
post or misstep on
Twitter can greatly
impact personal
branding and can
make candidates
less desirable to
employers."

Shawn Tubman, manager
of corporate employment,
Liberty Mutual

Source: Retrieved November 13,
2013, from www.boston.
com/business/technology/
innoeco/2011/09/social_media_
advice_for_job-se.html.

While building your social media online profile, here are some dos and don'ts to consider:

Do

1. Shine with best strengths: accomplishments and results first, then duties and responsibilities.
2. Use industry-, company-, or job-specific keywords throughout.
3. Monitor content on a regular basis.
4. Friend, endorse, and connect with credible individuals.
5. Keep it simple. Don't try to invent content or use underdeveloped content.
6. Add optional features only if you have quality content.
7. Use only appropriate pictures and images (content and size).
8. Use a profile photo of yourself (professional or business casual headshot).
9. Learn to use job search features.
10. Use the most updated tools to add, edit, or remove information.
11. Set your privacy setting for friends and family.
12. Tell friends and family about your job search, and ask them to restrict comments to your public page to professional comments that can support your job search, or ask them not to comment at all.

> *"Adding your picture to your LinkedIn profile makes your profile 7x more likely to be viewed by others."*
>
> LinkedIn Blog[1]

Don't

1. Use inappropriate photos (provocative, too casual; no group profile photos).
2. Use content about drinking or using drugs.
3. Bad-mouth a former or current employer.
4. Share confidential information from a previous employer.
5. Use poor communication skills.
6. Make discriminatory comments based on race, gender, or religion.
7. Lie about qualifications.

[1]Retrieved August 28, 2013, from http://blog.linkedin.com/2013/07/29/
five-simple-ways-to-boost-your-professional-brand-on-linkedin-infographic/.

8. Use a false or unprofessional name with any type of your online identity.
9. Friend, endorse, or connect with individuals with a poor reputation. You are judged by the company you keep.
10. Use illegal information.
11. Be afraid to approach industry professionals who know you for endorsements.
12. Wait until you graduate to upgrade your social media sites for professional use.

TIMING UPDATES

You should update your social media profiles when

- You have a new accomplishment to add.
- You have updated your resume.
- You are preparing for a job interview.
- You have earned a new degree.
- You have a new job.

Publish content only that you know will be viewed favorably by employers.

FACEBOOK AND LINKEDIN

Throughout your job search both Facebook and LinkedIn will likely be your major social media tools.

Because Facebook started out as strictly a tool for social networking, there may still be a tendency to designate it as your "personal social media site" and designate LinkedIn for professional networking. The reality is that this distinction no longer exists; Facebook is now an equal player when it comes to social media sites for professional use. So be sure to have Facebook at the top of your list when you begin editing sites for professional use. Similarly, LinkedIn started out strictly as a professional social media site. It has evolved to include special sections for students and recent graduates. As other social media sites gain popularity with employers, you will want to add them to your list of tools in your job search.

STUDENT LINKEDIN PROFILES

Sometimes students are reluctant to use LinkedIn because they think it works best for individuals with many years of work experience. Based on feedback from employers and students, a student LinkedIn profile now enables you to add sections that highlight some of your student experiences in and outside the classroom.

Here is an overview of some sections you may want to add to your profile:

- **Student Headline:** a short, memorable description of who you are professionally.
- **Experience:** internships, full- or part-time jobs, and volunteer or community service work.
- **Connections:** school's LinkedIn groups (alumni, clubs, and organizations, etc.), employers, teachers, advisors, internship coordinators, coworkers.
- **Projects:** projects that show that you can apply classroom learning to real-world challenges and work effectively in a team. Add compelling research or class projects to your profile—especially those that demonstrate experience relevant to your professional goals.
- **Honors & Awards:** provide objective validation for your accomplishments. Did you make the dean's list or earn a merit-based scholarship? Add it to your profile.
- **Organizations:** participation in on-campus or external organizations, showing your contributions outside the classroom. Your leadership abilities and contributions in making a positive impact within an organization are talents widely sought by employers and recruiters.

"Think about how you present yourself on all social media sites, including Facebook, especially when seeking a job. Be mindful about your wall postings and status updates: you wouldn't want a possible future employer to view inappropriate content or pictures on your wall."

Jennifer Ramcharan, Global Recruiter at TripAdvisor

Source: Retrieved November 5, 2013, from www.boston. com/business/technology/ innoeco/2011/09/social_media_ advice_for_job-se.html.

FIGURE 7.3

Student LinkedIn
Profiles

Add Sections   ✕

Featured
Overview

Sections
Certifications
Courses
Languages
Organizations
Projects
Patents
Test Scores

Preview

Organizations

Alpha Kappa Psi
Member
2008 | University of Southern California (USC)
A professional business fraternity working to develop the entrepreneurial mindset in our
members and to promote social and environmental responsibility.

Circle K

Add to Profile   Close Window

- **Test Scores:** test scores such as from standardized tests or your current grade point average (GPA). Employers often view strong test scores as indicators of good problem-solving skills. If you have excelled at standardized tests, or have a stellar GPA, include these in your profile.

- **Courses:** names of select courses that qualify you for positions you are seeking, or that demonstrate your commitment to expanding your academic horizons. Do you consistently push the envelope by enrolling in rigorous coursework? Many employers know your school's course catalogs as well as you do, so include the strongest courses of your college experience.

To add new student sections to your profile, go to your LinkedIn profile page in edit mode, and click the blue "Add sections" bar under your profile summary (Figure 7.3).

Progress Check Questions

1. What are the major accomplishments or results you currently want to highlight in your social media profile?

2. How often do you use updated tools to add, edit, or remove content from your social media sites?

7.3 KEYWORDS

Keywords are specific words or phrases that narrow online searches to result in best matches (Figure 7.4).

As you write your social media profiles, your goal should be to create a profile that is highly searchable by employers. You can do this by using keywords throughout different sections of your profiles. The *Career Directions Handbook* provides a one stop shop for sourcing relevant keywords.

FIGURE 7.4

Job-Related Keywords

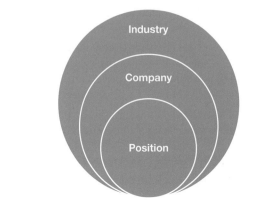

Industry

Company

Position

You also focus on the use of keywords when you write your resume. You can refer back to this discussion and the Career Directions Handbook when you write your resume in Chapter 10. The Career Directions Handbook contains a section of industry keywords and keyword phrases for easy reference.

KEYWORD CATEGORIES

Keywords important to a job search fall into three categories:

- Academic keywords
- Job-related keywords (including industry, company, and position)
- Diverse experience keywords

Keyword categories and examples are presented in the following table.

> Keywords can move you from a broad pool of job candidates to the finalists' list in a company.

Keyword Categories and Examples

Academic Keywords

Degrees
Concentrations
Certificates
Dean's list
Honors
Name of the university, college, institute
Internships, study abroad

Industry Keywords

Technical and transferable skills
Expertise
Certifications
Recognitions, honors, distinctions
Industry organizations and associations

Company Keywords

Company culture
Company mission and values
Customer base
Geographic reach
Strategic goals

Position Keywords

Job titles
Accomplishments and results
Duties and responsibilities
Technical and transferable skills
Degree requirement
Years of experience
Geographic location

Diverse Experience Keywords

Community service
Volunteer work
Languages
Extracurricular activities
Military experience

"Read job descriptions and identify the words that appear repeatedly. Then work these keywords into your profiles on LinkedIn, Twitter, Facebook, and Google+."

Miriam Salpeter, owner, Keppie Careers

Source: Retrieved November 16, 2013, from www.realsimple.com/work-life/life-strategies/job-career/social-media-job-search-job-hunt-00100000107873/.

EXAMPLE 1: KEYWORDS FOR A GRAPHIC DESIGN STUDENT

Academic

- Bachelor of arts degree in graphic arts
- Concentrations: graphic design, Web design
- GPA 3.5
- New Media College, Boston, MA

Industry

- *Technical skills:* Photoshop, Illustrator, Dreamweaver, Flash, HTML/CSS, JavaScript
- *Transferable skills:* team projects, training, leading, creating
- *Expertise:* nonprofit organization websites, corporate Facebook profiles, webinar presentations
- *Industry organizations and associations:* American Institute of Graphic Arts (AIGA), ArtBistro at Monster.com

Company

- *Company culture:* community engagement
- *Customer base:* nonprofit organizations, entrepreneurs
- *Geographic reach:* nationwide
- *Strategic goals:* grow Northeast Hispanic customer base

Position

- Graphic designer, Web designer, Web developer, interactive designer, communications specialist

Diverse Experience

- President, AIGA student group
- Hispanic Association of Student Entrepreneurs volunteer advisor
- Fluent in Spanish

EXAMPLE 2: KEYWORDS FOR A COMMUNICATIONS PROFESSIONAL IN A LINKEDIN PROFILE

Keywords that a communications professional would use in his or her LinkedIn profile to connect with potential employers include *crisis communications, community relations, media relations, speech writing, newsletter production, brainstorming,* and others. See Figure 7.5 for more suggested keywords.

In Chapter 10 you will use keywords in developing your resume.

> "LinkedIn allows you to fill in descriptions in your profile headline, personal interests, summary, job title, and career history. Make sure, when filling out these sections, to use keyword-rich descriptions that will draw in relevant search engine traffic."
>
> Jorgen Sundberg. CEO, Link Humans
>
> Source: Retrieved November 14, 2013, from http://jorgensundberg.net/linkedin-how-make-google-love-your-profile/.

FIGURE 7.5

LinkedIn Keywords for a Communications Professional

Skills & Expertise			
Crisis Communications	Event Planning	Media Relations	Media Spokesperson
Employee Communications	Employee Relations	Diversity Strategy	
Community Relations	InDesign	Microsoft Office	Writing	Speech Writing
Press Releases	Newsletter Writing	Newsletter Production	AP Style
Public Relations	Brainstorming	Social Media	

Progress Check Questions

1. What job search, industry, or company websites can you use to research targeted keywords?

2. Who are some industry professionals you can seek out to endorse some of your skills and expertise?

BUILDING AND RANKING YOUR KEYWORDS

Review the different categories of keywords shown below. For each category, write down some keywords that you think are important to include in your social media profiles. You can reference job descriptions and industry and company websites to help you.

Academic _____

_____

Industry _____

_____

Company _____

_____

Position _____

_____

Diverse experience _____

_____

Choose a total of five keywords that you think are most important to include in your social media profiles at this time. Rank them in importance with 5 being most important.

5. _____

4. _____

3. _____

2. _____

1. _____

Check your social media profiles to see how you have included these keywords in the appropriate sections.

ACTIVITY 7.2

Build and Rank Your List of Keywords

Real Life Stories

Sean and Lori: Handling Unemployment Status in Social Media Profiles

Sean was having trouble finding a job for some time after he graduated. He did not know how to refer to his unemployment status on his LinkedIn profile. He decided to use this as an opportunity to reach out to his LinkedIn network. In the Professional Headline section of his profile he wrote, "Recent College Grad Seeking Entry Level Accounting Position. Would appreciate appropriate referrals." In the Current Position section he wrote, "Recent Grad at (name of college).edu." He went one step further and shared the same with his college's LinkedIn Alumni Community Group and received three referrals within seven days.

Lori was laid off from her job after working for three years as a certified nursing assistant (CNA). In her LinkedIn profile she listed her Professional Headline as "Experienced CNA in transition." In the Summary section of her LinkedIn profile she mentioned her availability for work and contact information. She thought she was taking a risk exposing her unemployment status, but she knew that she had to be truthful. It is easy for employers to read through vague statements and to verify a questionable employment status. It's better to be truthful, and like Sean, work your LinkedIn and other career networks for leads to new opportunities.

FIGURE 7.6

Social Media Profile Rubric

CONTENT	POINT VALUE	Beginner	Developing	Well Developed	CAREER PROFESSIONAL	EARNED POINTS
PROFESSIONAL CONTENT	20	Existing Facebook or LinkedIn profile; other social profiles created.	Facebook, LinkedIn and other sites' professional content growing.	Facebook, LinkedIn and other sites' content mostly professional.	Facebook, LinkedIn and other sites' professional content strong and extensive.	
COMPLETENESS	20	Some main sections not complete.	Most main sections complete.	Most main sections complete with relevant, professional information.	All main sections complete with relevant, major professional accomplishments ordered first.	
PROFESSIONALISM	15	Unprofessional images/language. Many errors in grammar, capitalization, punctuation and spelling.	Some unprofessional images/language. Some errors in grammar, capitalization, punctuation and spelling.	Professional images/language. No errors in grammar, capitalization, punctuation and spelling.	Effective use of professional images/language; no errors in grammar, capitalization, punctuation and spelling in all sites.	
KEYWORDS	10	Minimum/random use of keywords. Keywords not consistently applied across all sites.	Most sites contain keywords.	All sites contain some keywords. Keywords consistently applied across all sites.	Keywords targeted to job, employer and industry consistently across all sites.	
SEARCHABILITY	10	Profiles are not clearly linked. None appear in a Google search.	Some profiles appear in a Google search.	Most profiles appear in a Google search and link to each other.	All profiles appear in a Google search and link to all professional online identity.	
CREATIVITY/ DISTINCTION	10	Key accomplishments/results not apparent.	Key accomplishments/results are distinct.	Hyperlinks provide distinct examples.	Online career portfolio linked to profiles.	
CONSISTENCY	5	All usernames are not the same. Information not same across sites.	Most usernames/URLs and information are consistent across sites.	All usernames/URLs and information are consistent across sites.	All usernames/URLs, domain name and information are consistent across sites.	
AUTHENTICITY	5	Sites contain misleading, exaggerated or false information.	Some sites contain misleading or exaggerated information.	Most sites contain verifiable information.	All sites contain verifiable information. No misleading/exaggerated content.	
RESULTS/ SCORES (KLOUT, KRED, TWEETGRADER, GOOGLE ANALYTICS)	5	Some random viewers and endorsements. No or low scores.	Targeted viewers and endorsements. Scores increasing.	Repeat targeted viewers and endorsements. Scores increasing.	Frequent, consistent, targeted viewers and endorsements. Strong scores.	

7.4 MEASURE YOUR PROGRESS AND STRENGTHEN YOUR SOCIAL MEDIA PROFILES

It is critically important that your social media profiles always leave a positive, lasting impression. In order to do this, you should have a plan to continually monitor and strengthen your profiles. The social media rubric (Figure 7.6) outlines stepping stones for growing and assessing key areas of your profiles. You can periodically ask your instructor or employer to evaluate your profiles using the rubric. Based on the feedback you receive, set goals for improvement. Activity 7.3 is a self-monitoring tool for managing the development of your social media sites. The checklist of questions will create awareness of areas that may need to be further developed to maintain a high-quality social media site. Correct grammar, spelling, and punctuation and accurate information are must-haves from the start, so make those edits immediately. Use this as a tool for periodic check-ins, and each time choose another area to improve on. It takes time to fully develop a social media profile. Be patient and don't present content until you know it is ready for public viewing. Both of these tools will enable you to successfully manage the use of social media profiles to advance your job and progress in your career.

> "When handled correctly, social media can help you professionally. The key is to be proactive about managing your activity and image."
>
> Amy Gallo, contributing editor, *Harvard Business Review*
>
> Source: Retrieved November 12, 2013, from http://blogs.hbr.org/2011/12/boost-your-career-with-social/.

ACTIVITY 7.3

Strengthen Your Social Media Profiles

Does your current social media content measure up for your job search? Do a self-check. Review your social media profiles, and look for opportunities to strengthen them.

Quality

1. Are your accomplishments and results in a lead position?
2. Are most of your skills and expertise industry relevant?
3. Are all images professional and of quality resolution? Do you include your profile photo?
4. Is your profile 100 percent error-free?
5. Is all of your information truthful and accurate?
6. Have you used relevant keywords in each profile section?

Relevance

7. Have you focused on job-related content?
8. Is all information current?

Consistency

9. Is your content consistent across sites?
10. Do you use the same images, including same profile photo, across all sites?
11. Do you use the same keywords?
12. Do your URLs consistently contain the same version of your name?
13. Do you update all sections of every site monthly or as needed?

Last Updates

Date _____ Type of update _____

Date _____ Type of update _____

Date _____ Type of update _____

Date _____ Type of update _____

As with your entire online identity, your social media profiles are living profiles of you that grow as you grow throughout your career. Managing their content will help ensure you always have your best foot forward and showcase your professional brand. Building content that matters most to employers will increase your opportunities to connect with jobs and employers that are a right match for you. Conveying quality and consistency will distinguish you and help build a solid professional reputation.

Regularly monitoring progress toward strengthening your profiles will ensure your social media profiles continue to be an asset to you as you pursue your next goal.

SOCIAL MEDIA PROFILES AND CAREER DECISION MAKING

Based on what you learned about social media profiles in this chapter, choose a career decision you are currently trying to make and practice the decision-making process by answering each of the following questions:

1. What am I trying to decide?

_____

_____

2. What do I need to know?

_____

_____

3. How will it help me make a more informed decision?

_____

_____

4. How can I obtain what I need to know?

_____

_____

People _____

Experience _____

Research _____

5. Who are the best resources for the information I need?

_____

_____

"The network is not just the people you know—
it's who your network knows."

Reid Hoffman, president, LinkedIn[1]

[1]http://www.thequotationstation.com/R/Reid-Hoffman/page1.html

Career Networking

After completing this chapter, you will:

1   **Develop** your own mini-message and career networking message

2   **Apply** career networking skills

3   **Identify** types of career networking

4   **Recognize** the best use of online career networking

5   **Prepare** a Career Portfolio entry

Career networking is the most widely used resource in successful job searches. According to a study conducted by the U.S. Department of Labor, 63.4 percent of people find their jobs through networking.[2]

Career networking helps you develop contact with people who can provide you with job leads or career advice. The most effective methods of career networking are person to person, networking events, and social and professional networks online. In this chapter, you will identify types of networking, create your own career networking message, learn how to network, document a helpful list of contacts and career networking events, and learn about various online networking tools.

CASE STUDY

Sarah Networks Her Way to a Job

Sarah wanted to learn more about different jobs in the criminal justice field. In her career development class, she learned about many different career paths. Her instructor told her that many of the jobs in criminal justice were not as easy to find as those in some other fields. There were jobs with the federal government that she applied for online, but Sarah knew that securing a job with the government involved a long process and felt that she was at a disadvantage because she did not know how she could personally contact any of the hiring managers directly. Sarah's instructor recommended that she put together a networking plan to get the word out that she was looking for a job in her field. Sarah remembered industry guest speakers she had met at the Criminal Justice Career Fair at her school and the recruiters she had met from some government agencies. She also made some contacts at a career fair sponsored

[2]Career Playbook. (2009). Job and Career Networking. Retrieved September 1, 2009, from www.careerplaybook.com/guide/networking.asp.

by the local chamber of commerce. When she was at her friend's house one day, she was talking about her job search. Her friend's father thought he could help and joined the conversation. He had been a police officer in their town for 10 years. Sarah talked about a job in loss prevention at a local department store that she had applied for online. She had not received any response. Her friend's father said he knew the manager of security at the company's home office which was located in a nearby state and offered to call the manager. This was a contact that Sarah needed but would probably never be able to make on her own. Because Sarah had already taken the initiative to apply for the job online, the manager knew she was seriously interested.

Sarah was interviewed and was offered the job. In the meantime, Sarah maintained her online profile and kept in touch with three of the contacts she had made at the career fairs. One of them asked if he could pass her information on to two colleagues he knew from a professional association he belonged to. A few weeks later, Sarah received a call for an interview for a position with a private security company. She did not get the job and decided to accept the loss prevention position at the department store. Sarah kept in touch with her other contacts and periodically learned of open positions she might be interested in. Sarah was grateful that her instructor had been honest with her about how difficult the job market could be and for encouraging her to develop and maintain a career network.

Discussion Questions

1. What things did Sarah do to build her career network?
2. Should Sarah have networked outside her field? Why or why not?
3. Was it important for Sarah to maintain her contacts once she began her new job? Why or why not?

8.1 YOUR CAREER NETWORKING MESSAGE

The first step to successful career networking is creating a message that clearly communicates why you are making the connection and briefly introduces you. For example, the reason you are making a connection might be to be hired for an internship or a full-time job, introduced to an employer, or advised on an industry or best strategies for your job search.

NOTES | Networking Goals

Internship or full-time position
Introduction to an employer
Industry information
Job search and career planning advice

MINI-MESSAGES

Develop a strong written and verbal message about your goals and qualifications to reach your networking goals. The following examples of mini-messages might help you communicate who you are, what your strengths are, and the benefits you offer.

Mini-Message #1: Student Seeking an Internship

My name is Cory Smith. I am a senior at Gateway College, majoring in accounting information technology. I am interested in your accounting internship to learn about preparing income tax statements for nonprofits. I have completed six courses in taxes and am an honors student with a 3.7 GPA. I have held a part-time job for two years at an accounting firm and am the team leader for my career capstone project. My contact information is included so that I can be easily reached after today's meeting.

Mini-Message #2: College Graduate Seeking a Career Position

My name is Kerry Gordon. I am graduating from County Community College with an Internet marketing degree and seeking an interview for a marketing position. During a three-month internship at BankOne, I prepared a customer service training manual now used to train new employees at the bank. I served as vice president of the marketing association on-campus. My Career Portfolio contains examples of my work, including the training manual and my Internet marketing project. I can be reached at the contact information provided and look forward to an interview.

Mini-Message #3: Student Seeking Career information at a Career Fair

My name is Valeria Rivera. I am seeking information about positions available with AS degrees in entrepreneurship and travel tourism management. I would like to learn the best path to becoming a partner in a small travel service. I organized a community outreach program for a nonprofit, start-up business. I am bilingual and looking for an opportunity to use my translation skills to build client relationships. I am providing my contact information so that I can be reached after today's meeting for a more detailed discussion.

> "First, you need to know what you are selling and to whom. Then you've got to package it up properly."
>
> Matt Youngquist, president, Career Horizons
>
> Source: www.npr.org/2011/02/08/133474431/a-successful-job-search-its-all-about-networking.

CAREER NEWORKING CARDS

Your career networking card conveys your uniqueness and should draw an employer's interest in you beyond your first contact. Take time building your message by planning the information you share and how you share it (Figure 8.1).

FIGURE 8.1

Sample Front and Back of Derek T. Thompsen Career Networking Card

DEREK T. THOMPSEN

Supports Web innovation and strategy to increase productivity of IT functions

WEB RESUME: www.dtthompsen2490.com/webres.html

EMAIL: dtthompson@xyz.com　**PHONE:** (412) 483-9730

PERSONAL WEBSITE: www.derektthompsen2490.com

CAREER PORTFOLIO: www.derektthompsendrktportfolio2490.com

DEREK T. THOMPSEN

CARDON COMMUNITY COLLEGE
B.S., Information Systems A.S., Web Development

- Web and Video Innovation in Design, Student Award 2012
- Web development and Web page design
- HTML, XHTML, JavaScript
- SQL, SQL/PL, Oracle, Access
- Unix and Windows XP
- Self-monitored projects generated new contracts totaling $200,000

CAPSTONE COURSE PROJECT:

"Publishing a Video" www.dtthompsenclassvideo.com

Card Style   The image you project on your career networking card should be a style consistent with the industry you are interested in. For example, if accounting is your career field, a conservative-style card is probably best. Marketing or graphics design majors would be expected to take a more creative approach. Designing your own card is one way to display your creativity if done professionally. You can select a business card template online or at a printing service. There are enough design choices to enable you to distinguish yourself.

Contact Information   Contact information should contain multiple ways to reach you and can also list links to more detailed information about you.

Professional Links   Links to your online resume, professional profiles, and Career Portfolio all help provide a complete picture of qualifications and accomplishments that distinguish you. A personal website is great way to host all components of your professional online presence in one place.

Skills and Education   List four to six bullets and always emphasize your expertise and skills. If you don't have a lot of work experience, select skills developed from volunteer work, work with clubs or organizations, or home–family management skills. Use a few education highlights to balance your skills list.

The samples shown in Figures 8.2 to 8.4 illustrate different ways to include your contact information, professional links, and skills and education on your card.

FIGURE 8.2

Sample Front and Back of Amanda Soto Career Networking Card

AMANDA SOTO

Job Ojective: Administrative Management for non-profits
Resume: www.asoto1resume.com
E-mail: amanda.soto1@xyz.com Phone: (206) 487-2976

SAMPLE WORK

www.acsseattlegiving.com
www.sotoam.com

AMANDA SOTO

B.S., ADMINISTRATIVE MANAGEMENT
Seattle Institute of Business and Technology

- American Cancer Society-10% increase online donations
- United Way-125 new donors
- Chair, City Year Youth Project
- Published training manual and video
- Blackbaud, Access, Photoshop, Blog Marketing

FIGURE 8.3

Sample Back of Kerry Gordon Career Networking Card

KERRY GORDON

Qualifications Summary

- BS, Internet marketing
- Marketing internship Go Great Computer Graphics
- Graphic design sample work
- Published training manual
- Vice president, Student Marketing Association
- Internet marketing business plan

www.kgordon.com

FIGURE 8.4

Sample Front of
Cory Smith Career
Networking Card

CORY SMITH

Seeking accounting internship for a nonprofit business
Career Goal: Nonprofit accounting consultant

- BS, accounting information technology
- 2 years' work at accounting firm
- Data storage systems
- Team leader—information security system implementation
- Career capstone accounting project

www.csmithportfolio.com

**CAREER
PORTFOLIO 8.1**

CREATE YOUR MINI-MESSAGE AND CAREER NETWORKING CARD

Career Networking Card

1. Create your own mini-message (60–90 words).

_____

_____

_____

_____

2. Prepare contact information for the FRONT SIDE of your card.

Full Name
Resume/Profile Link (e.g., LinkedIn, Monster, Google+, Twitter, etc.)
Portfolio Link
Personal Web Address
Phone
E-mail
Address

(Note: If you are not ready to list a personal Web address, you can add it later.)

3. Select keywords and phrases from your mini-message to highlight on the BACK SIDE of your card.

Career Goal   Professional Objective

_____   _____

_____   _____

_____   _____

8.2 CAREER NETWORKING SKILLS

Knowing how to network and practicing your networking skills will open many doors with people who can help you throughout your career. The following basic networking skills can be applied to most networking situations. Whether you plan to network person to person, through networking events, or online, show that you are prepared, can connect effectively, and can follow through with the connections you make.

PLAN

Know what you want. Are you looking for advice, a better job, a change in career, an introduction to a contact, perhaps someone at a higher level than you whom you can't connect with on your own?

- Be confident.
- Build a list of e-mail addresses.
- Plan your career networking message.
- Practice your presentation.

CONNECT

- *Call or write directly.* Even though your communication may be screened, there may be times when you will be able to reach the person directly. Some people will be impressed with the personal effort you make to connect.
- *Attend the same professional events as the people you want to network with.* Being seen regularly at these events provides an opportunity for you to get noticed and for you to establish ongoing contact.
- *Shake hands and introduce yourself.* Take the lead.
- *Work the room when attending networking events.* The following tips for working the room at a career fair explain how to use your time well at networking events and ensure you leave a positive, lasting impression.

ENGAGE

Engage the other person in a conversation about why you are interested in connecting with him or her. Ask questions that show you are interested in the person you are speaking with. Try to ask questions that are open-ended.

Open-Ended Questions   Invite the other person to take the lead in the conversation. You can ask open-ended questions that prompt the other person to talk about his or her personal interests, career, or the company he or she works for.

Here are examples of open-ended questions:

- "Tell me about . . ."
- "What do you think . . ."
- "What was your experience. . . ."
- "What do you do . . ."

There might not be a lot of time for small talk, and you want to be sure that you achieve your networking goal. Use your career networking card to shift the focus of the conversation to why the other person should be interested in you.

BUILD RELATIONSHIPS

Not all networking is a one-time activity. Some of the contacts you make will be important to grow and develop. Relationships are not built in a day. They take time and effort. Follow-up is key to deepening your relationship with key contacts.

- Make a list of the people you want to develop and maintain long-term relationships with.
- Create a schedule of activities that you initiate with them periodically.
- Call or e-mail them, inviting them to lunch, or plan to meet them at an upcoming social or professional event.

> "So build rapport with your contacts—by listening, seeking common ground, and helping out where possible."
>
> Judith Perle, co-author, "The Network Effect," Director, Management Advantage, Ltd

Source: Retrieved November 19, 2013 , from https://jobs.telegraph.co.uk/article/networking-the-key-to-a-successful-career/.

NETWORK AT A CAREER FAIR

You can increase your success with connections you make at a career fair by following this simple, step-by-step action plan:

1. *Update your networking goals.* Are you looking for an internship or a full-time job? Are you interested in career or company information? Do you need job search advice or an introduction to an employer?

2. *Research participating companies.* Research as many companies as you can prior to the event. This will help you manage time by weeding out those that do not match your career goals. Having some knowledge of companies you are interested in will make it easier to initiate conversation with them.

3. *Prepare a list of questions.* Develop a list of questions that cover three areas: company or industry information, job leads and referrals, and introductions to other companies.

4. *Update and print your resume.* Have printed copies of your resume to leave behind. Some companies do not accept printed resumes, and you need to apply online first before an interview can be scheduled. Be prepared to make an online copy of your resume available.

5. *Prepare and print your career networking cards.* Use your cards as leave behinds. It is a reminder of your meeting and provides company representatives easy access to you. The company representative will have something with your name on it and can write brief notes about some things to remember about your conversation at the career fair.

6. *Dress professionally.* Look serious about your career. This is probably your first introduction to these companies. Proper dress may vary according to industry and company culture. It is best for both men and women to wear a suit. If it turns out that business casual dress is appropriate for some companies, you can adjust your presentation once you have had one or more interviews with the company. Review the information in Chapter 4 on interview and workplace dress to create a great first impression.

NOTES   How to Work the Room at a Career Fair

1. Target people you want to meet.
2. Introduce yourself.
3. Get information that pertains to you.
4. Get them interested in what you do and who you are.
5. Make friends—find common ground.
6. Take notes to remember key points.
7. Try to schedule a time for another appointment.
8. Offer to leave your resume.
9. Thank the person.
10. Move on to the next person.

"Every interaction is a potential job interview. The best way to get that call for a great new position is to be the first person someone thinks of before they post that opening."

Laurie D. Battaglia, career and leadership coach and co-owner of Living the Dream Coaches, LLC

Source: Retrieved November 19, 2013, from http://blog.brazencareerist.com/2013/11/06/how-to-network-for-a-new-job-while-still-employed/.

Follow-Up after a Career Fair

1. Follow up within 24 hours or at the time you were asked to.
2. If you were referred to someone else in the company, follow up promptly and introduce yourself. Let the person who referred you know that you followed up.
3. Send a thank-you note to the company representative you spoke with.

. . . .

Progress Check Questions

1. Can you think of other ways to use your career networking card other than at a career fair?

2. What is the hardest part of career networking for you? What can you do to develop more confidence in that area?

. . . .

8.3 PERSON-TO-PERSON CAREER NETWORKING

Person-to-person networking involves direct contact one on one or in a group situation. Record a list of the career network contacts you already know and those you would like to develop. Some career network contacts might include the following types of people.

CAREER NETWORK CONTACTS

"Smart hiring managers will use technology to their benefit, but recognize the need for in-person meetings and phone calls to discover who the candidate behind the computer is."

Michele St. Laurent, HYPERLINK, Insight Performance

Source: Retrieved November 19, 2013, from www.tlnt. com/2012/11/01/9-ways-hr-recruiting-technology-will-evolve-in-next-4-years/.

Instructors. Many schools require instructors to stay current in their field by developing and maintaining industry contacts. Stay connected with them after you graduate. Alumni often seek career advice or connections to contacts, from former instructors, that help them make successful career moves.

Alumni. Former graduates of your school are a great resource of connections within their company or through professional and personal networks they have built. Many alumni return to campus to speak in the classroom or participate in career fairs. The hiring manager at the company you are interested in could be an alumnus of your school. Check your online alumni center to find alumni in hiring positions.

Counselors. Check to see if you have access to a career or academic counselor or advisor at your school. They may have industry contacts to share with you as well. Professional career counselors can also be a good resource. Their network may include people with career experience in your field willing to share career information with you.

Coworkers. The people you work with can provide valuable insight into which individuals at your company are best to connect with for career advice.

Community members. Within your local community, you may be a member of different social and professional groups. You probably became a member because you share common interests with the group. The community members you interact with are good sources of information that may result in job leads or new networking opportunities. Staying connected with your community is one way to build important networking relationships.

Relatives and friends. We often overlook relatives and friends as networking resources. If none of your relatives or friends are working in the field or at a company you are interested in, they may know someone that can help you. Don't forget to tell people about your job search. People you meet at church or other place of worship, the gym, the beauty salon, sporting events, and through volunteer work might make connections for you.

ACTIVITY 8.1

Create a List of Career Network Contacts

Names	Phone Numbers	E-mail Addresses

NETWORKING EVENTS

Networking events create opportunities to connect one on one with individuals who can help you in your job search. Three of the more popular types of career networking events include career fairs, professional association meetings, and professional conferences and workshops.

Career Fairs   Career fairs are excellent networking opportunities. If the list of participating companies is published, research in advance to determine which companies might best fit your career interests. Jot down notes about the company, and create a list of questions to ask. You may be most familiar with career fairs at your school, but you should also consider career fairs in your local community or on a regional or national level. The Internet lists career fairs held in different states or major cities.

Professional Association Meetings, Conferences, and Workshops   One-on-one contacts can be developed with members of professional associations you join. Belonging to professional associations is an effective way to connect with influential people in your career field. Through members you meet at conferences or workshops, you can explore job leads or career advice or obtain referrals to other helpful contacts. The *Career Directions Handbook* has lists of professional associations by career field to help you decide which organizations might benefit you most. Be sure to ask about student rates for memberships and conference attendance.

ACTIVITY 8.2

Create a Calendar of Career Networking Events

Date	Event	Location

"Your virtual handshake is just as important in making an initial impression as meeting someone face to face."

Sheryl Johnson, founder of BD-Pro Marketing Solutions

Source: Retrieved November 17, 2013, from www.weknownext. com/trends/amping-up-your-social-media-profile.

8.4 ONLINE CAREER NETWORKING

VIRTUAL INTRODUCTIONS

Virtual introductions have some advantages over face-to-face introductions. The biggest advantages are the ability to connect with contacts in different geographic locations and time to plan and review your message before sending it. One challenge is how to achieve the same feeling of personal connection as in a face-to-face introduction.

Virtual Handshake   A handshake is an important part of most introductions, often creating a lasting impression and connection between two people. In a physical handshake, nonverbal impressions such as eye contact, facial expression, and overall appearance influence the power of the handshake. How do you create a lasting impression and feeling of connection off-line? How can words and images in your online introduction bring you to a virtual handshake?

E-mails, Texts, and Tweets   Most online introductions start with an e-mail. The e-mail may refer to an online networking card, resume, portfolio, or website, but the content of the e-mail is what will draw someone to want to take a next step with you. A strong e-mail introduction rises to the top when it conveys you are the best fit for that specific job and company. Your career networking card is a good place to start. The skills and expertise in your e-mail should be consistent with those on your career networking card. Write to a specific person targeting the job and company. Find ways to convey your individuality and make a personal connection. Make the person feel comfortable with digging deeper to find out more about you. The trick with e-mails is conveying the strongest message you can concisely. Examples of strong e-mail introductions can be found in Chapter 11.

Be careful using texts or tweets to introduce yourself to an employer. If these are the tools a company uses to communicate with candidates, you will want to be sure to be professional in your text messages or tweets. Don't be hasty. Think beyond the informality and instant responses usually associated with these tools, and take time to think about what you say and how you say it.

MOBILE PHONE CAREER NETWORKING TOOLS

Mobile phone applications to manage your career networking activity save you time and make access to your contacts easier. These applications can help you design and send mobile career networking cards, make virtual introductions, and save career networking leads.

Design and Send Mobile Career Networking Cards   There are applications for designing and sending digital career networking cards directly from your mobile phone. You can create your digital card with a provided template or picture and can e-mail it directly to your contacts.

Make Virtual Introductions   You can introduce yourself online by allowing people to view your card. You can also ask selected contacts to use your card to introduce you to others online.

Save Career Networking Leads   Some applications allow you to take a picture of your contacts' business cards and read them using text recognition technology which automatically adds the information to your mobile phone's contact list.

LINKEDIN AND FACEBOOK CAREER NETWORKING TOOLS

LinkedIn Tools   LinkedIn is one of the most widely recognized social media sites for career networking. There are a number of career networking tools on LinkedIn that can help you build quality connections.

- *Connections and endorsements.* Click on a person you are connected with, and be invited to endorse that connection for multiple skills. Your connections can endorse your skills to help build a strong profile, but be sure the person you endorse and that endorses you is reputable.
- *LinkedIn groups.* You can access LinkedIn groups for the college(s) you attended and companies you have worked at by searching for the name of the school or organization so you can reconnect with selected individuals and check their current status. Some may become helpful new members of your career network. Some LinkedIn groups provide notifications and announcements, while others have a Jobs section that posts job opportunities.
- *"People You May Know"* tool. This tool displays potential contacts you might want to connect with on the top right of the screen where you log in. These contacts have something in common with you professionally that qualify them as potential members of your career network. You can choose to connect with them or not.
- *"Signals"* section. Signals tracks your contacts that are still active on LinkedIn. Review it to reconnect with individuals you may have lost touch with. Reconnecting with contacts keeps you up to date on what they are doing and reminds them you are actively networking on the site.
- *"Get Introduced"* section. This feature helps you get introduced to new, targeted contacts with the help of current contacts in your career network. You can send a message and ask your current contact to introduce you to a professional in his or her network that you want to know.
- *Recommendations* feature. You can receive and give professional recommendations on LinkedIn. A LinkedIn recommendation can interest an employer to dig deeper into your qualifications and pursue more detailed references. Be sure that those you ask for a recommendation are reputable and can be trusted to provide an accurate account of your qualifications Be careful making recommendations online. You want to be sure what you say accurately reflects the person you are recommending. If you embellish or falsify a recommendation for someone, it can reflect negatively on you. Do not agree to make a recommendation for someone you don't know or someone you can't honestly support in a positive way.
- *"Groups You May Like"* feature. You can also click on "Groups You May Like" to get group recommendations from LinkedIn. This feature provides you with a list of groups automatically selected for you based on similarities you may have with members of the groups. Similarities may include companies, schools, or industries common to both of you.

Facebook Tools

- *BranchOut.* BranchOut was the first Facebook application that enabled Facebook to be used for professional networking. Facebook users can develop a professional profile enabling them to do career networking through Facebook relationships. On BranchOut, you can search a company by name and connect with Facebook friends who work there. One of the basic premises of BranchOut is the ability to jumpstart a professional network through "friends" you already know on Facebook.

Connections and Endorsements
LinkedIn Groups
"People You May Know"
"Signals"
"Get Introduced"
Recommendations
"Groups You May Like"

"Surround yourself with only people who will bring you higher."

Oprah Winfrey[3]

[3]www.brainyquote.com/quotes/quotes/o/oprahwinfr383697.html.

- *BeKnown.* BeKnown is a Monster.com application for Facebook. Users can connect with professional contacts as well as Facebook friends. Personal and professional profiles are separate. Friends and work information help identify where you have inside connections. BeKnown is user-friendly to entry-level job seekers, making it a popular choice for career networking among college students. BeKnown has been key to bringing Facebook from a strictly social networking site to a popular option for professional networking.

Real Life Stories

Tom's Career as a Chef

With a new degree in culinary nutrition, Tom's career goal was to work as a chef preparing creative, healthy-choice spa menus. His dream job was to eventually work in a test kitchen for a large international hotel chain with resort properties featuring spa cuisine. Tom provided LinkedIn and Facebook profile links with his online applications. After receiving no responses, Tom asked his instructor for advice. Tom was embarrassed to learn that his Facebook public profile included photos of him on vacation playing at a club with his band. He had forgotten to apply the privacy setting for information he wanted to share only with friends and family.

Once a week, Tom spent 30 minutes online updating his profiles.

Tom's sister connected him with a chef manager she knew who told Tom about an online job site hosted by a leading culinary professional association. She told Tom to use the advanced search feature on the site. Here Tom could tailor his application to include position title, zip code, and his culinary-specific skills and specialization. Now, his revised online profiles and applications led to matches for several jobs that were the right fit for Tom.

"Attend the virtual event sneak preview to eliminate any potential computer problems or company firewall issues before the virtual job fair begins."

InXpo

Source: Retrieved November 19, 2013, from www.trainingmag. com/article/virtual-handshake-job-fairs-and-social-networks-aid-recruiting.

ONLINE CAREER EVENTS

Virtual career fairs, podcasts, webinars, and chat rooms are types of online career events. Online sites, including Facebook's built-in events application, are available to help you find and track conferences and events. Professional association websites post upcoming podcasts, webinars, and chat rooms. Be sure to combine your participation in both person-to-person and online career events to ensure you have a strong presence among a variety of prospective employers.

Progress Check Questions

1. Can you name online career networking sites that are targeted to your career field?
2. Do you feel more comfortable with networking online or in person?

Virtual Career Fairs   You can build your career network online by participating in virtual career fairs offered in a wide variety of career fields. It is not difficult to participate in a virtual career fair. The process usually involves accessing registration information for students and employers, a hot links page for companies that have preregistered, and examples of how the virtual booths might work. Booth information might contain job descriptions, company information, Web page links, and e-mail links. You can search the Internet for listings of virtual career fairs that pertain to your career interests.

Podcasts, Webinars, and Chat Rooms   A podcast is an audio broadcast on the Internet that allows you to listen or watch an audio or visual file. The most popular format of a podcast is your MP3 player; however, podcasts can also be accessed on your computer using certain software such as Media Player.

A webinar is a Web-based seminar that provides the ability to give, receive, and discuss career information. Often conference presentations or workshops are recorded when being delivered and then made available online as a webinar. You can also participate live in a webinar viewing a presentation online and share feedback and ask questions in real time.

A chat room is an online interactive discussion in real time. Your school's online alumni career center, professional associations, and company websites are all resources for participating in chat rooms specific to your career interests.

"By using connections and networks, you differentiate your name from the thousands of other online applications."

Dr. Lee Bowes, CEO, America Works of New York, Inc.

Source: Retrieved November 20, 2013, from www.huffngtonpost. com/dr-lee-bowes/getting-a-job-the-4-keys-to-mastering-networking_b_2341093.html.

ACTIVITY 8.3

Create Your Own List of Online Career Networking Resources

Virtual career fairs

_____

_____

Podcasts

_____

_____

Webinars

_____

_____

Chat rooms

_____

_____

Progress Check Questions

1. Can you identify one or two upcoming virtual career fairs in your field that you might like to participate in?

2. Can you identify one or two Webinars about career networking in your career field that you might want to participate in?

> **NOTES** | Tips for Managing a Professional Profile
>
> 1. Use a conservative photo of yourself.
> 2. Make your written profile brief and simple.
> 3. Focus the information you provide on your professional and career-related background.
> 4. Be careful what you say and how you say it. Avoid unprofessional or casual language, information, or comments.

CHAPTER SUMMARY

Effective career networking skills are among the most important job search skills you can develop. Setting networking goals is an important first step to a productive exchange with people you will connect with. Carefully planning your career networking message will make a difference in the way people respond to you and can set the stage for a successful exchange. You should use a combination of person-to-person and online networking to maximize the full potential of your contacts. In Chapter 9, you will see that one of the ways to use your networking skills is to find an internship position.

Networking is not a one-time event. It is an opportunity to build ongoing, valuable relationships. If you take the time to practice networking skills, you will develop the skill and confidence to manage professional relationships that can lead you to achieving, and maybe even exceeding, your career goals.

REFLECTION EXERCISE

NETWORKING AND CAREER DECISION MAKING

Based on what you learned about career networking in this chapter, answer the following questions.

1. What am I trying to decide?

_____

_____

2. What do I need to know?

_____

_____

3. How will it help me make a more informed decision?

_____

_____

4. How can I obtain what I need to know?

_____

_____

    People _____

    Experience _____

    Research _____

5. Who are my best resources for the information I need?

_____

_____

"Find that thing you are super passionate about."
Mark Zuckerberg, chair and CEO, Facebook, Inc.[1]

[1]www.ekaterinawalter.com/2013/01/12-most-profound-quotes-from-mark-zuckerberg/.

Internships and Co-op Programs

After completing this chapter, you will:

1 **Recognize** the value of internship and co-op programs to career success

2 **Create** learning goals for an internship or co-op experience

3 **Evaluate** and research different types of internship and co-op programs

4 **Define** your role in the success of your program

5 **Create** a Career Portfolio entry

As you prepare for your job search, you want to ensure that you have the strongest credentials to present to your prospective employer. This means being able to demonstrate on your resume and in your portfolio that you have acquired the skills and experiences that employers have said are most important to your career success. Employers want to know that you can apply the skills and knowledge you learn in the classroom through work experience. There are many forms of work experience ranging from part-time jobs and externships to internships and cooperative (co-op) education experiences. The two most commonly known types of formal work experience that employers look for are internships and co-ops. In this chapter, you will learn why internships and co-ops are important, and consider steps you can take to ensure that your internship or co-op experience is successful and becomes a valuable asset to your job search.

CASE STUDY

Liz's Competitive Edge

After enrolling in an interior design program at a local college, Liz learned about many career options in the interior design field. Not sure which path she really wanted to pursue, Liz took advantage of the school's co-op program. Liz completed two co-op experiences, one in retail and one in the commercial area.

Her retail co-op experience was with a home furnishings store. Unlike the sales work she did as her summer jobs, her co-op position was designed to be a learning experience and an opportunity to gain experience with the interior design function at the store. Much of her co-op experience was spent shadowing and assisting the store's interior designer.

Liz learned to coordinate colors and patterns. She used AutoCAD to practice designing floor plans using her knowledge of space planning. Liz scheduled home consultations and accompanied the interior designer on visits. She learned to work with clients to make recommendations on color schemes, fabric selection, and furniture layout that fit the clients' lifestyles and budgets. Liz also worked with a visual merchandising project. She assisted the interior designer with conducting weekly "power walks" through a few of the branch stores and participated in providing feedback to the merchandising department regarding showroom layouts.

Her second co-op experience was working with an architectural firm on two projects. Liz assisted the architects with small-scale commercial projects including a local fitness center. Her second assignment was assisting clients to determine space configuration and layout for a commercial office space using systems furniture. She used AutoCAD and Photoshop to edit floor plans. When the project was completed, she assisted with coordinating photo shoots and organized an opening event to promote the architectural firm's work.

In the office, Liz was responsible for keeping the architects' workspace organized and updating contact lists. When she graduated, she had a job offer from both of her co-op employers. The architects watched for co-op students who would be a possible fit for a full-time position with the firm. The firm extended a job offer to Liz at a higher starting salary than other entry-level hires and placed her directly into field work bypassing entry-level training. Liz accepted the position and credited her co-op experiences with helping her decide the type of work she wanted to do and helping her gain a competitive edge over most graduates applying for the same job.

Discussion Questions

1. Can you make a list of some specific skills Liz gained from her co-op experiences?
2. Can you identify technical and transferable skills that Liz learned in the classroom and applied on the job?
3. How can the real-world skills gained from a co-op experience help with making career decisions?

9.1 THE VALUE OF INTERNSHIPS AND CO-OP PROGRAMS

Internship and co-op programs provide experience that many employers look for in college graduates. The National Association of Colleges and Employers conducted research to support how highly employers value this type of work experience. The results showed that more than three-fourths of employers say they would prefer to hire new college graduates who have relevant work experience gained through an internship or co-op.[2]

An internship or co-op can help you build self-confidence, acquire or enhance skills, broaden your knowledge, or even evaluate a company as a potential employer. You become better qualified for the first job you want, and you enhance your long-term career potential.

Internship and co-op programs can slightly vary across institutions, so it is best for you to meet with a faculty or career advisor to discuss how these programs work at your school.

Generally the following distinguishes internship and co-op programs:

Internship: Internships are typically one-time work experiences related to your program of study or career goal. Students work in a professional setting with on-site supervision. Internships can be paid or unpaid and can grant academic credit or no credit.

Cooperative (co-op) education: Cooperative education generally describes multiple work experiences a student may have with one or more companies. The student alternates

---

[2]International Association of Employment Web Sites. (2009). "Work Experience Key for New College Grads Seeking Employment." Retrieved September 1, 2009, from www.employmentwebsites.org/work-experience-key-new-college-grads-seeking-employment.

terms of work experience in his or her field of study, usually full time, with classroom study. Almost all co-op positions are paid and grant academic credit. Internship and co-op programs are not the only forms of learning in the workplace, but they are the most widely recognized.

Some important things to consider when looking for the right program for yourself include your learning goals, whether the position is paid or unpaid, whether it offers academic credit or no academic credit, and if the work experience is full or part time.

BENEFITS OF INTERNSHIP AND CO-OP EXPERIENCES

There are many benefits to participating in a co-op or internship program. For example, you can:
* Improve basic work skills.
* Develop an understanding of the professional demands and requirements within your particular field.
* Test theories you learned in the classroom.
* Sometimes gain financial assistance to help defray educational expenses.
* Obtain job experience without a permanent commitment to the company.
* Gain exposure to facilities, equipment, and situations not available in the classroom.
* Build opportunities for higher starting salaries.
* Develop potential contacts for employment after graduation.
* Build your ongoing career network.
* Develop your Career Portfolio.

9.2 CREATING LEARNING GOALS FOR YOUR EXPERIENCE

Deciding your learning goals before selecting an internship or co-op experience creates a foundation for an experience that is right for you. Many schools require students to have written learning agreements prior to program participation.

Work with your faculty or career advisor to determine the goals that best fit your interests and level of experience. Some things to consider when identifying your learning goals:

How will I apply what I learned in class?

Do I want to learn or enhance a skill?

Do I want to further my knowledge or awareness about a career field and the positions within it?

Do I want to explore my fit with a particular type of organization?

Do I want to explore my interest in working with this company full time after graduation?

Do I want to learn about networking opportunities in my field?

These are only a few examples. The point is that there are many different reasons for doing an internship or co-op, and you should determine what you hope to gain from your experience. You should meet with a faculty member to get help in forming your learning goals.

> "An internship is à very long interview,' a 10-week interview. It takes into account the whole person. We see how well you perform and whether you will be good in a full-time position."
>
> Karen Fox, talent attraction manager, The Vanguard Group
>
> Source: Retrieved November 20, 2013, from www.austincollege. edu/wp-content/uploads/2012/10/Employers-and-Internships.pdf.

ACTIVITY 9.1

Writing Learning Goals

> **SAMPLE LEARNING GOALS**
> 1. Expand my use of technology by learning two new Excel applications by January 15.
> 2. Learn the new online system for patient registration by June 10.
> 3. Learn two different career paths in my field and document them in my journal by March 1.

ACTIVITY 9.2

Set a SMART Learning Goal for Internships and Co-ops

Using the SMART method for setting goals you learned in Chapter 3, write a learning goal statement for your co-op or internship experience.

Goal: _____

Write how your goal is:

*S*pecific _____

*M*easurable _____

*A*chievable _____

*R*ealistic _____

*T*imely _____

Write three other possible learning goals for a co-op or internship experience using the SMART method:

1. _____
   _____

2. _____
   _____

3. _____
   _____

"It's important to base your decision on whether or not a position is a good fit with your future interests, as well as with your financial situation."

Suzanna de Baca, vice president, Wealth Strategies

Source: Retrieved November 20, 2013, from www.huffngtonpost. com/suzanna-de-baca/ paid-job-vs-unpaid-internship_b_3610555.html.

9.3 EVALUATE AND RESEARCH THE RIGHT PROGRAM FOR YOU

You can learn about internship and co-op programs available to you from your instructors, professional association members, or career advisors; or at career fairs and information sessions or on the Internet.

Start with your school's resources to tap into the opportunities available to you. In most cases, your school is working through established relationships with employers who understand the type of experiences that best fit your degree program and background. These ongoing relationships with industry often provide the opportunity for feedback between the employer and faculty that helps to improve these experiences for both you and your employer. Online resources are also helpful with researching available positions by industry, geographic location, company, or position and providing a wide range of information and advice about these programs.

PAID OR UNPAID EXPERIENCES

Most internship and co-op experiences are paid. There are industries in which it is not customary to pay students. When developing a pay structure, an employer may consider your year of study. Some calculate a percentage of the starting salary being offered to graduates that year to determine an hourly rate. It is up to the employer to decide whether the experience will be paid or not. In some cases, the decision is influenced by state labor laws pertaining to certain industries. While pay most certainly will be an important consideration in your choice of program, you should first consider the quality of the experience you will have, if you can. Some of the best learning experiences are unpaid.

Most employers do not offer benefits, but some may provide paid holidays or relocation assistance. Talk with your faculty or career advisor to evaluate options that are best for you.

ACADEMIC CREDIT OR NO CREDIT

Schools have different approaches to granting academic credit for work experience programs. In almost all cases, co-op positions have some form of academic credit attached to the experience. These are typically more structured experiences. Students may or may not receive academic credit for internships. Talk with your faculty or career advisor to evaluate whether or not academic credit is associated with your experience at your school.

FULL TIME OR PART TIME

You should consider whether it will be best for you to participate in an experience that is full time for a term or runs part time, in conjunction with your classroom work throughout the academic year.

Full-time opportunities can be available year-round, but many companies structure their programs to run during the summer. If you are interested in a full-time experience, you have the option of traveling to and living in another geographic location. If you choose to relocate for your experience, be sure to budget the cost of travel, housing, and living expenses to ensure you can afford the related expenses. Many students choose to stay local for their experience due to financial concerns with relocating, or family commitments. Some students who live on campus choose to stay local, not to lose the opportunity to stay connected to campus activities such as clubs and organizations, career fairs, and on-campus recruiting. Part-time internships and co-ops allow you to continue taking other classes during your experience.

NOTES | A Day in the Life of Accounting Intern, Leah

CPA Firm

8:00 a.m.–9:00 a.m.	Observe staff meeting with partners.
9:00 a.m.–11:00 a.m.	Assist CPAs with work related to preparing tax returns.
11:00 a.m.–12:00 noon	Call clients to obtain missing information needed to complete their tax return.
12:00 noon–1:00 p.m.	Lunch with intern advisor.
1:00 p.m.–2:00 p.m.	Present update on intern project and receive feedback from supervisor.
2:00 p.m.–3:00 p.m.	Finalize internship project, "Offce Procedures Manual."
3:00 p.m.–4:30 p.m.	Attend training on new computer system.

NOTES | A Day in the Life of an Ad Sales Associate Intern, Carla

Theme Park

9:00 a.m.–10:00 a.m.	Register sales associates for executive management meeting.
10:00 a.m.–12:00 noon	Assist with media planning project.
12:00 noon–1:00 p.m.	Take calls at the reception desk.
1:00 p.m.–2:00 p.m.	Lunch with graphic designer.
2:00 p.m.–2:30 p.m.	Update client profiles in client database.
2:30 p.m.–4:00 p.m.	Summarize customer survey results for morning meeting.
4:00 p.m.–5:00 p.m.	Organize approved work samples from media planning project for career portfolio.

"Internship programs are a great way to generate more work samples for your professional portfolio and give you real accomplishment stories for your resume and online profiles."

Heather R. Huhman, president & founder, Come Recommended

Source: Retrieved November 20, 2013, from http://money.usnews.com/money/blogs/outside-voices-careers/2011/04/29/why-you-should-get-a-summer-internship.

> **NOTES** | A Day in the Life of a Merchandising Co-op Student, Anthony
>
> **Discount Retail Store**
>
> | | |
> |---|---|
> | 7:30 a.m.–9:00 a.m. | Meet other co-op students and travel to home offce. |
> | 9:00 a.m.–11:00 a.m. | Tour the distribution center. |
> | 11:00 a.m.–12:30 p.m. | Participate in panel discussion: logistics team and co-op students. |
> | 12:30 p.m.–1:30 p.m. | Have working lunch: orientation on mystery shopping assignment. |
> | 1:30 p.m.–3:30 p.m. | Do mystery shopping at area competitors. |
> | 3:30 p.m.–5:00 p.m. | Write and turn in mystery shopping reports. |
> | 5:00 p.m. | Co-op students travel home. |

ACTIVITY 9.3

Internship and Co-op Research

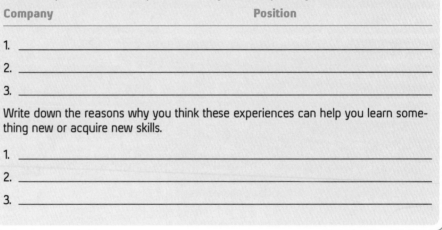

Using the Internet, research sites that provide information on how and where to obtain a co-op or internship experience, including actual position postings. You can use information on Weblinks in the Career Resources section for this chapter on the online learning center or explore other sites on your own. Write down the names of three companies and intern positions that you could possibly be interested in:

Company   Position

1. _____
2. _____
3. _____

Write down the reasons why you think these experiences can help you learn something new or acquire new skills.

1. _____
2. _____
3. _____

> "We also find that our interns move faster in our organization."
>
> Maura Quinn, director of university relations, Liberty Mutual Insurance Company
>
> Source: Retrieved November 20, 2013, from www.austincollege. edu/wp-content/ uploads/2012/10/Employers- and-Internships.pdf.

Real Life Stories

Rachel's Internship in Human Resources

Rachel obtained an internship in human resources at a leading financial company. The ad that she read on Twitter suggested that the intern would assist the training coordinator with promoting the company's training programs to all department heads, conducting and analyzing surveys to evaluate the programs, and matching new trainees with mentors. It also read that there would be opportunities to work on projects with the benefits coordinator. This sounded ideal to Rachel who wanted to know the ins and outs of human resources, which was her concentration in school.

During her first week on the job she met a number of people and became familiar with the training schedule and survey tool to be used. She noticed that some program sessions were filled and some still had many open slots. She immediately proposed some ideas of how to promote the sessions to increase enrollment. She was told not to worry about that, and that she was needed to help organize the sessions already scheduled. Her supervisor gave her a checklist of daily tasks.

Rachel was disappointed to see that her work consisted of making copies, setting out refreshments for breaks, and ensuring that the audiovisual equipment was up and running properly each day. She could not observe the sessions because she had to answer the phones while the human resources assistant participated.

While she was in the office, she was given survey forms to sort and then turn over to someone to consolidate and analyze the data. She had a weekly appointment scheduled with the director of human resources to talk about career paths in human resources, discuss her progress, and provide feedback on her experience.

Rachel met with her instructor for a midway progress report and said her disappointment was causing her to rethink her major. Her instructor advised Rachel to take the lead and speak with her supervisor to correct the situation. Rachel's initiative paid off. The last six weeks became a better learning experience.

Progress Check Questions

1. What are some things Rachel could have done to try to get her experience on track?

2. What are some actions you have taken to turn a disappointing work experience around?

9.4 YOUR SUCCESS WITH YOUR PROGRAM

Once you have been selected for your internship or co-op position, there are some things you can do both during and after your assignment to gain the most from your experience.

DURING YOUR EXPERIENCE

Set Goals   Your learning goals will keep you focused throughout your experience. Keep referring back to them.

Project Professional Image   Maintain a professional look and communication style.

Immerse Yourself   Spend time observing how people and positions relate to one another.

Take the Initiative   Look for opportunities to volunteer to do more than you are assigned if you are able.

Be Willing to Learn   Look for opportunities to ask others to show you how something, other than your work, is done and why it is important.

Be Willing to Work Hard   Show that you will do what it takes to get the job done.

Locate a Mentor   If a mentor is not assigned to you, seek someone out who can help guide you through the company culture and provide career advice.

Monitor Your Progress   You will have formal performance reviews that will tell you how well you are performing. Take the extra step and ask your supervisor if you can complete a pre-performance self-appraisal in advance of your performance review meeting. This will provide the opportunity for you to initiate conversation with your supervisor about how you both feel about the progress you are making.

> "Meet with your supervisor and lay out projects you'd like to tackle and skills you'd like to master by the end of your internship."
>
> Susan Adams, Forbes Staff

Source: Retrieved November 20, 2013, from www.forbes.com/sites/susanadams/2012/07/25/odds-are-your-internship-will-get-you-a-job/.

"Break out of your shell and build relationships with your fellow interns, coworkers, and managers."

Ashley Mosley, community engagement manager, InternMatch

Source: Retrieved November 20, 2013, from www.careerbliss.com/advice/how-to-turn-that-internship-into-a-fulltime-job/.

Obtain Feedback   Ask for input from your supervisors and peers along the way. Their feedback will help you know if you are on track and in what areas you could improve. It may also open opportunities for you to discover more challenging work sooner than planned.

Build Career Network Contacts   Some companies offer opportunities to build connections with students. These can include anything from having students observe weekly management meetings; "lunch and learn events"; presentations by key departments within the company; breakfast, lunch, or dinner meetings with key executives; executive speakers or any other exchange that connects students with the company at a business level. Keep a journal of people you are meeting who might be helpful to you long after your experience is over.

AFTER YOUR EXPERIENCE

Once you have completed your internship or co-op assignment you should take the time to reflect on your areas of improvement as a result of the experience. With your ideas well formulated, you should then set up a meeting with your faculty and/or career advisor to discuss the experience. This meeting is often referred to as an exit interview. Be sure to send a thank-you letter to your site supervisor. Finally, be sure to update your resume and your Career Portfolio to reflect your newest experience.

ACTIVITY 9.4

Reflect on Your Accomplishment

"You grow, you develop, you build relationships. You are inspired to stay."

Karen Fox, college relations and recruiting, Vanguard

Source: Retrieved November 20, 2013, from www.austincollege.edu/wp-content/uploads/2012/10/Employers-and-Internships.pdf.

Answer the following questions:

What have I learned? _____

_____

Work-related skills _____

_____

Insight into my personality and work style

_____

_____

Insight into my strengths and weaknesses

_____

_____

Did I achieve my learning goals?

_____

_____

Did I enjoy the position/experience that I was exposed to?

_____

_____

Would I want to do this work full time?

_____

_____

Is this the industry or career field I want to be in?

_____

_____

Would I want to work for this employer again?

_____

_____

Would I recommend this experience to another student?

_____

_____

Has this experience confirmed, or caused me to rethink, my original career goal?

_____

_____

_____

Debrief with Your Faculty and/or Career Advisor   This is an opportunity to confirm how your experience helped you achieve your learning goals. This is important because if you have any areas of concern about the value of the experience or other issues pertaining to the employer you worked with, your feedback can help improve the experience for other students.

Send a Thank-You Letter   You should always send a thank-you letter to your site supervisor. This is the person in the company who has committed the most time and energy with you and with whom you have likely developed the closest relationship. Even if the experience was not all that you expected, you should be courteous and acknowledge his or her work with you. This is particularly important if you think that you would like this person to serve as a reference for you or if you are considering the company for a full-time position. Figure 11.8 in Chapter 11 is an example of a format for an application letter for an internship or co-op program.

Update Your Resume   Update your resume to reflect, not just the work experience, but also new skills or knowledge you gained. Review your career objective on your resume. You may want to adjust your objective based on what you learned about your career goals during your internship or co-op.

Update Your Career Portfolio   You may want to update your Career Portfolio if you have new evidence of your skills from your work. You may have completed a project, developed a new procedure, implemented a new computer system, received a certificate of merit or recognition, or have other examples of work that will add value to your Career Portfolio. For example, Figure 9.1 shows an orientation manual that a student created while doing an internship.

FIGURE 9.1

Sample Internship Project

"[The internships] are about producing a product that can be implemented within the departments."

Leith Sharp, director of the Green Campus Initiative

Source: Retrieved November 20, 2013, from www.ulsf.org/pub_declaration_opsvol51.htm.

BRITTANY SMITH

233 South Andover Street

Burlington, Massachusetts

Cell phone: 508-396-7725

E-mail: smith.brittany@xyz.com

Gplus.to/smithbrittany

Web: smithbrittany.com

Tollgate Technical Institute

Manchester, New Hamsphire

Candidate: B.S., Medical Imaging

COMMUNITY HOSPITAL ORIENTATION MANUAL

FEBRUARY 2016

CAREER PORTFOLIO 9.1

"New media writing sample examples—blog posts, tweets and Facebook posts are great—no, not your personal ones, but rather ones you wrote on behalf of an organization."

Jeremy Porter, director of social and content marketing at Definition6.

Source: Retrieved November 20, 2013, from http://blog.journalistics.com/2013/skills-entry-level-pr-hires-should-have/.

●● INTERNSHIP AND CO-OP WORK SAMPLES ●● AND ACCOMPLISHMEMTS

Select Career Portfolio Entries from Your Internship or Co-op Experience

1. Work samples: written projects, websites, videos

_____
_____
_____

2. Recognitions: awards, certificates, commendations, endorsements

_____
_____
_____

3. Special distinctions

_____
_____
_____

4. Write brief descriptions that provide context for what you selected

_____
_____
_____
_____

While there are many different types of work experience that can contribute to your career success, internship and co-op programs can provide a more structured learning experience that clearly connects your classroom learning to workplace performance. Employers rate these experiences as very important when considering candidates at hiring time. You can improve your chances of obtaining a meaningful job in your career field at graduation by participating in work programs offered at your school. You need to be well prepared for your experience by knowing your goals and researching companies and positions that fit your qualifications and meet your career interests. You might talk with an instructor as you go through that process and inquire about availability of a co-op or internship advisor to help you make the most of your experience. Once you have been hired for a position, it is important for you to know how to take ownership of your experience. Finally, when you have completed your assignment, take time to reflect on how your experience may influence your current and future career decisions.

INTERNSHIP AND CO-OP PROGRAMS AND CAREER DECISION MAKING

Based on what you have learned about the value of internship and co-ops programs to your career success, complete the following exercise.

1. What am I trying to decide?

_____

_____

2. What do I need to know?

_____

_____

3. How will it help me make a more informed decision?

_____

_____

4. How can I obtain the information I need to know?

People _____

Experience _____

Research _____

5. Who are my best resources for the information I need?

_____

_____

"Employers today expect a clean, polished and professional resume that is full of keywords."

David Kiger, CEO and founder, Worldwide Express[1]

[1]http://finance.yahoo.com/news/worldwide-express-ceo-discusses-resumes-131700022.html.

Resumes and Job Applications

10

After completing this chapter, you will:

1   **Know** how to use multiple resume versions

2   **Select** your best resume format

3   **Differentiate** between the three versions of resumes

4   **Describe** the types of visual resumes

5   **Understand** how to complete job applications

6   **Create** a Career Portfolio entry

When preparing your resume, the most important thing to remember is that the employer is your main audience. Your resume will get better results when you target it to a specific industry and employer. This includes knowing which digital version of your resume an employer wants and having a quality print copy available for certain situations. It also includes knowing how to select and apply industry-, employer-, and job-specific keywords and power words when creating your resume. This will increase the probability of your resume rising to the top during an interview screening process. Knowing the difference between a chronological and functional resume will help you think about how to order your information on your resume to factually emphasize your strengths and accomplishments.

Like your resume, a job application should provide a professional and accurate picture of you. Understanding how your answers on a job application impact your job search will help you prepare a best approach to filling out an application factually and completely.

CASE STUDY

Jack took one last look at his resume before going to the career fair scheduled the next day. Jack first learned how to write a resume in his freshman year Professional Development class. At the time, he had developed a chronological resume. He had limited work experience to tout on his resume. His various jobs as a waiter, camp counselor, and part-time worker at the volunteer center developed nicely into a chronological resume that neatly showed his work history. Over time, Jack developed new transferable and technical skills from his internship, volunteer work and specialized courses. He was pleased to now be able to write a functional resume highlighting his more advanced and varied skills. He was sure to reference his language skills. He spoke and wrote both Spanish and Italian very well. He listed special accomplishments, including being selected to represent his school at a special ceremony recognizing outstanding service to AmeriCorp. Jack also provided a short, bulleted list of technical skills he had gained from work and through his coursework.

It was time to graduate, and Jack wanted to create a wide range of job options in case an offer from one of his top five companies didn't come through. All five companies would be at the career fair. He printed multiple copies of his paper resume to bring with him. He had taken the time to create targeted resumes for the five companies he was most interested in. Jack was able to do this by using keywords from each company's website and job posting that best fit his qualifications. He had also uploaded his e-resume into several online tracking systems.

At the career fair, Jack first went to the companies that he had applied to online. Only one of the company representatives was aware of his online application. He introduced himself to the others and gave them a hard copy of his resume. Two said they were interested in interviewing Jack now that they had met him and seen his resume. Several companies didn't take a paper copy of Jack's resume but asked him to post his resume on their company's resume bank. These companies had a policy to not accept paper resumes. Two companies preferred receiving an e-mail with a resume attachment, and one small business only wanted a paper copy. The company was too small to use an electronic system.

By the time Jack connected with all the companies he was interested in, he was pleased that he was prepared to follow up so quickly with each of these different requests. He received a call a few days later asking for a reference that could be contacted. When Jack said that his references were listed on his resume, he learned that two of them couldn't be reached at the contact information he had provided. When he asked if his e-resume had been received, he was told that it had not arrived and that occasionally e-mails with attachments were filtered out as junk mail. Jack received three interviews and two job offers, including an offer from one his five targeted companies.

Discussion Questions

1. What things did Jack do to make his resume stand out?
2. Do you think Jack's impressive background could stand out as clearly as he did in person at the career fair? Why or why not?
3. Do you know how the companies you are interested in will prefer you to submit your resume?

10.1 TODAY'S TRADITIONAL RESUME

"Resumes aren't dead but they are changing."

Chris Fields, HR professional, resume writer, and career coach[2]

In today's job market, you need different versions of your resume to respond to individual employer preferences. The basic print resume was known as the traditional resume. It was common to prepare a single version and send it to different employers during a job search. A resume is no longer limited to one document. Today's traditional resume is created in different versions for both digital and print distribution and targets specific positions using keywords.

The way to prepare and distribute a resume changes, but the reason for writing a resume stays the same. The purpose of a resume is to obtain an interview.

[2]Retrieved April 23, 2013, from www.jobsite.com/blog/resumes-are-not-dead-yet/.

MULTIPLE VERSIONS

The three essential versions of your resume are an edit-ready document, a PDF file, and a plain-text file. These will enable you to send your resume to an employer online or print a quality hard copy.

Following are some examples of different employer requests for resumes:

"Please resend your resume as a PDF. The format was jumbled when I opened your attachment."

"Copy and paste your plain-text resume in an e-mail."

"Do you have a resume in HTML format?"

"Do you have a Web resume?"

"Please enter a keyword-optimized resume into the online job application."

"The attachment you sent will not open. Please send me the ASCII version of your resume."

"Please just send me the traditional version of your resume."

"Can you bring a print copy of your resume?"

Details on when and how to use different resume versions are discussed later in this chapter. In any version, your resume must be well prepared and show that you are a fit for the position you are applying for. The best way to show fit is to use keywords and power words to complete the sections in your resume.

> *Today's traditional resume is created in different versions for both digital and print distribution and targets specific positions using keywords.*

KEYWORDS AND POWER WORDS

Keywords and power words in your resume help employers identify how well you match the requirements for a specific position. Whether an employer is scanning your resume with the human eye or the digital eye, keywords usually determine how far your resume may go in the interview screening process. This makes keywords a critical component in all versions of your resume.

Keywords are specific words or phrases that narrow online searches to result in best matches. You already practiced using keywords to create or update your social media profile in Chapter 7. You will find that many of the same keywords will apply to certain sections of your resume. Try to be consistent with the keywords you use in your professional social media profile(s) and your resume.

Resume Keyword Examples	Resume Power Word Examples
B.S., Administrative Management	Increased
Administrative Assistant	Raised
Liaison	Recruited
Dean's list	Developed
GPA	Trained
Blackbaud fundraising software	Managed
Access databases	Earned
Blog writing	Promoted
Photoshop	Coordinated
Microsoft Office 2013	Updated

A power word is an action verb that communicates the ability to do something. Some power words are stronger than others. Strong power words describe an accomplishment or result as opposed to only a job duty or responsibility. Listing both accomplishments or results and job duties or responsibilities is important in your resume.

> *WORDS MATTER: Every word on your resume should take you one step closer to an interview.*

You can refer back to the list of transferable or functional skills in Chapter 2 for some potential power words. As you work through writing the different sections in your resume, focus on using appropriate keywords and power words and remember to lead your sections with those indicating your greatest strengths. The Career Directions Handbook contains a section of industry keywords and keyword phrases for easy reference.

Progress Check Questions

1. What are the most important keywords you will include in your resume?
2. What are some power words you might use to lead a description of your accomplishments or results?

CORE RESUME SECTIONS

> "Identify exactly what you want your resume to do and convey before you get started. Put together the content once your target message is clear."
>
> Sylvia Flores, Partner, Adler Koten Institute
>
> Source: Retrieved December 1, 2013 from www.alderkoten. com/institute/2013/10/10-basic-guidelines-to-a-high-impact-executive-resume/

Identification   The identification section includes your name, address, phone number, and e-mail address.

1. Use your proper name in your e-mail address. Remember, the name part in your e-mail address is case sensitive. Be consistent with your use of uppercase and lowercase letters. Use a reputable domain. Gmail, Yahoo, or AOL are examples. The domain part of your e-mail is not case sensitive.
2. It is best to list your cell phone number if you are listing one phone number. You can list both your home and cell phone numbers if you choose. Don't use a business phone number.
3. If you are a student living on campus, you do not need to list your campus address. Most employers will contact you at your phone number or e-mail address.

Profile, Summary of Skills, or Professional Objective   There are different viewpoints about the use of professional objectives on a resume. A broad objective may indicate you don't have a well-thought-out career goal. A narrow objective may help you emphasize your fit for a targeted job, but a narrow objective can also limit you.

1. A resume profile is a descriptive summary of your major strengths, special accomplishments, and experience that would be of interest to a specific employer. It can be written in two or three sentences or presented in bulleted form.
2. A summary of skills is a short list of industry- or job-specific major skills, usually technical skills, presented in bulleted form.
3. A professional objective is a one- or two-sentence statement summarizing your career goal.

In general, a resume profile works best for someone with previous work experience. If you use a resume profile and have a professional social media profile, the two should be aligned. A professional objective is best for a recent graduate or for targeting a job with very specific requirements. Today, a summary of skills in a resume works well for most job seekers because it emphasizes keywords at the top of your resume.

EXAMPLE: SUMMARY OF SKILLS

- Blackbaud fundraising software
- Access database
- Photoshop
- Blog development
- Microsoft Office 2013

Use the Internet to research examples of resume profiles, summary of skills, and professional objectives by career field.

Education   The education section contains your institution's name, city, state, and zip code; your graduation date; and the name of your degree and major or concentration.

1. If you have not yet graduated, you can indicate when you expect to graduate in a few ways:

EXAMPLES

Expected graduation date 20__ or Expected graduation June 20__

September 2010–present

> Do not use the term *graduation pending* as this usually means your graduation date may be delayed because of an issue with your grades.

2. If you are receiving a master's degree, list both the awarding institution and your undergraduate institution.
3. List any relevant certifications or licenses you received as part of your degree.

EXAMPLE

Education:

2011–2015 Seattle Institute of Business and Technology, Seattle, WA 98101

B.S., Administrative Management

Dean's list, GPA 3.6

For alternatives to these examples, the presentation of your education can:

1. List the degree first followed by the institution.
2. Spell out the full name of the degree and a concentration.

EXAMPLE

Bachelor of Arts, Communications

Concentration in Professional Writing

3. List both an associate's degree and a bachelor's degree if the associate's degree relates a relevant specialization.

EXAMPLES

B.S., Internet Marketing

A.S., Advertising and Public Relations

Work Experience   The work experience section includes current and past work experience. If you have many years of work experience, there is no need to go back further than seven years. If all of your work experience has been with the same company, list the different positions you have held. If you are a recent graduate with limited work experience, you can list your internship and part-time and seasonal jobs in this section. What is most important in the work experience section is how you describe the work performed in particular positions. Lead each position description with accomplishments and results, and then describe specific job responsibilities. In the following example, accomplishments and results are listed first starting with a power word. Increasing online donations is a quantifiable result. The ability to increase results adds the greatest value to an employer, followed by the ability to manage, followed by the ability to update. All are important to list, but the order creates the right emphasis.

1. Lead with accomplishments and results.
2. Quantify or explain results qualitatively.
3. Target keywords from job descriptions.
4. Start each description with an action verb or power word.

"Turn accomplishments into numbers."

Suzanne Lucas
MoneyWatch

Source: Retrieved December 1, 2013 from www.cbsnews.com/news/how-to-write-a-resume-dos-and-donts/

> Today, a summary of skills in a resume works well for most job seekers because it emphasizes keywords at the top of your resume.

EXAMPLE
Work Experience:
9/2013–12/2013 Administrative Assistant Intern
American Cancer Society, Seattle, WA 98101

- Increased online donations by 10% in twelve months by creating new online giving system with project team (www.acsseattle.giving)
- Managed 300 major donor profiles using Blackbaud fundraising software
- Updated American Cancer Society's Facebook profile

CUSTOM OR OPTIONAL RESUME SECTIONS

Custom or optional resume sections can help you build on the strong foundation in the core section of your resume. If used selectively, custom options in your resume can help employers see a clearer picture of your unique qualifications.

Support Claims	Excellence	Diverse Experience
Career Portolios	GPA	Internships
References	Honors	Community service
Hyperlinks	Awards	Volunteer work
	Special recognitions	International study or work
	Certifications or licenses	Languages
		Extracurricular activities
		Homemaker experience
		Military experience
		Professional affiliations

Custom resume sections

When to Use Custom or Optional Sections   Custom or optional sections can help you communicate diverse experience, excellence, or support claims in your resume. Your resume can say, "I did more," "I did it better," "I can prove it." These claims should be used only to add meaningful and relevant information that pertains to the job you are looking for. Don't include stretched information to try to make it sound more important than it is. For example, traveling abroad once for vacation does not qualify as an international experience.

Once you have completed preparing your Career Portfolio, you can refer to it at the bottom of your resume page as "Career Portfolio Available upon Request." If your portfolio is online, you can list the URL. If you choose to list the URL, test the hyperlink to be sure it works.

Today, references are not usually included on the resume. Employers assume you will have references available if they ask for them. The common practice is to create a separate sheet listing references that can be given to employers who request it.

Examples of how to incorporate the previously discussed sections into your resume are provided in the resume samples (Figures 10.1 to 10.10).

"Every resume is a one-of-a-kind marketing communication with both explicit and implicit messages. It should be appropriate to your situation and focused on the story you want to tell."

Sylvia Flores, Partner, Adler Koten Institute

Source: Retrieved December 1, 2013 from www.alderkoten. com/institute/2013/10/10-basic-guidelines-to-a-high-impact-executive-resume/

Custom sections in your resume can help employers see a clearer picture of your more unique qualifications.

ACTIVITY 10.1

Draft Sections of Your Resume

Use the worksheets below to draft the core sections of your resume and then identify custom sections that are relevant to your targeted resume. Copy the blank education or work experience sections to accommodate additional entries.

RESUME SECTIONS WORKSHEET

CORE RESUME SECTIONS

IDENTIFICATION

Name_____

Address_____

_____

Phone number_____

E-mail address_____

PROFILE, SUMMARY OF SKILLS, OR PROFESSIONAL OBJECTIVE

_____

_____

_____

EDUCATION

Name and address of institution

_____

_____

Degree _____

Dates _____

WORK EXPERIENCE

Job title_____

Company name and address

_____

_____

Bulleted list of accomplishments or results and duties or responsibilities

_____

_____

_____

_____

_____

_____

_____

_____

_____

_____

Progress Check Questions

1. Do you think a profile, summary of skills, or professional objective is best for you? Why?

2. What custom sections do you think are most relevant and meaningful to include on your resume?

RESUME SECTIONS WORKSHEET

CUSTOM RESUME SECTIONS

DIVERSE EXPERIENCE

Internships_____

Community service_____

Volunteer work_____

International study or work_____

Languages_____

Extracurricular activities_____

Homemaker experience_____

Military_____

Professional affiliations_____

EXCELLENCE

GPA above 3.5_____

Honors_____

Awards_____

Special recognitions_____

Certifications or licenses_____

SUPPORT YOUR CLAIMS

Career Portfolios_____

References_____

Hyperlinks_____

10.2 RESUME FORMATS

Choosing a resume format is an important decision because the format organizes your information to emphasize your strengths. Chronological and functional resume formats are the most commonly used.

CHRONOLOGICAL RESUMES

The chronological resume lists your education and work experience in reverse chronological order, that is, by most recent dates first. This type of resume is excellent if you are entering the job market for the first time. It can be used when changing jobs within the same career field because it clearly shows a concentration of related jobs and experiences.

FIGURE 10.1

Sample Chronological Resume #1, Amanda Soto

AMANDA SOTO

234 Lindmore Road, Seattle, WA 98101
(206)487-2976
amanda.soto1@xyz.com

EDUCATION:

September 2011– present
Seattle Institute of Business and Technology, Seattle, WA 98101
B.S., Administrative Management Dean's List, GPA 3.6

SUMMARY OF SKILLS:

- Blackbaud fundraising software
- Access database
- Photoshop
- Blog marketing
- Microsoft Office 2013

WORK EXPERIENCE:

September 2013 – December 2013
Internship, AMERICAN CANCER SOCIETY, Seattle, WA 98101
- Created new online giving system which increased online donations by 10% in 12 months www.acsseattlegiving.com
- Managed 300 major donor profiles using Blackbaud fundraising software
- Updated organization's Facebook profile

June 2013 – September 2013
Administrative Assistant, UNITED WAY OF SEATTLE, Seattle, WA 98101
- Recruited 125 new donors by publishing a new donors' blog to promote United Way success stories in the local community
- Liaison with photographers, printers and media to develop marketing materials
- Scheduled United Way presentations at local businesses
- Coordinated staff schedules and travel arrangements
- Trained four clerical staff on use of Access database

COMMUNITY SERVICE:

June 2012 – September 2012
Chair, CITY YEAR YOUTH PROJECT
- Recruited and trained 20 new volunteers using online video "Growing Team Spirit" by Amanda Soto www.sotoam.com
- Recognition certificate for leadership of City Year Youth Project
- Team earned Top Performance Award
- Managed schedules, budget and promotion

CAREER PORTFOLIO:

www.sotoamportfolio.com

FIGURE 10.2

Sample Chronological Resume #2, Ramone D. J. Munoz

RAMONE D.J. MUNOZ　　ramonedj.munoz@xyz.com
1463 Trighton Park Place | Dedham, MA 73082 | (517) 629-8365

EDUCATION

TRIGHTON TECH INSTITUTE　　　　　　　　　　9/2011-12/2015
Dedham, MA 73082
B.S., Software Engineering
Concentration in Web Services and Applications

WORK EXPERIENCE

MAXIM SOFTWARE FUTURES　　　　　　　　　9/2011-12/2015
Boston, MA 02120
Software Specialist Intern:
- Maintain PC software and hardware systems
- Analyze company software needs
- Assist with review of data structures, algorithms and software design
- Worked on iOS and Android development team project
- Lead project presenter at weekly department meeting
- Experience with Postgres and MySql

TRIGHTON TECH INSTITUTE　　　　　　　　　9/2011– 5/2012
Dedham, MA 73082
Lab Assistant/Help Desk:
- Troubleshooter for help requests
- Identified, documented and reported network connectivity issues
- Updated equipment inventory records
- Coordinated with vendors for warranty repairs
- Trained department heads on company and IT department guidelines

ALTA POINT TECHNOLOGY SERVICES　　　　5/2011– 9/2011
Boston, MA 02120
Coder: Coding skill in C, C++, Java, Python

DIGITAL GAMES FOR YOUTH　　　　　　　　5/2011– 9/2011
Dedham, MA 73082
Online Tutorial Assistant

PROFESSIONAL ASSOCIATIONS:

Member, AITP (Association of Information Technology Professionals) Student Organization; Member, Trighton Tech Institute Student Advisory Group

VOLUNTEER WORK:

Boston Green Technology
Admissions Ambassador, Trighton Tech Institute
Student Advisor, Junior Achievement of Greater Boston

CAREER PORTFOLIO:

www.rdjmunozeng.com

FIGURE 10.3

Sample Chronological Resume #3, Judy P. Epstein

JUDY P. EPSTEIN   (508) 675-9387   jpepstein@xyz.com

89 Stallworth Drive, Boston, MA 08948

PROFESSIONAL OBJECTIVE

Junior Staff Accountant position with a national insurance or financial services firm.

EDUCATION

Collins College, Boston, MA 89498 B.S., Accounting, 2015

SUMMARY OF SKILLS

- Cloud computing
- SOA (Service-oriented architecture)
- SaaS desktop applications
- QuickBooks online
- Intuit Payroll Service
- Strikelron and Xignite
- BidMagic Proposal and Project Management Software

WORK EXPERIENCE

Goldcircle Bank, Quincy, MA 89457 2012 — Present

Lead Customer Relations Associate

- Match appropriate products to customer needs
- Advise customers on alternate banking solutions
- Perform routine account management functions
- Assist junior associates with product education and bank processing systems
- Three year recipient of Goldcircle Customer Relations Award.

Brinker's Insurance Company, Boston, MA 89498 Summer 2012

Summer Internship

- Performed bookkeeping functions and monitored monthly budget reports
- Assisted with processing insurance claims
- Maintained updates to client profiles in Access database
- Worked with clients to ensure all necessary paperwork was available to process claims
- Updated employee handbook
- Performed general office work as needed.

Collins College Purchasing & Student Payroll Departments

Boston, MA 89498 September 2011 — May 2012

Student Assistant/College Work-Study Program

- Managed bid proposals for smart classroom equipment including Hitachi Starboard annotating monitors, Creston touch panel control system, and Wolfvision high definition document cameras.
- Coordinated classroom equipment inventories with facilities department to ensure classrooms were properly equipped.
- Completed purchase orders.
- Assisted with processing student payroll.

Camino's Italian Restaurant, Boston, MA 89498 Summer 2011

Hostess

COMMUNITY SERVICE/VOLUNTEER WORK

Boys and Girls Clubs of America, Quincy, MA 89457

EXTRACURRICULAR ACTIVITIES

Vice President of the Accounting Club
Member of DECA (Distributive Education Clubs of America)
Coach for girls' volleyball team
Fitness Trainer

REFERENCES: Available Upon Request

FIGURE 10.4

Sample Chronological Resume #4, Brittany Smith

———————————————— **BRITTANY SMITH** ————————————————

395 Lake Garden Drive East Lansing, MI 48823

(508)396-7725 smith.brittany@xyz.com

EDUCATION:

September 2011 - May 2015 Tollgate Technical Institute, Manchester, NH 03103

B.S., Nursing

June 2010 - January 2011 East Lansing Institute, East Lansing, MI 48823

Certifications: CNA (Certified Nursing Assistant), 12 Lead EKG, Certified Emergency Room Technician

Licenses: EMT (Emergency Medical Technician) and Paramedic

WORK EXPERIENCE:

December 2014 - May 2015 Community Hospital Burlington, MA 01803

ER Training Department/Intern:

- Reduced ER patient waiting time by 30% by simplifying admission process
- Assisted with training 25 CNAs on hospital medication administration policies
- Code Grey response training
- Organized and promoted 15 new employee orientation sessions
- Trained to provide intubation and IV procedures and triage intake
- Created updated emergency room staff orientation manual to include current OSHA (Occupational Safety and Health Administration) regulations and current CDC (Center for Disease Control) Guideline for Infection Control in Hospital Personnel
- Received annual Quality in Health Care Award

August 2014 - December 2014 Tollgate Hospital, Manchester, NH 03103

Clinical Experience:

- Applied IntelliView Telemetry System to assist with patient care on telemetry units
- Completed TLS (Trauma Life Support), ACLS (Advanced Cardiac Life Support) and LIFEPAK 20e defibrillator training
- Applied CDSS (Clinical Decision Support System) to determine diagnosis of patient data
- Completed rotations in operating room, emergency room, and intensive care unit to observe and assist with select patient procedures under direct supervision of nurse or doctor
- Planned, provided and evaluated care for patients with a variety of medical or surgical problems

January 2011 - August 2011 Crestwood Nursing Villa, East Lansing, MI 48823

CNA:

- Admitted and transferred patients
- Worked with physical therapy department to plan and assess patient care plans
- Assisted patients with daily living tasks
- Coordinated patient lab work
- Charted daily vital signs and meal intake

February 2009 - June 2010 Northstead Veterinary Clinic, Northstead, MI 48822

Intake Coordinator

COMMUNITY SERVICE:

Elder Helpers online eldercare community volunteer; Red Cross Chapter blog coordinator; PAWS for Pets events volunteer-Top Volunteer; Lansing Theater Project

PROFESSIONAL ASSOCIATIONS:

Member, National Association of Health Care Assistants; Member, GROWS (Grass Roots Organization for the Well-being of Seniors)

REFERENCES AVAILABLE UPON REQUEST

CAREER PORTFOLIO: www.smithbrittany0283.com

FIGURE 10.5

Sample Chronological Resume #5, Allison McKenzie

ALLISON MCKENZIE

56 Seaver Street San Francisco, CA 94110 *(415)555-2555* allie.mckenzie@xyz.com

EDUCATION

CA College of Graphic Design and Creative Technologies   1/2011-1/2015
San Francisco, CA 94110
B.S., Graphic Design

SUMMARY OF SKILLS:

- *Adobe Creative Suite*
- *CSS Cascading Style Sheets*
- *MAC-based software (CS, Xpress)*
- *Corel CorelDraw Graphics Suite*
- *HTML and JavaScript*
- *Photo Imaging Software*

WEB AND MULTIMEDIA	PHOTOGRAPHY	PRINT
WEBSITE DESIGN	*BLACK AND WHITE PHOTOGRAPHY*	*BROCHURES*
VIDEO EDITING	*LITHOGRAPHY*	*LOGOS AND BUSINESS CARDS*
VIDEOMONTAGES	*RETOUCHING*	*POSTERS AND POST CARDS*
SOCIAL MEDIA IMAGE DESIGN	*PHOTOGRAPH RESTORATION*	*STATIONERY*

WORK EXPERIENCE

Alphamedia Productions   6/2014-1/2015
San Francisco, CA 94110
Graphic Design Capstone Internship
Consulted with prospective customers to plan and design projects based on
business objectives. Assisted with obtaining quotes and bids and preparing
budgets. Led design and production functions throughout project implementation.
Assisted with corporate website design. Created design theme and graphics
for marketing and sales presentations and training video. Coordinated planning
meetings with freelancers and in-house publications teams to develop team
project plans. Monitored strict adherence to project deadlines. Conducted client
satisfaction surveys and made recommendations to better meet client expectations.
KEY RESULT: New team projects generated $150,000.

CA College of Graphic Design and Creative Technologies
San Francisco, CA 94110
Admissions Marketing Student Assistant   6/2013-6/2014
Worked with vendors to create new design themes for Admissions Marketing.
Participated in production of print and digital promotional communication for
all campuses. Coordinated publications schedule to ensure on time delivery of
marketing materials to the Admissions department.

PROFESSIONAL ASSOCIATIONS:

Member, Excellence in Graphic Design Student Association
Member, AIGA (American Institute of Graphic Arts) Student Chapter

CAREER PORTFOLIO: www.allie34mck.com

FUNCTIONAL RESUMES

The functional resume organizes your experience according to specific skills or functions. This format is appropriate if you are changing your career or reentering the workforce after a period of absence, because it emphasizes your skills and abilities and downplays any gaps in employment or unrelated work experience. This format is especially effective if you have a lengthy work history. Emphasizing skills acquired in an unrelated field can help demonstrate you can apply those same skills to a new situation.

FIGURE 10.6

Sample Functional Resume #1, Derek T. Thompsen

DEREK T. THOMPSEN   **(412) 438-9730)**
962 Summerdale Pittsburg, PA 15122
dtthompsen@xyz.com

Professional Objective   To obtain a Web Developer position to support growth and development, and increased productivity of IT functions.

Relevant Experience and Skills

Web Development	Knowledge of Section 508 and W3C Standards
Web Page Design	Architecture and Accessibility Techniques
Programming/Scripting Languages:	HTML, XHTML, JavaScript
Database Applications:	SQL, SQL/PL, Oracle, Access
Operating System/Platforms:	Unix and Windows 8.1
Software:	Adobe Image Ready, Photoshop, Dreamweaver, MS Front Page, Microsoft Visio

Professional Experience

Cyrus Systems, Denver, CO 80239 (2010-present)

<u>Web Developer</u>: Manage the maintenance, development, and enhancement of applications that interface with an Oracle database. Create, update, and maintain Web pages. Perform JavaScript and PDF conversions. Train staff in Flash and Fireworks applications.

<u>Junior Systems Programmer</u>: Developed and coded Web-based applications and user interfaces. Technical team member responsible for developing Web, database, data search and retrieval applications.

Code Systems Securities, Pittsburgh, PA 15122 (2008-2010)

<u>Technical Support Assistant</u>: Generally assisted IT department with requests and interfaces with user groups. Monitored monthly Help Desk maintenance reports and tracked trouble shooting results.

Special Distinctions

Web and Video Innovation in Design, Student Award 2012; Employee of the Month, June 2010, Cyrus Systems; Tech Support, Cardon Church of Denver; Mentor, Boys and Girls Clubs of America

Education

Cardon Community College, Denver, CO 80239 (2010-2014) B.S., Information Systems A.S., Web Development	<u>Lead Lab Teaching Assistant</u> Trained and supervised 22 computer lab, work-study students.	Capstone Course Project: "Publishing a Video" www.dtthompsenclassvideo2490.com "Publishing a Video" Presentation Guide

Career Portfolio

www.thompsendrktportfolio2490.com
Web resume: www.dtthompsen2490.com/webres.html
Video resume: www.dtthompsenvideoresume2490.com
Personal Website: www.derektthompsen2490.com

FIGURE 10.7
Sample Functional Resume #2, Louis Ricci

LOUIS RICCI
900 Brayton Point
Manchester, NH 03109
(603)893-9187
louis.ricci@xyz.com

PROFILE:
*Marketing Manager
with eight years
experience improving
business results
applying online
and Social Media
marketing strategies*

Special Distinctions:
Cityview Institute
New Alumni
Program Award
*"New Alumni
to Alumni
Recruitment
Program."*

WORK EXPERIENCE:

Multichannel Marketing Manager
Alpha Brand Resources, Manchester, NH 03109
October 2008 – Present
- New proposals increased business with existing clients by 20%, and reduced new business start-up costs by 30%
- Reduced project expenses by 30% over previous two years
- Led plan to grow company ranking to one of the Top 20 New Hampshire businesses
- Conducted competitive analysis used for company strategic planning
- Managed $10M marketing budget
- Led benchmark study to measure the effectiveness of social media vs. print materials for in-bound marketing
- Outsourced marketing content creation to customize messaging for targeted customer groups

Interactive Marketing Assistant
The Funds First Group, Manchester, NH 03109
October 2006 – September 2008
- Increased company Website traffic by 25%
- Coordinated company presentations to demonstrate SEO capabilities
- Created online and social media marketing content
- Tracked, monitored and analyzed use of social media programs to drive continuous improvement
- Conducted customer surveys to determine preferred product lines and marketing channels
- Assisted Marketing Manager with managing department budget
- Coordinated logistics for company events
- Managed calendars and schedules

Customer Service Representative
Dover Bank, Manchester, NH 03109
Summer 2006
- Processed routine bank transactions
- Represented the bank hosting local Business to Business event – event participation increased 20%
- Generated 15 new accounts in two months

EDUCATION

Cityview Business Institute, Manchester, NH 03109
September 2010 – June 2014
B.S., Internet Marketing
A.S., Marketing

FIGURE 10.8

Sample Functional Resume #3, Dina Bartnett

DINA BARTNETT
84 Commander's Way Annapolis, MD 02203
(410) 782-9184 dbartnett@xyz.edu

SUMMARY OF SKILLS:
- ES3 file explorer file manager
- CAT (Computer-assisted translation) software
- XLNT writing and proofreading
- Time Matter docketing/calendar software
- Videoconferencing
- ADP payroll system

WORK EXPERIENCE:
Framingham and Tyson Attorneys at Law Annapolis, MD 02203
Paralegal Assistant/Intern 9/2015 – PRESENT
- Assist with deposition preparation work
- Responsible for selected document organization and management
- Created e-file system for paralegals using ES3 file explorer file manager
- Translate legal notes using CAT software
- Apply XLNT writing and proofreading (skills)
- Manage client databases
- Track attorney's billable time
- Manage software to track projects and deadlines
- Coordinated weekly "lunch and learn" sessions with lawyers and other legal staff and interns

Town's Clerk's Office Annapolis, MD 02203
Legal Assistant/Intern 6/2015 – 9/2015
- Processed document drafts for Town Clerk review
- Researched and logged updates on local ordinances
- Maintained Town Clerk's Office Website
- Fielded routine legal inquiries
- Used judgment to either handle complaints or refer to the Town Clerk
- Prepared licenses and official documents for issue
- Coordinated outsourcing of data entry with virtual legal assistant services
- Created and distributed e-newsletter
- Assisted with voter registration

Starbuck's Coffee Company Annapolis, MD 02203
Shift Supervisor 9/2014 – 5/2015

Home Depot Annapolis, MD 02203
Part-time Payroll Assistant 5/2013 – 5/2014

EDUCATION:
The Legal School of Business Annapolis, MD 02203
B.S., Paralegal Studies A.S., Legal Assistant
9/2011 – PRESENT GPA 3.7

CERTIFICATION: CLA (Certified Legal Assistant)

VOLUNTEER WORK:
Church Services of Maryland, Event Coordinator
Hospital Group of Annapolis, Annual Telethon Coordinator

CAREER PORTFOLIO: Available Upon Request

FIGURE 10.9

Sample Functional Resume #4, Elizabeth A. Cole

Elizabeth A. Cole | (317) 492-8309

eacole@xyz.com | 2 Morris Street Indianapolis, IN 46214

PROFESSIONAL OBJECTIVE:

To create and implement training and development programs for international event management.

SUMMARY OF SKILLS:

- Cisco TelePresence and WebEx videoconferencing systems
- Office Suite cloud-based phone system
- MOS (Microsoft Office Specialist)
- REMARK Tour Operator reservation software
- Event Day software
- Certified Event Planner

SPECIAL DISTINCTIONS:

Fluent in Italian and Spanish

WORK EXPERIENCE:

September 2008-present

Globe Enterprises, Indianapolis, IN 46214

ASSOCIATE DIRECTOR, EMPLOYEE DEVELOPMENT: Increased employee satisfaction with Employee In-Service programs by 25%. Reduced program cost by 20%, by creating first video-conference training program for satellite offices. Coordinate employee continuing education program with local institutions. Outsource company Wellness Program by contracting with local health care providers and other community resources. Advise employees on company career paths and individual career plans. Coordinate employee awards programs. Prepare and manage department budget. Supervise and train ten department employees.

TRAINING CONSULTANT

www.eacoleabctrain.com

February 2004-September 2008

Globe Enterprises, Indianapolis, IN 46214

ADMINISTRATIVE ASSISTANT II: Coordinated Executive Committee meetings and prepared meeting minutes. Coordinated travel for quarterly Corporate Board meetings. Responsible for vendor relations. Managed employee database and job description inventory. Prepared routine correspondence and maintained electronic file system.

August 1999-February 2004

Fresh Concepts in Sales, Indianapolis, IN 46214

ADMINISTRATIVE ASSISTANT I: Responsible for processing customer orders and providing product feedback. Coordinated bi-weekly payroll with department heads. Prepared routine correspondence. Provided support services to other departments as needed. Knowledgeable in MS Office Suite and PBAX phone system.

February 1998-July 1999

T & T Travel and Tours, Indianapolis, IN 46214

TOUR GUIDE: Assisted with corporate group travel to Italy, Spain and England. Booked reservations, confirmed itineraries and led group travel from departure through return. Conducted post-trip customer satisfaction surveys.

PROFESSIONAL ASSOCIATIONS:

Member, Virtual Association for Administrative Professionals (VAAP)

Member, National Staff Development and Training Association (NSDTA)

Member, American Travel Association

EDUCATION:

September 2010-June 2014

L & L Community College, Indianapolis, IN 46214

B.S., Sports, Entertainment and Events Management

September 2008-June 2010

Administrative Assistants' Institute, Indianapolis, IN 46214

A.S., Administrative Assistant

REFERENCES: AVAILABLE UPON REQUEST   **CAREER PORTFOLIO:** AVAILABLE UPON REQUEST

FIGURE 10.10

Sample Functional Resume #5, Lorinda Messina, MT (ASCP)

LORINDA MESSINA, MT (ASCP)

231 Maple Avenue Long Island NY 11111

(555)555-5555   lmessina@xyz.com

PROFESSIONAL OBJECTIVE:

Medical Technologist's position at a leading medical center

SPECIAL DISTINCTIONS:

Experienced medical technologist with ASCP certification, three years of experience as an NYU Medical Center Lab technologist and bachelor's degree in medical terminology. Excellent clinical laboratory skills, with commended performance conducting/analyzing laboratory assays and resolving complex clinical and instrument problems. Accurate, reliable, diligent and focused on the timely, quality completion of all lab procedures. Work well under pressure and time constraints within high-volume environments.

WORK EXPERIENCE:

Medical Technologist

5/2010-Present, NYU Medical Center, New York, NY

Collect and prepare specimens and perform laboratory procedures used in the diagnosis, treatment, and prevention of disease. Verify, record, and report lab results on all performed tests. Ensure compliance with government requirements, hospital policies, and laboratory procedures, including maintaining the cleanliness of lab equipment, instruments and work area.

KEY CONTRIBUTIONS:

Executed and analyzed tests in areas including chemistry, hematology, urinalysis, serology, histology, and bacteriology to aid physicians in diagnosing and treating disease.

Consistently commended for the timely, high-quality completion of both routine and special laboratory assays of patient specimens (including blood and other body fluids, skin scrapings, and surgical specimens). Ensured test-result validity before recording/reporting results, earning a reputation for meticulous attention to detail. Demonstrated the ability to communicate test results effectively with physicians, pathologists, and nursing staff as a member of an interdisciplinary team focused on providing exemplary quality of care. Evaluated quality control within laboratory using standard laboratory test and measurement controls, and maintained compliance with CLIA, OSHA, safety, and risk-management guidelines.

CLINICAL TRAINING

2/2009-5/2010 St. Vincent's Hospital Medical Center, New York, NY

Completed 15-month clinical training program at St. Vincent's Microbiology Department.

KEY CONTRIBUTIONS:

Operated and calibrated an assortment of laboratory/testing equipment and performed various chemical, microscopic, and bacteriologic tests. Performed stat and routine testing on a variety of specimens quickly and accurately. Maintained lab equipment and troubleshot/resolved instrument problems. Quickly mastered Meditech system.

EDUCATION

9/2006-5/2010 College of Long Island, Staten Island, NY

B.S. Degree in Medical Technology with honors (GPA 3.6)

CERTIFICATIONS

American Society for Clinical Pathology (ASCP)

Medical Technologist (MT), 2010, Chicago,IL

Basic Life Support (BLS), 2010, New York, NY

CPR and First Aid Certification, 2010, New York, NY

SKILLS (INTERMEDIATE LEVELS)

Clinical assays

Clinical microbiology

Lab equipment calibration

CLIA and OSHA compliance

Test result validity verification

Lab testing and reporting

Quality control

ADDITIONAL INFORMATION

Available for all shifts and extended work hours. Relocating to Chicago, IL

Real Life Stories

Eric

Eric had just lost his job with a high-tech start-up company he had been with for two years. He was actively seeking a new job, using his expertise in the data storage industry. Eric circulated his resume with members of his industry trade group, an important part of his career network, and also posted his resume online. He also decided to file for unemployment. When he did, he did not realize that his resume automatically was sent to an online job resource developed by the Department of Labor. Eric received a job offer for a software engineer's position that was posted on the job bank. He accepted the offer and started the job within three weeks of posting his resume online. Eric's experience is an example of how applicant tracking systems can work well to electronically match job seekers' skills and experiences with specific job requirements.

Lisa

Lisa successfully used her online resume and job search follow-up advice she had received to obtain the internship she wanted with a public relations agency. The agency specifically requested applicants to submit plain-text resumes online. After posting her plain-text resume, Lisa received a call for an interview. After her interview, she was told that she would be contacted directly by the hiring manager for a second interview. Lisa asked for the name and e-mail address of the hiring manager. When she did not hear anything for a few days, Lisa e-mailed the hiring manager explaining she was following up from her first interview. She attached an MS Word document copy of her resume to the e-mail. She was asked back for a second interview. During the interview, Lisa noticed that the hiring manager had a printed copy of the MS Word version of her resume as opposed to the plain-text version that prompted her first interview. Lisa was offered the internship position and later reflected on how important it was to be prepared to forward her resume in multiple formats to accommodate different situations in her job search.

Source: Accessed September 4, 2009, from http://money.cnn.com/magazines/moneymag/moneymag_archive/2004/04/01/365028/.

··

Progress Check Questions

1. Do you think a chronological or functional resume format works best for you?
2. How will you handle any information about your work history that is a challenge to explain?

··

> "The reports of my death are greatly exaggerated."
>
> *Mark Twain*[3]

PRINT VERSIONS

Much of what you read about resumes today talks about the eventual elimination of a resume in print form. While digital resumes are certainly more the norm, there is still a traditional job market where a print resume is appropriate. A quality print copy of your resume is appropriate for targeted situations.

You can take a print copy with you to interviews, career fairs, networking events, and resume coaching sessions or send it via the U.S. mail. You can place your resume with a cover letter and reference sheet in a folder for presenting in face-to-face situations, but when you send it by U.S. mail, it's best to include only the paper copies with no folder. It's true that a nice folder will protect your documents and make an initial impression, but the

[3]www.brainyquote.com/quotes/quotes/m/marktwain141773.html.

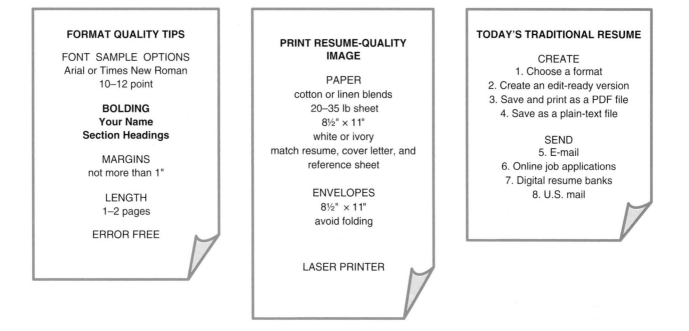

FORMAT QUALITY TIPS

FONT SAMPLE OPTIONS
Arial or Times New Roman
10–12 point

BOLDING
Your Name
Section Headings

MARGINS
not more than 1"

LENGTH
1–2 pages

ERROR FREE

PRINT RESUME-QUALITY IMAGE

PAPER
cotton or linen blends
20–35 lb sheet
8½" × 11"
white or ivory
match resume, cover letter, and
reference sheet

ENVELOPES
8½" × 11"
avoid folding

LASER PRINTER

TODAY'S TRADITIONAL RESUME

CREATE
1. Choose a format
2. Create an edit-ready version
3. Save and print as a PDF file
4. Save as a plain-text file

SEND
5. E-mail
6. Online job applications
7. Digital resume banks
8. U.S. mail

recipient will likely place your documents in a stack with others who are their top picks (be positive!), and the folder may be discarded—one more step for the employer. Either way is fine; you decide.

10.3 EDIT-READY, PDF, AND PLAIN-TEXT RESUMES

An edit-ready version of your resume is considered your "working resume" because it is in a form that allows changes to be made as needed. Saving it in portable document format (PDF) preserves the words, format, images, and layout of your resume when it is sent online. A plain-text resume is a format-free version of your resume that is compatible with most online application systems. These three versions of your resume will enable you to respond to different employer requirements.

EDIT-READY AND PDF VERSIONS

Most resumes start as an edit-ready version using word processing software such as Google Docs, OpenOffice, or Microsoft Word. A resume prepared in edit-ready form can be printed as a hard copy or sent online with an e-mail. If a recipient of an edit-ready resume does not have compatible software, the person may not be able to open the document or may open it but find the format jumbled. To avoid this, you should save the edit-ready version of your resume as a PDF file. To create a PDF file version of your resume, you can use Adobe Reader or other software that enables a document to be converted to a PDF version. You should verify how your resume looks in print form before sending it to anyone. E-mail yourself a copy, and open and print it as your own test.

CAREER PORTFOLIO 10.1

⠿ WRITE YOUR RESUME

The goal of this activity is to prepare a final version of your resume. You have already done most of the work. Your edit-ready version will be the foundation for creating multiple versions of your resume, as needed, throughout your job search.

STEP 1. Review what you have learned about creating a resume in this chapter:

- Multiple resume versions.
- Keywords and power words to target your resume.
- Core and custom sections.
- Resume formats.

STEP 2. Choose a chronological or functional resume format: _____

STEP 3. Select your targeted job: _____

STEP 4. Using the draft copy for sections of your resume, prepare your edit-ready version.

STEP 5. Have someone review your resume before saving as a final copy.

PLAIN-TEXT VERSIONS

For online use, resumes are usually converted to ASCII, or plain-text, format. To avoid formatting issues, employers often prefer receiving an e-mail with a plain-text version of a resume pasted in the body of the e-mail. This enables the resume to be entered directly into a digital applicant tracking system. You can also paste your resume directly into some online job applications.

You can prepare your plain-text version of your resume with or without line breaks as part of the formatting. To paste your resume into the body of an e-mail message, you need to use line breaks. Plain-text resumes prepared without line breaks are compatible for uploading to resume banks online. There are many websites that provide detailed instructions on how to prepare a plain-text resume using the plain-text drop down in the Save As file in Microsoft Word (Figure 10.11).

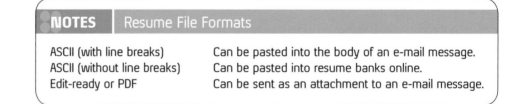

NOTES	Resume File Formats
ASCII (with line breaks)	Can be pasted into the body of an e-mail message.
ASCII (without line breaks)	Can be pasted into resume banks online.
Edit-ready or PDF	Can be sent as an attachment to an e-mail message.

Keywords are most important in plain-text resumes. If the keywords in your resume match those in a job description, your resume is selected and ranked by the computer. Those selected and ranked are read by a person who decides whether to invite you in for an interview.

FIGURE 10.11

Sample Plain-Text Resume, Derek T. Thompsen

```
DEREK T. THOMPSEN
962 Summerdale Drive
Pittsburg, PA 15122
412*483*9730
dtthompsen@xyz.com

PROFESSIONAL OBJECTIVE To obtain a Web Developer position to support growth and
development, and increased productivity of IT functions

RELEVANT EXPERIENCE AND SKILLS
Web Development
Knowledge of Section 508 and W3C Standards
Web Page Design
Architecture and Accessibility Techniques
Programming/Scripting Languages HTML, XHTML, JavaScript
Database Applications SQL, SQL/PL, Oracle, Access
Operating System/Platforms Unix and Windows 8.1
Software Adobe Image Ready, Photoshop, Dreamweaver, MS Front Page, Microsoft Visio

PROFESSIONAL EXPERIENCE
Cyrus Systems, Denver, CO 80239 2010 to present
Web Developer: Manage the maintenance, development, and enhancement of applications
that interface with an Oracle database
Create, update, and maintain Web pages
Train staff in Flash and Fireworks applications
Perform JavaScript and PDF conversions
Junior Systems Programmer: Developed and coded Web-based applications and user
interfaces
Technical team member responsible for developing Web, database, data search and
retrieval applications

Code Systems Securities, Pittsburg, PA 15122 2008 to 2010
Technical Support Assistant: Generally assisted IT department with requests and
interfaces with user groups
Monitored monthly Help Desk maintenance reports and tracked trouble shooting
results

SPECIAL DISTINCTIONS
Web and Video Innovation in Design, Student Award 2012; Employee of the Month, June
2010, Cyrus Systems; Tech Support, Cardon Church of Denver; Mentor, Boys and Girls
Clubs of America

EDUCATION
Cardon Community College, Denver, CO 80239 2010 to 2014
BS Information Systems
AS Web Development
Lead Lab Teaching Assistant Trained and supervised 22 computer lab, work-study
students
Capstone Course Project
Publishing a Video www.dtthompsenclassvideo2490.com
Publishing a Video Presentation Guide

CAREER PORTFOLIO www.thompsendrktportfolio2490.com
WEB RESUME www.dtthompsen2490.com/webres.html
VIDEO RESUME www.dtthompsenvideoresume2490.com
PERSONAL WEBSITE www.derektthompsen2490.com
```

FIGURE 10.12

E-mail with Pasted Plain-Text Resume

ACTIVITY 10.2

Prepare a Plain-Text Resume

Using the Internet, research online resume tutorials that provide detailed instructions on how to prepare a plain-text resume. Career websites like www.careerperfect.com, www.monster.com/, and http://quintcareers.com/ are examples of online resources that you can also refer to. Use the space below to write or copy notes on the steps to convert your edit-ready resume to a plain-text version. Use this information and convert the edit-ready version of your resume to a plain-text version. You can work with an instructor to be sure your conversion is successful.

_____

_____

_____

_____

_____

_____

10.4 VISUAL RESUMES

A visual resume is a digital resume that uses visual images and multimedia tools to describe who you are to a prospective employer. Types of visual resumes can include video, Web, social, or infographic resumes.

Visual resumes generally have a specific use in a job search. They work well in certain career fields where it is important to demonstrate the ability to combine creativity and technology to reach a certain audience. Graduates majoring in public relations, advertising, marketing, communications, journalism, technology, graphic design, culinary arts, and media are likely to benefit most from a well-done visual resume.

Keep in mind that visual resumes are not usually scannable into applicant tracking systems. If you decide to use a visual resume, you will also need a resume saved in a PDF file and a plain-text version to use in e-mails and print for certain situations. Following are some examples of visual resumes.

BOTTOM LINE: An infographic resume can't completely replace your traditional resume.

You still need a strong traditional resume for certain situations. The infographic resume just gives you another tool to use when the situation calls for something more creative.[4]

VIDEO RESUME

A video resume is a short summary of a job candidate's experience and qualifications prepared for employers in video form (Figure 10.13). A video resume is fairly easy to edit to target specific employers. It can be used to demonstrate skills or qualities not picked up with a traditional resume such as your verbal communication skills, personality, and professionalism. It can also be used to describe examples that support claims on your traditional resume.

It is best to have a professional help you prepare a video resume to ensure its quality. As you build your online presence, a video resume can be placed on your professional social media profile, online portfolio, or on your personal website. It can also be housed on the Internet at its own URL.

FIGURE 10.13

Sample Image of a Video Resume

WEB RESUME

A Web resume is a resume in HTML format. It can also be uploaded to your professional social media profiles, online portfolio, personal website or housed on the Internet at its own URL (Figures 10.14 and 10.15).

FIGURE 10.14

Sample Personal Website Hosting a Web Resume: Nicola Rider

---

[4]Retrieved June 15, 2013, from http://biginterview.com/blog/2013/06/infographic-resumes.html.

FIGURE 10.15

Sample Web (HTML) Resume Hosted on a Personal Website, Derek T. Thompsen

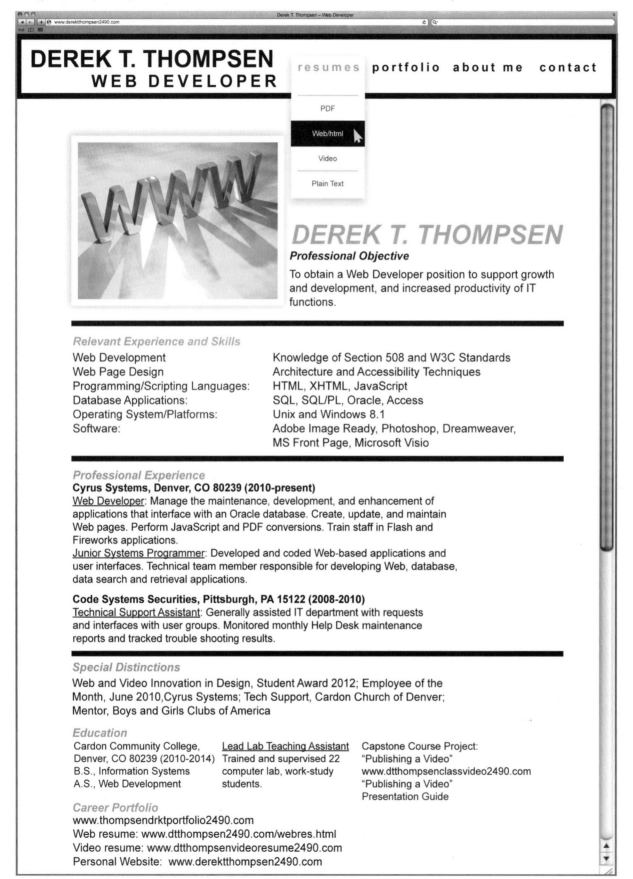

SOCIAL RESUME

A social resume is a combination of your professional social networks and profiles and includes a summary of your work history, education, and professional skills. If you contribute to a blog or have written or contributed to any professional articles online, this may be part of your social resume. Endorsements may also be included (Figure 10.16).

INFOGRAPHIC RESUME

An infographic resume is a visual presentation that details work history and professional skills. Infographic resumes often contain images, data charts, text, and color that describe work experience and expertise. Most often this information is presented in a time line (Figure 10.17).

NOTES   Guidelines for Using a Visual Resume

1. Is it appropriate for your industry or specific employer?
2. Do you have the verbal communication skills?
3. Do you have the technical skills?
4. Is your story ready to tell?
5. Is this the best way to tell it?

If done well and presented to the right audience, a visual resume can promote your qualifications in a unique way. Review the guidelines presented earlier to help you decide if this is the right choice for you.

MANAGING RESUME VERSIONS

When using multiple versions of your resume, it is important to update and edit all versions consistently and remove old versions from the Internet. While you are conducting your job search, you want to be sure only the most current version of your resume is public. Once you have accepted a position, you do not want to give your new employer the impression that you are still job hunting. You can go online to find specific instructions on how to edit or remove digital versions of your resume.

10.5 JOB APPLICATIONS

Take as much care preparing a job application as you do your resume. It is a screening device employers use to determine which candidates to interview. When an employer screens your job application, two questions will be answered. *"Can I hire you?"* and *"Do I want to interview you?"* Your job application should stand out above the crowd and cause an employer to say, *"This one is a definite interview!"* Here are some ways to do that.

KNOW YOUR GAME PLAN

Have a game plan for how you will approach completing sections of the job application.

1. Target your answers to the specific job.
2. Handle difficult questions.
3. Account for your time.

   A quality document reflects a quality candidate

"It's all right to stand out, but always be ready to share a simplified version of your resume.

When I send out my resume, I always send both the infographic and Word version."

Jonha Revesencio, social media consultant, Top 500 Community Managers Globally, infographics curator[5]

---

[5]Retrieved June 15, 2013, from http://biginterview.com/blog/2013/06/infographic-resumes.html.

FIGURE 10.16

Sample Social Resume, Amanda Wills

social resume

Amanda Wills

 Lives in New York, New York   Social Media Editor

Studied Journalism and Electronic Media and Spanish at the University of Tennessee

 Earth911.com, Earth911 Inc.

Managing Editor | March 2009 – Present | New York, New York

- Helped to increase social media following by 300 percent over 12 months
- Monitor audience behavior using analytics programs for social media
- Manage a staff of seven writers, both in–house and freelancers
- Write and publish daily content (news, features, blog posts)
- Design infographics, logos and supporting graphics for stories
- Oversee final rounds of editing and publishing for all news, feature content
- Implemented advertorial model to increase department revenue
- Developed new content production model to increase efficiency on budget
- Increased site traffic by 30 percent in one year
- Assisted in creating a content plan for Android and iPhone applications

About

A multimedia journalist with both print and Web experience, my love of social media was born in the fast-paced newsroom.

 Scripps Networks Interactive, HGTV.com

Editor, Reporter (Contract) | Aug. 2008 – Jan. 2009
Knoxville, Tennessee

- Managed and copy edited freelance content for HGTV's FrontDoor.com
- Filed daily articles covering home and garden and the the real estate market
- Designed and created content packages for FrontDoor.com and HGTV.com
- Loaded content and wrote HTML code on CMS

Contact

718-300-0313
amandakwills@gmai.com

 @AmandaWills

 /in/amandakwills

amandawills.com

amandawills.
tumblr.com

amandakwills
@gmail.com

 Playboy Magazine

Editorial Intern | May 2008 – Aug. 2008 | New York, New York

- Contributed to various sections of magazine, byline published in print, Web
- Reported on local events, off–Broadway plays, fashion and pop culture for Playboy.com and its Editor's Blog
- Worked with copy editing, fact–checking and design for print issues

Skills

- Adobe Creative Suite
- Microsoft Office
- Google Analytics
- WordPress
- Social media (Twitter, Klout, Facebook, Tumblr)
- HTML
- AP Style
- Photo editing, graphic design
- Fluent in Spanish

Education

University of Tennessee, 2008
B.S. Journalism and Electronic Media, Spanish

- Studied South American Journalism at Universidad del Salvador, Buenos Aires
- Studied Spanish language in program at Universidad de Malaga, Spain
- Led a breaking–news team as the editor in chief of the Tennessee Journalist (TNJN.com), UT's first online news platform.
- Took first place in SPJ Mark of Excellence Awards for coverage of Darfur
- Awarded prestigious Alex Haley/Playboy Interview Scholarship, highest honor in the College

FIGURE 10.17
Sample Infographic Resume, Tina Chen

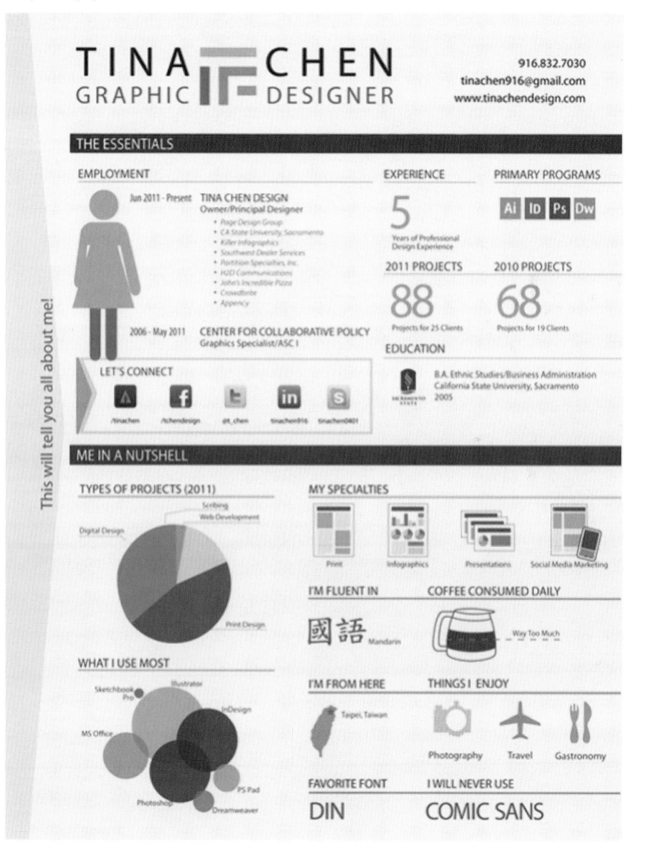

Own the Job Application   The job application determines whether you meet hiring guidelines and if you can do the job based on what you know and can do. Questions on the job application are based on employment screening guidelines set by the Equal Employment Opportunity Commission (EEOC) . Employers need to comply with these guidelines. That is why you need to complete the full application. The goal is to protect both you and the employer in the process. Answer truthfully and look for ways to insert special skills and accomplishments that relate to the job. While you don't own the questions, you own the answers.

NOTES   Anticipate Questions and Plan Answers

Google yourself. See what employers can access about you, and be sure it matches what you put on your job application. Remove or edit any dated or conflicting information online.

Be informed. Go online to the EEOC website for the latest regulations affecting employment screenings.

Think ahead. Based on what you learn, practice how you will truthfully answer any difficult questions.

Be truthful. Falsifying information to cover up a problem area is worse than revealing the problem. Revealing a problem area will not necessarily rule you out. How you answer the question might.

Get advice. Test your thinking about how you plan to handle any difficult questions. Go to a trusted member of your career network for advice on your own situation.

IDENTIFICATION QUESTIONS

Name.   Write your proper first and last name with your middle initial. Do not use an alias (false) name.

Mailing address.   Write the mailing address that applies during your job search. This should be your permanent address. If you are in transition, forward your mail to an established PO box number or in care of (c/o) a reliable person. Be sure to check in regularly to a PO box or forwarded address. If you are a student living on or off campus, list both your permanent address and your student address.

Telephone number.   List your cell phone number first, and indicate the word *cell* next to it. If you list an alternate phone number, be sure the person taking the call is reliable and will answer the call properly.

E-mail.   Use your personal e-mail address, not your employer's e-mail address or a casual version you use with friends. Use the same e-mail address as on your resume.

If under 18, list age.   Labor laws prohibit the employment of minors in particular settings. This is the reason for the question.

Social Security number.   List your correct Social Security number.

BACKGROUND AND GENERAL QUESTIONS

Background and general questions are generally set up for yes or no responses. Some of them provide space to explain. Use that space wisely.

Citizenship. Are you authorized to work in the United States? I certify that I am a U.S. citizen, permanent resident, or a foreign national with authorization to work in the

United States. All employers are required to complete an Immigration and Naturalization Form I-9 for each new employee. The hiring of an unauthorized alien can subject an employer to fines and imprisonment.

Convictions. Have you ever been convicted of a crime? A yes answer to this question does not always disqualify you from being hired. It depends on the nature of the job, nature and seriousness of the offense, and length of time since the conviction. If you have been convicted of a crime you need to reply yes on the job application, but you have the opportunity to explain if one of the following applies to you:

- The conviction was expunged.
- You contest accuracy of the report.
- You can show full rehabilitation.

This is when a current reference can help you. Choose a person who can attest to how you have changed to overcome your past issue. The longer the period of time after the conviction, and the better the credibility of the person providing the reference, the more confidence the employer will have with the recommendation.

Drug and tobacco use. Do you use drugs or tobacco? It is permissible to ask you if you use drugs or smoke. This section is used to obtain agreement to comply with the company's drug and smoking policies and agreement to submit to drug testing. Understand that if you are found to be in violation of the company policy, you will not be hired or will be terminated.

Special accommodation. Are you able to perform the essential functions of the job you are applying for, with or without reasonable accommodation? Reasonable accommodation is a modification or an adjustment to a job or the work environment to make it possible for a qualified applicant or employee with a disability to participate in the application process or to perform the functions of a job. If you have a disability and are able to perform the essential functions of the job with or without accommodation, answer yes to the question. If you need an accommodation, you can briefly describe it or you can wait to discuss it face to face with the employer. To receive a special accommodation, you need to request it of your employer. You are protected from discrimination. An employer does not have to hire you if you are unable to perform all of the essential functions of the job, even with reasonable accommodation.

Current employees. Do you have any relatives or friends who work at this company? If you have friends or relatives working for the company, you cannot be given preference over other applicants. List the names of any friends or relatives you know work for the company. An employer may be able to find this information through public records if needed.

Other Background and General Questions

- Can you meet the work schedule requirements of the job?
- Do you have transportation to work?
- Can you travel if required for the job?
- Are you seeking full-time, part-time, or temporary work?
- Can you work nights and weekends?
- Have you ever worked at this company?
- How did you learn about this company?
- Do you have a driver's license? If yes, provide license number and state issued in.
- Have you had any accidents or moving violations during the past three years? If yes, how many?

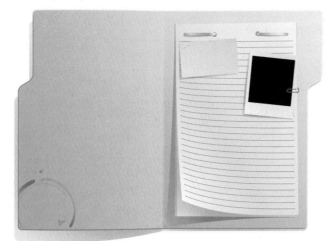

JOB QUALIFICATION QUESTIONS

Position desired. Write in the correct title of the position you are applying for. If there is an ID code for that specific position, list it along with the job title. Use the same spelling and uppercase and lowercase for the title as appears in the job posting.

Salary desired. It is usually best to leave desired salary as a topic for face-to-face discussion. Write *open* or *negotiable* instead of indicating a specific salary or salary range. Be prepared to discuss salary in person in case you are interviewed after you turn in your application.

Education

1. List institutions you attend(ed) in reverse chronological order along with dates attended and degree received.
2. If you attended, but did not graduate from, another institution, list it if you spent more than six months taking courses. It is better to account for your time than to show an unexplained gap. Don't list it if you attended only a few classes or took a few courses. If you took a special interest course that pertains to your career field, you can list it here if there is enough space. The other option is to mention it in the Brief Statement section if appropriate.
3. List licenses, certifications, or registrations, with those that pertain to the specific job you are applying for first.
4. A skills checklist may be provided. If you are asked to write a list of your skills, list those that pertain to the specific job you are applying for first.
5. If there is not a section on the application that asks about special recognitions, awards, honors, or GPA and you have special accomplishments worth noting, use the Brief Statement section to highlight them.

Work Experience

1. *Reason for leaving:* If you were laid off due to downsizing, say it. Another option is to say your job was eliminated due to company cutbacks. If you were fired due to a reorganization or your old position was redefined, use those terms, but be prepared to discuss this in an interview. Use a positive tone. In the interview you can emphasize your focus on the future and how the experience you gained can now be applied to a new job. Of course there are many other reasons for voluntarily leaving a job. Going back to school, changing jobs, or relocating are some.
2. *Current salary:* Accurately list your current salary. Inflating it to influence a salary offer is falsifying your application and would likely disqualify you from a job offer.
3. If you have recently completed an internship, you can include this and designate it as an internship, not a full-time job.

Brief statement. Why are you interested in or qualified for the job? Use this section to briefly describe any additional information about you that did not have a place somewhere else on the job application such as special recognitions, awards, honors, or your GPA. Briefly incorporate a few reasons why you would like to work for this particular company.

References. Many job seekers think that employers do not contact references. This is not generally true. Employers often contact references—especially when the job includes significant responsibilities. Be sure to get an individual's permission before naming that person as a reference. You want to be sure to have his or her most recent contact information. It is best to let the person know what jobs you are applying for so he or she can be prepared to be contacted.

Targeted questions. Some companies include a few targeted questions to see how much you know about the company. These questions are often intended to determine how well you might fit the company culture. The following section of the Starbucks Coffee Company job application is an example:

Have you ever visited a Starbucks Coffee location? Where? Describe your experience:
_____
_____

What do you like about coffee? _____
_____

Why would you like to work for Starbucks Coffee Company?_____
_____
_____

Describe a specific situation where you have provided excellent customer service in your most recent position. Why was this effective? _____
_____

Other Job Qualification Questions

- Honors?
- Awards?
- GPA?
- Special accomplishments?
- Volunteer work?
- Extracurricular activities, hobbies, and interests?

QUALITY DOCUMENT

Like with your resume, you should ensure that your completed job application has a professional look.

- Follow all instructions.
- Be truthful.
- Be consistent. Bring your resume to be sure the information you put on the application matches what is on your resume.
- Fill in every section, leaving no blank spaces.
- Use a high-quality black pen.

- Print your responses in each section, except for the signature section where you sign your name.
- Make no errors. Check your spelling, punctuation, and grammar. This is a formal document.

ONLINE JOB APPLICATIONS

Most companies have an online job application system and information from it is stored in an applicant tracking system. Fewer employers require a print copy. Some employers require you or offer the option to download a printable version of the application. If you can download a company's application, print a copy and practice filling it out before completing a final copy. Whether you complete a print or online copy, ensure the content and consistency of your answers, and you should have no problem.

ACTIVITY 10.3
Sample Job Application

Study the following application for employment to get an idea of what a typical job application looks like. Fill in each section accurately. Make sure you understand the questions you are required to answer, and be sure you feel comfortable with each response.

Once you have completed the job application, give it to someone to review. Discuss which sections you had the most diffculty with and why. Get input from others on how to handle any sections about which you are uncertain.

XYZ CORPORATION
Application for Employment
Incomplete Applications will not be Considered

IDENTIFICATION

NAME (Last First Middle)				Date		
Mailing Address				Area Code	Phone Number	Cell Number
Street	City	State	Zip			
Temporary Address				E-mail Address		
Street	City	State	Zip			
If under age 18, list birth date.				Social Security Number		

Are you applying for Full-Time ❏   Part-Time ❏   Seasonal ❏   Other? ❏

BACKGROUND AND GENERAL QUESTIONS

Are you authorized to work in the U.S.?   Yes ❏   No ❏
I certify that I am a U.S. citizen, permanent resident or a foreign national with authorization to work in the U.S. Yes ❏   No ❏
Are you able to perform the essential function of the job you are applying for, with or without reasonable accommodation?   Yes ❏   No ❏
Have you ever been convicted of any crime?   Yes ❏   No ❏

If yes, explain.
Do you use drugs or tobacco?
Do you have any relatives or acquaintances employed by XYZ Corporation?   Yes ❑   No ❑   Location:

JOB INTEREST

Have you ever been employed by XYZ Corporation?   Yes ❑   No ❑

Have you ever applied to XYZ Corporation?   Yes ❑   No ❑

Position Desired:	Starting wage expected? $ per

How were you referred?	How did you learn about this company?

Why are you interested in or qualified for this job?

_____

_____

Can you work:

Saturday ❑ Yes   Sunday ❑ Yes   Weekdays ❑ Yes   Evenings ❑ Yes   Holidays ❑ Yes   Daytime ❑ Yes
    ❑ No   ❑ No   ❑ No   ❑ No   ❑ No   ❑ No
or Night Hours? ❑ Yes
        ❑ No

Can you meet the work schedule requirements of the job? Yes ❑   No ❑

Do you have transportation to work? Yes ❑   No ❑

Do you have a driver's license? Yes ❑   No ❑
If yes, provide license number and state issued in.

Have you had any accidents or moving violations during the past three years? Yes ❑   No ❑
If yes, how many?

EDUCATIONAL HISTORY

School	Name and Location	Major	Honors, Awards, Special Recognitions	Circle Highest Grade Completed	Type of Degree or Certificate Received	Completion Date
High				9 10 11 12		
Trade/ Technical				1 2 3 4		
College				1 2 3 4		
Postgrad				List Degree(s) _____ _____		
Other training or skills (factory or office equipment, special courses)						
List computer skills (such as competency with software packages)						
Licenses, Certifications, or Registration						

WE ARE AN EQUAL OPPORTUNITY EMPLOYER

EMPLOYMENT HISTORY

READ CAREFULLY: Starting with your present or most recent job, working backward, account for all time, including periods of unemployment (include five-year employment history).

Name, Address, Phone		Dates		Position, Duties, Supervisor	Base Wage/Salary	Reason for Leaving
		Month	Year			
	From				Starting	
	To				Final	
	From				Starting	
	To				Final	
	From				Starting	
	To				Final	
	From				Starting	
	To				Final	

Reference:

Name _____   Phone _____

Title _____   E-mail _____

Association: _____

_____

I certify the information in this application is true, correct, and complete, to the best of my knowledge. I understand that, should this application contain any false or misleading information, my application may be rejected or my employment with this company terminated.

SIGNATURE: _____

DATE: _____

Sections in a job application may vary by company, but the sample shown in Activity 10.3 represents information employers are allowed to use to screen candidates. You can use this sample form to practice completing a job application.

A professionally prepared resume is essential to any job search. Next to the interview, it is the tool most widely used by employers to screen job candidates.

Starting with a well prepared edit-ready version of your resume will ensure you can meet today's minimum requirements to provide a PDF and plain-text version of your resume to an employer. Once you have covered these basics, you can consider other resume options, including the use of a visual resume if appropriate for your industry and your individual style and skill set. Most employers in industries where a visual resume is appropriate will also expect you to have a PDF or plain-text version of your resume.

If you haven't written many resumes, you will benefit from practicing writing your resume a few times and having someone else read it before you print or post your final copy. Based on what you learned in this chapter, you can consider your resume is well prepared if you included industry- and job-specific keywords that target specific employers and have chosen a resume format that best emphasizes your strengths and accomplishments. Your resume will become one of your most important tools in your Career Portfolio.

You should pay as much attention to completing a job application as you do to preparing your resume. Think ahead about the best way to answer any questions that might concern you. The information you provide should match information in your resume and professional social media profile.

RESUMES AND JOB APPLICATIONS

Based on what you learned about resumes and job applications in this chapter, answer the following questions.

1. What am I trying to decide?

_____

_____

2. What do I need to know? _____

_____

3. How will it help me make a more informed decision? _____

_____

4. How can I obtain what I need to know? _____

People _____

Experience _____

Research _____

5. Who are the best resources for the information I need? _____

_____

"It's about storytelling and the cover letter shines the spotlight while the resume tells the broader story."

Jen Steinmann, chief talent offcer, Deloitte LLP[1]

[1]Retrieved July 27, 2013, from http://jobs.aol.com/articles/2012/12/17/deloitte-secrets-getting-job/.

Letters

11

After completing this chapter, you will:

1 **Identify** guidelines for writing job search letters

2 **Recognize** and effectively write cover letters you may use during your job search

3 **Write** effective follow-up letters

4 **Create** a Career Portfolio entry

During your job search, letter writing is an important form of communicating with an employer. In your written letters, you reveal information about your professional goals and your personality. The prime reason for writing a cover letter is to secure a job interview. If your background and work experience are comparable to those of other candidates, your cover letter can distinguish you from everyone else. The most effective cover letters are targeted to specific employers or positions. The cover letter communicates the reason you want to work for the company and highlights some of your qualifications. The clarity, conciseness, and professionalism of your letter can make a positive first impression on an employer who has not met you in person. Throughout the application process, different types of cover letters may include a letter to apply for a specific position or to an internship or cooperative education program; networking letters; career change letters; or a letter to request a recommendation. With each of these letters, you would typically be including your resume.

The other important group of letters in your job search is follow-up letters. Follow-up letters may include a thank-you letter after an interview, a letter accepting a position or declining a position, or a letter of resignation. It is also helpful to know how to best incorporate letters into your online job search.

CASE STUDY

Maura Learns Targeted Letters Capture Interest

Maura learned the importance of a well-written cover letter to her job search in her career development and business communications classes. Now that she was preparing for her job search, Maura wanted to focus on preparing letters that would capture employers' interest in her unique qualifications.

Maura selected 10 companies she was really interested in working for. For each company, Maura targeted her cover letters by including the company name, the title of the position she was interested in, and some reasons why she wanted to work for that company. She researched the job descriptions posted on the company websites to identify keywords to use in her letter that matched some of her own skills and other qualifications. She researched the names and correct titles of the contact people she was writing to and their mailing and e-mail addresses. Maura had a head start on correct contact information with the business cards she had collected at a career fair. If she did not have all the contact information, she either called the company directly or went online to research it. She found most of the contact information she needed on LinkedIn. Maura used online editing tools to avoid spelling, punctuation, or grammar errors and also had her business communications instructor review her documents for accuracy and correctness. She was prepared to send her letters online or by U.S. mail, depending on the requirements specified by the company.

After sending her targeted letters to the 10 companies that were her first choice, Maura prepared another short list of other companies that interested her and regularly monitored their job postings online. Her plan was to use the general cover letter she had prepared in her career development class to respond to other opportunities as they became available.

Maura heard back from several of her targeted companies and received a job offer from one she was most interested in. In addition to the fact that Maura was very qualified for the job, the hiring manager was impressed with the time Maura took to learn about the company and the job and communicate how she might be a good fit.

Discussion Questions

1. What steps did Maura take to ensure her cover letters to her preferred employers were targeted to attract their attention?
2. Was Maura's strategy to use her general cover letter for the rest of her job search a good decision?
3. Do you think that Maura was right to include highlights of her skills and qualifications in her cover letter, in addition to including them on her resume?

11.1 GUIDELINES FOR WRITING JOB SEARCH LETTERS

NOTES Types of Letters	
Cover Letters	**Follow-Up Letters**
Letter of application for a specific position	Thank-you letter following an interview
Letter of inquiry	Letter accepting a position
Networking letter	Letter declining a position
Letter to request a recommendation	Letter of resignation
Application letter for an internship or cooperative education position	Career change letter
E-mail Letters	
Application e-mail with attached cover letter and resume	E-mail cover letter with attached resume

Writing effective letters as part of your job search can be one of your most valuable efforts. Your letters can help distinguish your unique qualifications and capture employers' interest in meeting you in person. Both the content and the form of your letters are equally important to making a positive impression. Here are some basic guidelines for writing job search letters.

CONTENT GUIDELINES

Be brief and to the point. Think about what you want to say before you compose your letter. Present information about yourself that will really spark interest in learning more about you. Don't repeat the detailed experience listed in your resume; summarize it. Balance brief statements about skills, personal qualities, and the job or company details that interest you.

It takes practice to create a well-written letter. Don't get frustrated if writing doesn't come easy to you and you have trouble with your cover letter at first. Seek out some help from an instructor, or professional contacts, and you will be sure to end up with a document you are proud of.

Links to further information. If you have a presence online and there is an example of something you referred to in your letter that can be accessed, refer to the link and provide the URL. This is a great way to draw the employer in a little closer to learn more about you professionally.

FORMAT GUIDELINES

Use standard letter business format.

Your letters should be formatted as a formal business correspondence letter. There are sample formats for you to follow in this chapter. If you are not accustomed to business writing, these formats provide basic guidelines for you to follow. There are many reference resources in print and online on effective business letter writing that give helpful hints on how to compose a letter that has a proper business format. Reviewing the sample formats in this chapter and completing the activities, you will be able to structure your letters professionally. Some basic tips:

- Use left-justified text.
- Single-space.
- Use conservative, black font; font size 12 works best.
- Use the same font style for your letters that you used for your resume.
- Avoid bolding text.
- Insert your own handwritten signature whenever possible; try to reserve using digital signatures unless you need to forward your document online.

Address the letter to the proper individual.

Personalize the salutation. It is important to personalize your letter by addressing it directly to the appropriate individual and using his or her proper title. If the name of the contact person is not listed, or if you have heard about the job from another source, call the company and ask for the name and title of the person to write to. You may also want to ask for the person's proper mailing address, because he or she may not be located at the main address listed for the company. Many times a company has offices or buildings spread out in various locations. At all costs, avoid writing letters that begin with "Dear Hiring Manager" or "To Whom It May Concern." This type of general salutation may cause the reader to feel you have not taken much time to research the company or that you are not seriously considering that particular company in your job search. We all like to be acknowledged by name, and we all like our names to be spelled correctly; your prospective employer is no different. Online, LinkedIn is a widely used resource for finding up-to-date contact information.

Make absolutely no errors.

Your letter must be error-free. Most employers view the quality of your letters as a reflection of your professionalism, attention to detail, and written communication skills. Even one error can cause an employer to pass on your application. Do not depend on only your own eyes to proofread your letter. You may be too close to your own work to see your mistakes. Have one or two other people read your letter and make necessary corrections. Do not rely only on spell check. A word that is spelled properly but used out of context in your letter might be accepted by spell check and leave you with a grammatical error in your letter.

Progress Check Questions

1. Have you composed a business letter before using standard business format? Can you use this as an example for the format to follow to write your job search letters?

2. Do you know how to use automatic formatting tools on your computer to format your letters and proof them for correct spelling, punctuation, and grammar?

11.2 COVER LETTERS

A cover letter is a letter that accompanies your resume. It is the main letter used in a job search. The purpose of the cover letter is to promote your qualifications to an employer so that you can obtain an interview. Employers receive hundreds of resumes for a single job opening. When the resumes received show similar backgrounds among many candidates, employers look for some way to narrow down the field of applicants to be interviewed. A well-prepared cover letter can make you stand out favorably among other applicants and lead to you being selected for an interview.

Look at the sample format for cover letters in Figure 11.1. By using this as a guide for preparing your own cover letters, you will be sure to convey all the important information your prospective employer needs to know.

There are different types of cover letters. These include application letters for a specific position or to an internship program, inquiry letters, requests for recommendations, career change letters, and networking letters. Different types of cover letters have one thing in common and that is to secure a job interview. While these letters all have a common purpose, they are each written in a different way to emphasize key points.

> *Different types of cover letters have one thing in common—to secure a job interview.*

FIGURE 11.1

Format for Cover Letters

Return address → 123 Oak Street
New Town, NJ 01234
Telephone number → (201) 597-0049
E-mail address → t.smith@bus.edu
Date → July 8, 20__

Inside address →
Ms. Mary Jones
Vice President
American Insurers
2500 Brook Avenue
Boston, MA 00215

Salutation → Dear Ms. Jones:

First paragraph: State your reason for writing → In your initial paragraph state the reason for the letter, name the specific position or type of work for which you are applying, and indicate from which source (career services office, news media, friend, employment service) you learned of the opening.

Second paragraph: Describe your qualifications → Indicate why you are interested in the position, the company, its products or services. Above all, note what you can do for the employer. If you are a recent graduate, explain how your academic background makes you a qualified candidate for the position. If you have some practical work experience, point out your specific achievements or unique qualifications. Avoid repeating the information the reader will find in the resume.

Third paragraph: Refer to enclosed resume or application → Refer the reader to the enclosed resume or application form, which summarizes your qualifications, training, and experiences.

Final paragraph: Indicate your plan for follow-up → In the closing paragraph, indicate your desire for a personal interview and your flexibility as to the time and place. Repeat your phone number in the letter, and offer any assistance to help in a speedy response. Finally, close your letter with a statement or question that will encourage a response. For example, state that you will be in the city where the company is located on a certain date and would like to set up an interview. Or state that you will call on a certain date to set up an interview. Or ask if the company will be recruiting in your area, or if additional information or references are desired.

Closing → Sincerely,
Your written signature →
Your name typed → Thomas L. Smith

LETTER OF APPLICATION FOR A SPECIFIC POSITION

This letter states your specific qualifications for the job for which you are applying (Figure 11.2). Always begin by addressing the letter to a specific person, using his or her full name and title. Be sure to enclose a, copy of your resume. Say in the letter that you did so, and include the word *Enclosures* at the bottom of the letter. State the title of the specific position you are applying for, and mention where you found out about the job (career services, online, referral, etc.). Relate how your education or experience has made you qualified for this position. State what you can offer rather than what you hope to gain. Unless requested, do not mention a salary requirement in your letter. This is because by being too high or too low, you can eliminate your chance for an interview. Request an interview at the employer's convenience, and follow up in approximately one week with a telephone call.

FIGURE 11.2
Sample Letter of Application for a Specific Position

234 Lindmore Road
Seattle, WA 98101
(206) 487-2976
amanda.soto1@xyz.com
May 3, 20__

Mr. Brent Addison
Executive Director
The Community Fund
42 Central Boulevard
Seattle, WA 98101

Dear Mr. Addison:

I am writing in response to your ad in the *Seattle Times on Sunday,* April 22, for an administrative assistant.

I have followed the progress The Community Fund is making on establishing two new programs in conjunction with City Year. The network your organization continues to build in the local area seems ready to support these efforts. I am interested in being part of the team raising the needed program funds.

I have experience creating Access databases and have worked with Blackbaud fundraising software while on an internship with the American Cancer Society. I also worked on the team to create a new online giving system which helped increase online donations by 10 percent last year.

Enclosed is my resume which includes a link to the online giving page on the American Cancer Society website and how I can be contacted for an interview.

I look forward to speaking to you soon.

Sincerely,

Amanda Soto

Amanda Soto
Enclosure

LETTER OF INQUIRY

Use the letter of inquiry as part of a general mailing to employers (Figures 11.3 and 11.4). You are writing to inquire whether or not the company is hiring someone with your background and skills. To your knowledge, there is not a specific position available. Address your letter to a specific person, and use his or her name and full title. Enclose a copy of your resume, and say that you did so in the letter. Briefly state how your background may

FIGURE 11.3

Sample Letter of Inquiry #1

---

900 Brayton Point
Manchester, NH 03109
(603) 893-9187
louis.ricci@xyz.com
May 18, 20__

Ms. Maura Sengel
Vice President
Coast One Bank
328 East Mountain Highway
Manchester, NH 03109

Dear Ms. Sengel:

I am writing to inquire about a career opportunity in marketing with Coast One Bank.

At a recent career fair at Cityview Business Institute, I learned that Coast One Bank is expanding branches in the Northeast. I have read about your profits over the past five years and see that your bank has a solid history of growth.

I decided to continue my education after working in the marketing field for eight years at a local company. To date, my work has involved improving business results by applying online and social media marketing strategies. The bank representative I met at the career fair shared some of the current challenges your bank is having with increased local competition. I am interested in learning how the skills I have developed in my previous job can be applied to the banking industry and help Coast One Bank maintain the leadership position you currently hold.

My resume is enclosed for your information and details my work experience.

I would like the opportunity to discuss the bank's goals and how I might contribute. Please contact me at (603) 893-9187.

I look forward to speaking to you soon.

Sincerely,

Louis Ricci

Louis Ricci
Enclosure

---

benefit the company, mentioning your education and any skills gained through outside activities and previous jobs. Ask for the opportunity to discuss your qualifications in person, at the employer's convenience. Even if a company is not hiring, a letter of inquiry creates visibility about you as a potential candidate down the road.

FIGURE 11.4

Sample Letter of Inquiry #2

962 Summerdale Drive
Pittsburgh, PA 15122
(412) 438-9730
dtthompsen@xyz.com
April 10, 20__

Mr. James Fitzgerald
Vice President of Information Technology
Webs Spark Results, Inc.
1967 East Boulder Highway
Denver, CO 80239

Dear Mr. Fitzgerald:

I am writing to apply for the Web developer position at Webs Spark Results, Inc. recently posted on the Cardon Community College online Alumni Career Center.

While pursuing my BS degree in information systems, I have gained experience working as a Web developer with Cyrus Systems. One of my proudest accomplishments is successfully completing three independent projects for Cyrus that resulted in new contracts totaling $200,000. I especially enjoy building client relationships and determining creative technology solutions to improve business results. The position at Web Sparks Results requires significant time customizing proposals targeted to small business owners. The position would provide me the opportunity to become familiar with technology challenges unique to small businesses.

You can learn about my special projects and view my Career Portfolio by visiting my personal website at www.derektthompsen2490.com. I look forward to an interview.

Sincerely,

Derek T. Thompsen

Derek T. Thompsen

NETWORKING LETTER

Someone in your career network may have suggested you write to another person. Your purpose might be to obtain information or to ask for a job lead or interview. Networking letters (Figures 11.5 and 11.6) are among the most effective job search letters because employers generally like to hire someone referred by someone they know.

FIGURE 11.5

Sample Networking Letter #1

1463 Trighton Park Place
Dedham, MA 73082
(517) 629-8367
ramonedj.munoz@xyz.com
October 20, 20__

Mr. Cameron Bready
Vice President of Information Technology
Merckel, Inc.
1293 Cloud Business Park
Boston, MA 02120

Dear Mr. Bready:

I am writing at the recommendation of Kyra Olsen who suggested I contact you regarding my job search. I will graduate in December with my bachelor's degree in software engineering. I learned from Kyra that you and I are both graduates of Tech Institute and that there are many graduates from our school working at Merckel, Inc.

My goal is to eventually be a software engineer for Merckel. I have four years of part-time work experience in various technology-related positions. There are a number of positions posted on your company website's career center that currently fit my qualifications. In addition to completing the online application for those positions, I am enclosing my resume which includes my contact information. My Career Portfolio is also available for review at www.rdjmunozeng.com.

If there is another individual within the company whom you think I should connect with directly, please be sure to let me know. I look forward to an interview.

Sincerely,

Ramone D.J. Munoz

Ramone D.J. Munoz
Enclosure

FIGURE 11.6

Sample Networking Letter #2

84 Commanders Way
Annapolis, MD 02203
(410) 782-9184
d.bartnett@xyz.com
November 7, 20__

Ms. Erica Downing, Esquire
Crane and Crane, Attorneys at Law
486 Regal Parkway
Baltimore, MD 21206

Dear Ms. Downing:

Tom Lester suggested I write you regarding the possibility of a position for a paralegal at the new law office you will open in January. I am interested in working with Crane and Crane because of the fine reputation the firm has as the leading law firm in Maryland for bankruptcy and foreclosure work.

I am confident that my paralegal degree and work experience gained through two internships have provided me with specific skills needed by your firm.

Skills/qualifications	Examples
• legal research	researching legal journals to draft motions
• legal writing	writing case notes
• computer skills	XLNT writing
• meeting deadlines	filing papers on deadline with courts

I have assisted attorneys with preparing for hearings and have the ability to prioritize work to accommodate case load requirements. I have experience with maintaining client databases. I created a new e-files system for the paralegals at one of my internship sites. The opening of your second office presents an opportunity for me to use my experience to establish a well-organized, client-friendly office that reflects Crane and Crane's standards for quality.

Being part of your new office opening team would be an exciting and challenging experience for me. My resume, with contact information, is enclosed. Knowing you are frequently out of the office at hearings and with clients, I have copied Ms. Terri Burke, your office manager, should she be scheduling interview times with candidates. I will call next week if I do not hear from you or Ms. Burke sooner.

Thank you for your time.

Sincerely,

Dina Bartnett

Dina Bartnett
cc: Ms. Terri Burke
Enclosure

Real Life Stories

Craig's Career Networking Letters

Craig was about to graduate with a degree in homeland security and public safety.

His goal was to obtain an entry-level position with the Department of Homeland Security. He knew that it might be diffcult to stand out among the thousands of candidates applying each year. After Craig followed the instructions to apply online on the department's website, he wanted to draw attention to his application. He took advantage of his career network and wrote a letter to a friend currently working at the department, who had graduated from his school the year before. Craig asked his friend for the recruiting manager's contact information and then wrote her a targeted letter of application.

Craig also wrote a letter to his friend and e-mailed his resume and asked her to share it directly with the recruiting manager. His friend said that she would be sure to communicate that Craig was one of the top graduates from the school's program that year and that Craig had already completed his application online.

Craig did receive a call for an interview and later received a job offer, which he accepted. He recognized the value of his personalized career networking letters and made a commitment to use targeted letters as a way to maintain and develop connections in his career network.

Progress Check Questions

1. How many different situations can you think of where you might use a networking letter?

2. Have you updated your contact information in your career network recently?

"One way to customize a cover letter is to reference an employer's products or services or point out content on its Web site."

Sarah E. Needleman, writer, the *Wall Street Journal*[2]

LETTER TO REQUEST A RECOMMENDATION

This letter is written to people who have enough knowledge about your qualifications to feel comfortable recommending you for a position (Figure 11.7). Make a personal call in addition to writing the letter. Choose people you are sure can recommend you favorably. Identify yourself by name and make mention of how you know the person. If your name has changed since the time you first knew this person, mention your previous name. Ask permission to use this person's name as a reference. Make the contact cordial, but convince the other person that his or her support is important to you.

Send a copy of your resume to each person you would like to serve as a reference, and send updates as you make them. This will enable the person to be more comfortable and/or specific when talking about you to an employer.

APPLICATION LETTER FOR AN INTERNSHIP OR COOPERATIVE EDUCATION PROGRAM

Address this letter using the name of the hiring manager and/or persons involved in the selection process (Figure 11.8). Enclose a copy of your resume, and include references on a separate page. State why you would like to be considered for the program along with your qualifications. State the kind of professional experience you hope to gain and how you will apply this experience to reach your goal.

[2]Retrieved July 29, 2013, from http://online.wsj.com/article/SB10001424052748704187204575101940175633 532.html.

FIGURE 11.7

Sample Letter to Request a Recommendation

19 Bridge Street
Detroit, MI 48213
(313) 458-9287
tyrone.trenton@xyz.com
May 1, 20__

Mr. Garrett Fowler
Assistant Manager
The Sports Authority
All Star Mall
415 Tyson's Corner
Detroit, MI 48213

Dear Mr. Fowler:

I am currently conducting a job search and would like permission to provide your name as reference to prospective employers.

I value the experience I gained when working for you last summer. Since you were my direct supervisor, you have firsthand knowledge of my skills, dependability, and ability to work well with others. Would you be willing to write a letter of recommendation for me to include in my Career Portfolio?

If you agree, please forward your letter to me at the above address. I am forwarding you a copy of my current resume so you will have a complete picture of my education and experience to date. please contact me if I can answer any questions.

Thank you for your continued support.

Sincerely,

Tyrone Trenton

Tyrone Trenton
Enclosure

FIGURE 11.8

Sample Application Letter for Internship or Cooperative Education Program

395 Lake Garden Drive
East Lansing, MI 48823
(508) 396-7725
smith.brittany@xyz.com
April 2, 20___

Dr. Julian Suarez
Director of Medical Services
Community Hospital
893 Canton Street
Burlington, MA 01803

Dear Dr. Suarez:

I am writing to apply for the internship position posted at Community Hospital.

I am pursuing my degree in nursing, and this position would better familiarize me with day-to-day experiences I would be exposed to in a community hospital emergency center. I am required to complete a project that would contribute to the hospital's quality improvement program. I think an area I can contribute to is employee development and training. My goal would be to review the current employee onboarding process and create an updated employee orientation manual that could be used to implement a new employee training program.

Enclosed is my resume. I look forward to the interviewing process and the opportunity to make a positive contribution should I be selected.

Sincerely,

Brittany Smith

Brittany Smith
Enclosure

CAREER CHANGE LETTER

This type of letter is usually written by people who have returned to school to pursue a new career after already being in the workforce (Figures 11.9 and 11.10). This letter should include the additional skills and qualifications acquired by advancing your education and the benefits of your previous work experience. Use this letter to tie everything together by emphasizing your transferable skills. The use of bulleted points within the letter accentuates the transferable skills and how they match specific skill requirements for the job.

FIGURE 11.9

Sample Career Change Letter #1

2 Morris Street
Indianapolis, IN 46214
(317) 492-8309
eacole@xyz.com
June 8, 20__

Mrs. Tynetta Jackson
Operations Manager
Cranmore Industries
492 Seamore Street
Indianapolis, IN 46214

Dear Mrs. Jackson:

I am writing in response to the corporate event planner position posted on your website. Cranmore Industries has always been an employer of choice for me. I have followed your growing list of corporate clients. While the opportunity to open your first international location in Italy, the site of the 2016 World Sports Competition, is exciting, I am sure it will present some challenges. I know that it will take much advanced planning, staffing, and training to prepare for operating an event of this magnitude.

I am about to graduate with my degree in sports, entertainment, and event management. I decided to obtain a new degree to pursue my passion for a career as an events coordinator for a large, multinational company. I have worked as an administrative assistant in a corporate environment for sixteen years. My proudest accomplishment is organizing an employee development program for my company.

Enclosed is my resume. I am available for an interview upon request and look forward to the opportunity to speak with you in person. I feel confident that we will discover that Cranmore Industries and I are a right fit.

Sincerely,

Elizabeth A. Cole

Elizabeth A. Cole
Enclosure

FIGURE 11.10
Sample Career Change Letter #2

62 Indian Bend Court
Phoenix, AZ 85008
(480) 849-9624
l.diaz@xyz.edu
March 24, 20__

Mr. Felipe Estrada
Vice President of Operations
Delta Pharmacy Corporation
1498 Comstock Parkway
Miami, FL 33154

Dear Mr. Estrada:

I am writing to apply for the regional store manager's position posted on Monster.com on March 22nd. I have been following Delta Pharmacy's expansion plan to the Phoenix area and am impressed with the company's strategic plan to be ranked among the top five pharmacy companies in the United States. Below are examples of my skills that match some of the job requirements.

Skills/qualifications	Examples
• speak and read Spanish fluently	translated pharmaceutical representative's training manuals from English to Spanish
• pharmaceutical product knowledge	semiannual pharmaceutical sales convention
• time management	Mind Tools software and personal digital assistant (PDA)
• cost control and revenue generation	monitor generic drug prices vs. name brands three-year consecutive lead sales award

After spending fifteen years in pharmaceutical sales for Blake and Blake, I returned to school to pursue my degree in business management. After completing my degree in June, I am interested in applying my management skills and my sales experience to move from sales to a lead operations role. I am confident that I can build a strong team and manage the financial success of Delta's Southwest group of stores.

I look forward to the opportunity to discuss this with you in person. I can be reached at the above phone number or e-mail address. My resume is enclosed.

Sincerely,

Lior Diaz

Lior Diaz
Enclosure

Progress Check Questions

1. Would you send a letter of application for a specific position if you already applied for the position online? Why or why not?

2. If you are currently employed, what precautions should you take when sending letters in search of another job?

E-MAIL COVER LETTERS

E-mail is the most common way cover letters are sent to employers during a job search.

First, you should create an edit-ready version of your letter that you can access and edit as needed. Google Docs, OpenOffice Writer, and Microsoft Word are examples of word processing software you can use to create an edit-ready version. Then save it as a PDF file, and use the PDF version if you are attaching your letter to an e-mail. Follow the employer's instructions on how to submit your cover letter.

An e-mail cover letter should be written as well as any other business correspondence. Because it is easier and faster to communicate by e-mail, you might be tempted to rush your writing and compromise the quality of your communication.

Guidelines for E-mail Cover Letters   When attaching a cover letter to an e-mail message addressed to an employer, follow the guidelines provided in this chapter for text and format for traditional letters.

The guidelines for writing your message in the body of your e-mail are somewhat different. For example, the content of a letter in the body of an e-mail should be briefer than in a traditional letter.

The following are tips for writing an effective e-mail cover letter.

Use your personal e-mail account.

Do not use your current employer's mail system for your job search. Most employers use e-mail scanning systems to monitor employees' e-mails. You may not want your employer to know you are seeking a new position, and you should not use your time on your current job to look for a new one. Doing this could put your current job at risk.

Send your message from a serious e-mail address.

Use an e-mail address like louis.ricci@xyz.com. If you want to tell something about you, use an address like louis.riccimkt@xyz.com. Here Louis Ricci is highlighting his marketing degree. Don't use your bigboozer@xyz.com account for your job search. Messages from informal e-mail addresses may look like junk e-mail (or jokes) and can be deleted or ignored.

Have an effective subject.

Target your message in the subject line to catch the reader's attention. For example, for Louis Ricci, an effective follow-up to a job interview for a marketing position at Coast One Bank might be louis.riccic1bkmkt as opposed to "Interview Follow-up."

Send your message to the appropriate addresses.

If there is a specified recipient in the job posting or instructions on the website, use that addressee. Otherwise, try to obtain a person's name and e-mail address to use, preferably the hiring manager or human resources recruiter.

Use short paragraphs.

E-mail messages need plenty of white space to be easy to read. Break big paragraphs into smaller ones. Summarize important points.

Keep the message short.

Long messages are not likely to be read, especially in e-mail form.

E-MAIL WITH ATTACHED COVER LETTER AND RESUME

When an employer indicates that you should send an e-mail with your cover letter and resume attached (Figure 11.11), take these simple steps:

1. Prepare an edit-ready version of your letter.
2. Save as a PDF file to ensure formatting is protected.
3. Attach the PDF versions of your cover letter and resume to your e-mail.
4. Target your message in the subject line.
5. Send your e-mail.

As an extra precaution, just before you press the Send button, open the attachments and review them to be sure you have included the right documents and that the formats remain intact.

E-MAIL COVER LETTER WITH ATTACHED RESUME

Another option is to include the text of your cover letter directly in the body of your e-mail message addressed to the employer and then attach a PDF version of your resume (Figure 11.12).

FIGURE 11.11

Sample E-mail with Attached Cover Letter and Resume

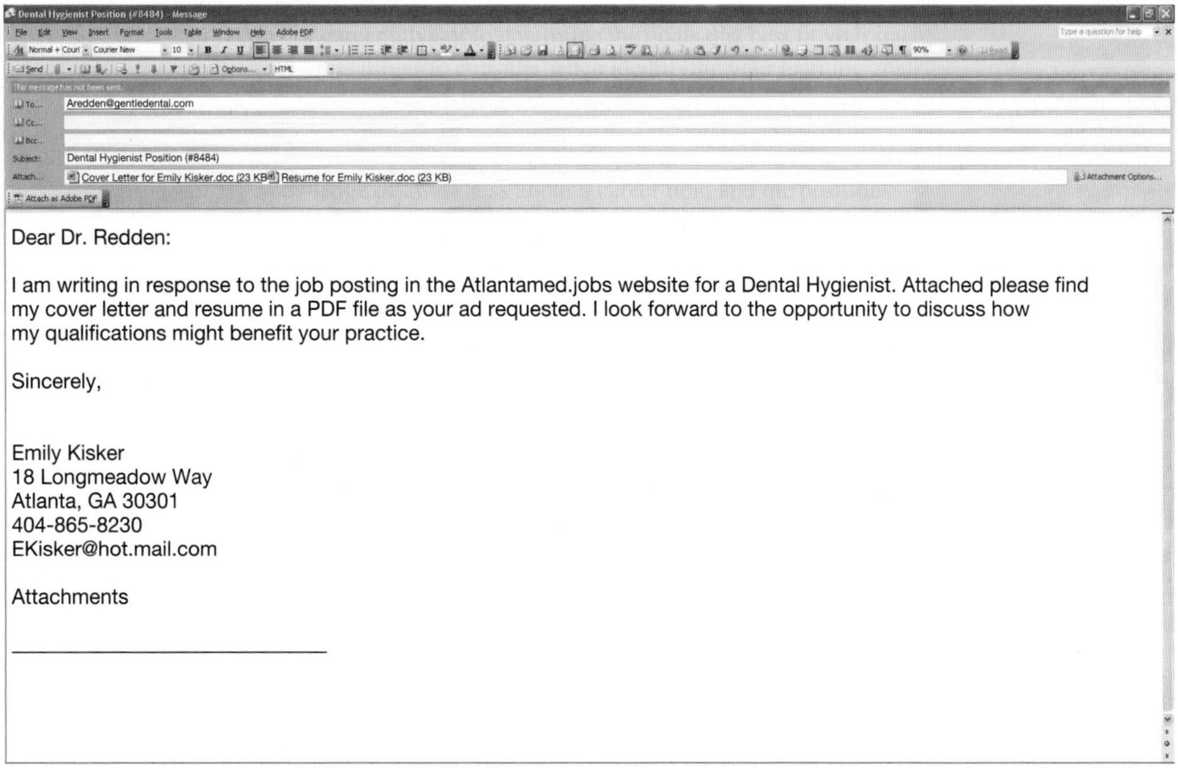

Dental Hygienist Position (#8484) - Message

To... Aredden@gentledental.com

Subject: Dental Hygienist Position (#8484)

Attach... Cover Letter for Emily Kisker.doc (23 KB); Resume for Emily Kisker.doc (23 KB)

Dear Dr. Redden:

I am writing in response to the job posting in the Atlantamed.jobs website for a Dental Hygienist. Attached please find my cover letter and resume in a PDF file as your ad requested. I look forward to the opportunity to discuss how my qualifications might benefit your practice.

Sincerely,

Emily Kisker
18 Longmeadow Way
Atlanta, GA 30301
404-865-8230
EKisker@hot.mail.com

Attachments

CAREER PORTFOLIO 11.1

⚬⚬ WRITE A COVER LETTER

Preparing your own cover letter is easy if you take the time to organize your thoughts and plan what you want to say in each part of the letter.

Select an employer to write to concerning your interest in employment. Decide what you want to say to your prospective employer. Then fill in each section below to create your own cover letter.

Return address ——— •

Telephone number ——— •
E-mail address ——— •
Date ——— •

Inside address ——— •

Salutation ——— •

First paragraph:
State your reason ——— •
for writing

Second paragraph:
Describe your ——— •
qualifications

Third paragraph:
Refer to enclosed ——— •
resume or application

Final paragraph:
Indicate your plan ——— •
for follow-up

Closing ——— •

Your written signature ——— •

Your name typed ——— •

FIGURE 11.12

Sample E-mail Cover Letter with Attached Resume

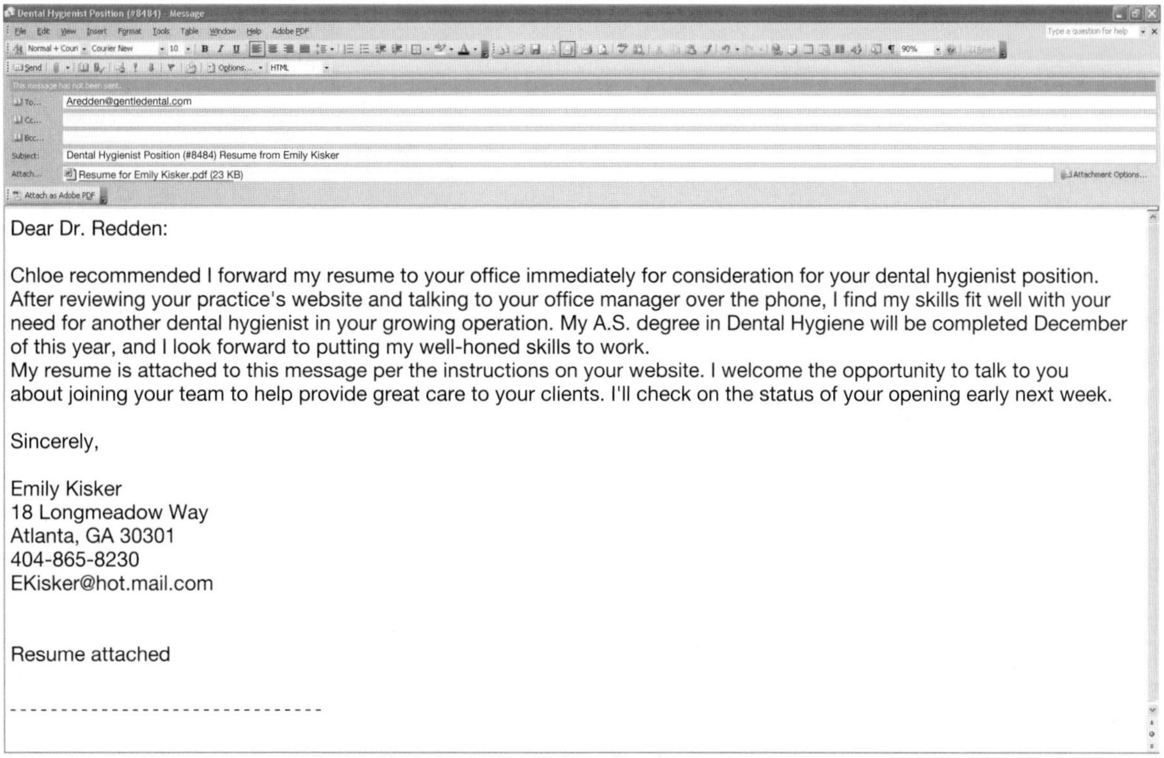

To: Aredden@gentledental.com

Subject: Dental Hygienist Position (#8484) Resume from Emily Kisker

Attach: Resume for Emily Kisker.pdf (23 KB)

Dear Dr. Redden:

Chloe recommended I forward my resume to your office immediately for consideration for your dental hygienist position. After reviewing your practice's website and talking to your office manager over the phone, I find my skills fit well with your need for another dental hygienist in your growing operation. My A.S. degree in Dental Hygiene will be completed December of this year, and I look forward to putting my well-honed skills to work.

My resume is attached to this message per the instructions on your website. I welcome the opportunity to talk to you about joining your team to help provide great care to your clients. I'll check on the status of your opening early next week.

Sincerely,

Emily Kisker
18 Longmeadow Way
Atlanta, GA 30301
404-865-8230
EKisker@hot.mail.com

Resume attached

11.3 FOLLOW-UP LETTERS

Writing follow-up letters is an important part of acting on decisions throughout your job search. A timely thank-you letter after an interview can keep you in the running for a job you just interviewed for. If you are still interested in a job after your interview, confirming it in writing shows initiative and tells the employer you took the interview seriously. Personalize your connection with your interviewer by sending a handwritten thank-you note. This shouldn't substitute for a formal letter to follow, but it can be especially effective right after the interview when you are really serious about pursuing next steps. Even when an outcome is not what you expected and you do not receive a job offer or you decide the job is not for you, sending an appropriate letter demonstrates courtesy and professionalism. Don't forget to send thank-you letters to those who agreed to be a reference and to those in your career network who provided you the names of individuals to write to.

Follow the same guidelines for writing and transmitting e-mail follow-up letters as described earlier for e-mail cover letters.

The following discussion describes basic follow-up letters with tips on when and how to write them.

THANK-YOU LETTER FOLLOWING AN INTERVIEW

This letter is written after the interview to acknowledge the interviewer's time and information shared during the interview (Figure 11.13). This is a good way to help your interviewer remember you. Be sure to send the letter right after the interview.

In addition to thanking the interviewer for his or her time, state the position you interviewed for and provide the date and place of the interview (campus interview, career fair, company location, etc.). If you are interested in the job after the interview, express your enthusiasm for the job and the company. Be sure to include your telephone number, your mailing address, and your e-mail address. Without this information, an employer may not

FIGURE 11.13

Sample Thank-You Letter Following an Interview

98 Towerplane Drive
Dallas, TX 75216
(214) 503-0458
keith.douglas@xyz.com
May 18, 20__

Ms. Myra Seigel
Regional Territory Manager
Healthy Way Foods, Inc.
10600 Major Highway
Dallas, TX 75216

Dear Ms. Seigel:

I appreciated the opportunity to interview with you on May 16 about the account representative position for the Dallas territory. The update you shared with me about the company was informative, and I left the interview excited about the position.

I am confident that my sales experience with ABC Food Marketing the last three summers has prepared me for transitioning to a full-time role in sales. I pride myself on my time management and organizational skills and ability to adapt to new situations. These are particularly important skills for someone responsible for self-monitoring work on a daily basis. Having firsthand experience with what a sales position involves will help me hit the ground running. I am sure that I can generate new accounts while working to retain current business.

If I can provide you with any additional information, please let me know. I look forward to hearing from you soon.

Sincerely,

Keith Douglas

Keith Douglas

be able to contact you and you could lose a job offer. Even though you have provided this information previously, it is worth another reminder to ensure the employer can easily reach you. To help with writing thank-you letters, make sure you keep current and accurate records of every interview: the date, time, location, interviewer, and any special information concerning the company or the job itself.

LETTER ACCEPTING A POSITION

Once you decide to accept a position, writing a letter of acceptance not only confirms your decision but also shows your employer that you take the new job seriously and that your professional approach does not end once you have the job (Figure 11.14). Whether the job offer comes to you verbally or in writing, answer the employer immediately if you are sure you are accepting the job. Be direct about your acceptance and restate the specific position you are accepting. Be sure to express your appreciation for the opportunity you have been given, and express your eagerness to begin your new job.

FIGURE 11.14

Sample Letter Accepting a Position

56 Seaver Street
San Francisco, CA 94110
(415) 555-2555
allie.mckenzie@xyz.com
January 5, 20___.

Mrs. Connie Hu
Partner
Infographics and Web Development Specialists
429 Reed Street
San Francisco, CA 94110

Dear Mrs. Hu:

I am very pleased to accept the position of lead graphics designer as outlined in your offer letter of January 3rd, 20___. I understand that I will be located at the main office on Reed Street but will travel to branch locations as needed. As you requested, I will bring the completed forms you need when I arrive on Monday, January 10.

I have a phone call scheduled with Anna Lee in Human Resources this week to clarify first-day logistics. I appreciate the confidence you have expressed in me, and I intend to meet or exceed your expectations.

I am especially eager to begin working with the team. I look forward to a great start!

Sincerely,

Allison McKenzie

Allison McKenzie

LETTER DECLINING A POSITION

First, think carefully before deciding not to accept a job offer. If you have given it your full consideration, and are in a secure enough situation that allows you to refuse the offer, you should write a letter to communicate your decision (Figure 11.15). Be direct, but soften your tone to show appreciation for the offer. Be concise and make the letter simple. Even though you are not taking the job, you want to leave a favorable impression. Someday you may be applying for another job at the same company, and it is good to be remembered for your professional approach in communicating your previous decision.

FIGURE 11.15

Sample Letter Declining a Position

15 Hope Avenue
Aurora, CO 80014
(303) 919-6346
john.lester@xyz.com
December 2, 20__

Mr. Paoblo Mendez
Director of Administration
Orson and Blinn CPA Firm
345 Trail Road
Denver, CO 80202

Dear Mr. Mendez:

Thank you for your letter of November 26 offering me an accounting position with your firm.

After considerable thought, I have decided not to accept the position at this time. I have accepted an accounting position with a nonprofit organization in the local area.

This has been a very difficult decision for me. However, I feel I have made the right choice at this point in my career.

Thank you for your time, effort, and consideration. Your confidence in me is very much appreciated.

Sincerely,

John Lester

John Lester

LETTER OF RESIGNATION

This letter can be written to officially notify your employer of your decision to leave your company (Figure 11.16). Regardless of the reason you are leaving, you should write a resignation in a positive tone. For example, if you are leaving to begin a new job or to relocate to another city, and you are leaving the company on good terms, you can indicate the reason for your leaving in the letter. If you have not had the best experience, avoid mentioning any details, especially referring negatively to the company or your boss or coworkers. Once your letter is received, it is a permanent record of one of the last forms of your communication with the company. In the future, a negative letter could hurt your chances of ever returning to the company or obtaining a good reference.

FIGURE 11.16

Sample Letter of Resignation

24 Terrace Street
Boston, MA 02982
(617) 592-9567
reaton@xyz.com
April 30, 20___

Ms. Carol Faulkner
Director of Management Information Systems
Tech Corp
1818 Tech Parkway
Boston, MA 02982

Dear Ms. Faulkner:

This letter is to confirm my decision to leave Tech Corp on May 30, 20___. I have accepted a management position at Software Inc. I feel this career opportunity provides me new growth potential. My experience with Tech Corp has been an asset to my career. I have learned technical skills and developed new, improved leadership skills through my work with members of the operations team.

Thank you for the career opportunity Tech Corp has provided me. Best wishes!

Sincerely,

Richard D. Eaton

Richard D. Eaton

"Manners matter. Some 88 percent of executives say a thank you note can influence a hiring decision."

Money Magazine[3]

Personalize your connection with your interviewer by sending a short, handwritten thank-you note after your interview. Follow up later with a formal thank-you letter.

[3]Retrieved July 29, 2013, from www.nytimes.com/2007/11/10/business/10offline.html?_r=0.

ACTIVITY 11.1

Practice Writing Follow-Up Letters

The following is a list of the types of follow-up letters discussed in this chapter. Place a check next to the type of letter you would like to practice writing; then fill in each section of the letter format provided.

❑ Thank-you letter following an interview

❑ Letter accepting a position

❑ Letter declining a position

❑ Letter of resignation

Return address _____

Telephone number _____
E-mail address _____
Date _____

Inside address _____

Salutation _____

First paragraph:
State your reason _____
for writing

Second paragraph: _____
Provide details

Third paragraph:
Express appreciation _____
for the experience/
job offer.

Final paragraph:
Indicate your plan _____
for follow-up if
appropriate.

Closing _____

Your written signature _____

Your name typed _____

Have someone critique your letter for content and check for grammar, punctuation, and spelling.

Progress Check Questions

1. Would you send a thank-you note after an interview even if you are no longer interested in the job or company as a result of the interview? Why or why not?

2. What things should you think about before sending a letter declining a position?

The letters you create during your job search are critical because they sell your resume and ultimately help differentiate you from other candidates with similar backgrounds. You should recognize that there are many opportunities, in addition to a letter of application, for letters to help you connect effectively with companies that are potential employers now, and in the future.

Whether you are searching for an internship, asking for a recommendation, or applying for a job, a well-composed letter can give you a competitive edge. You should remember, however, that your letter must always be a truthful representation of your qualifications and background. To create a letter that promotes your strengths, you must first have acquired competitive skills and qualifications from your educational and work experiences. Letters give you the opportunity to emphasize your work experience, highlight your interest in a particular company, and express your unique personality. In many ways, the letters you write are the most critical elements of a successful job search, because they can reveal more about you as a person than your resume can. Whether sent as hard copy or transmitted electronically, a well-put-together letter during your job search can draw the favorable attention you need to obtain a job interview.

LETTERS AND CAREER DECISION MAKING

Based on what you learned about job search letters in this chapter, answer the following questions.

1. What am I trying to decide?
   _____
   _____

2. What do I need to know? _____
   _____

3. How will it help me make a more informed decision? _____
   _____

4. How can I obtain what I need to know? _____
   _____

   People _____
   Experience _____
   Research _____

5. Who are the best resources for the information I need? _____
   _____

"Most everything you want is just outside your comfort zone."

Jack Canfield, author[1]

[1]Retrieved July 13, 2013, from www.goodreads.com/
quotes/57134-most-everything-that-you-want-is-just-outside-your-comfort.

Successful Interviews

After completing this chapter, you will:

1 **Understand** the different types of interviews

2 **Practice** interview questions

3 **Prepare** for an interview

4 **Know** how to manage the interview and follow up

5 **Understand** how to evaluate job offers

6 **Create** a Career Portfolio entry

It is important to understand different types of interviews. Depending on the company and position, it is possible to experience more than one type of interview. For all interviews, questions and answers are the most important part. Strong answers to different types of questions takes practice, especially for questions you might find difficult to answer. In addition to answering questions well, you can take the lead and shine by accentuating your major strengths and giving examples. Knowing ways you can manage certain parts of the interview will build confidence and help you stand out from other candidates. Follow-up after the interview may include a simple thank-you to your interviewer and completing the next steps you agreed to in the interview. The last step is evaluating a job offer for fit and the experience it can provide to help you reach your future goals.

CASE STUDY

Naomi's Interview: Turning Stumbling Blocks into Stepping Stones

Naomi spent five years working as a guide with a tour company. She was doing extremely well. When the company offered her a promotion with a significant salary increase, she declined. She realized that she was tired of the demanding schedule that consisted of constant travel. Deciding to make a career change, Naomi enrolled in college to pursue a degree in art.

Naomi applied for a job online, using her Web resume, at the corporate office of a greeting card company. She posted selected photos she had taken of many of the international travel destinations she had traveled to. Naomi learned that she loved photography and used her photo collection to create a card collection. At first she presented the cards as gifts to relatives and friends. Eventually her collection was sold at several tourist and airport gift shops. She saw the entry-level job in the art department as an opportunity to further develop an interest, gain some experience in a new field, and earn money to pay for her tuition. She followed up her online application with a telephone call to the company to secure a job interview. Though she did not know the full scope of the company's plans, goals, financial stability, or customer base, she felt she knew enough from the job posting to go on her interview.

When she arrived, she was surprised to see the company had a much more formal environment than she expected. Two other candidates in the reception area were dressed more professionally than Naomi. She assumed that because the position was in the art department, she would be interviewing in a more casual environment.

Her interviewer began by telling Naomi how impressed she was with her photography samples posted on her Web resume. She remarked that they demonstrated her artistic talent and that her card collection revealed her creative side. When she asked Naomi why she was interested in the company, Naomi explained that she was most interested in a job to help pay for her tuition. Naomi explained her previous salary and said she hoped to earn the same in a new job.

Within a week, Naomi was contacted by the company and told she was not being asked back for a second interview. Naomi was disappointed and surprised. She thought the interviewer was really impressed with her.

Naomi called the interviewer and asked if she would be willing to provide feedback on her interview. She was told that her salary expectations were too high and that she was probably better suited for a more casual work environment. Members of the art department frequently participated in meetings in-house and off-site, and often interfaced with current and prospective clients running focus groups on proposed art copy and messaging. They needed to know how to dress professionally on these occasions, even though the art department itself was very casual.

The interviewer was impressed with her follow-up and invited her back for a second interview. When they met the second time, Naomi learned that the lower salary was not negotiable. She had to face the fact that she was switching career paths and sometimes that meant having to accept an adjusted salary to gain entry into a new field. She learned that the company had a tuition reimbursement program that could cover much of her tuition expense. Naomi agreed to stay with the company after completing her degree if the company provided educational assistance. Naomi was now on a new career path that she was more passionate about with a plan on how to accomplish her goal.

Discussion Questions

1. How could Naomi have been better prepared for her first interview?
2. Why do you think Naomi was finally offered a second interview?
3. What decisions did Naomi have to make as she changed her career path?

12.1 TYPES OF JOB INTERVIEWS

Job interviews range from a structured face-to-face interview to a technology-driven format such as a video or Web-based interview. The type of interview conducted depends on the company and the job. Some companies use more than one format to interview for a position. The first step may be Web-based, followed by a telephone or face-to-face interview. Most employers consider the structured face-to-face interview as the most effective.

STRUCTURED FACE-TO-FACE INTERVIEWS

Most face-to-face interviews are structured to have any interviewer ask the same questions of all candidates and apply a standard rating system. Some hiring decisions are based on one interview while others involve a second or third interview.

The First Interview   The purpose of the first interview is to evaluate whether the candidate is qualified for the job. Beyond the job qualifications, the interviewer tries to get a sense about the applicant's fit for the company culture. Based on the outcome, the candidate may be referred to a second or third interview.

Some first interviews are the only interview. The first interview is also sometimes referred to as the initial interview, the first round interview, or the screening interview.

Second and Third Interviews   Once you make a favorable impression on an initial interview, you may be asked back for a second or third interview. These follow-up interviews are usually held to have others who are part of the hiring decision meet you and further evaluate your fit for the job. For example, you might meet with the department head for the area you would be working in. As the specialist, this person might focus more on how well you can perform specific functions of the job and how well you would fit in with the rest of the team.

NOTES | **Advantages of Face-to-Face Interviews**

- Can probe with follow-up questions to incomplete or unclear responses.
- Provides the candidate a forum to ask follow-up questions.
- Can observe the candidate's thought process while answering questions.
- Can observe body language.
- Can ask questions that require lengthy response times.
- Can observe how a candidate communicates.
- Provides information not on the job application.

"You're being evaluated the moment you get off the elevator and come into our lobby."

Jim French, executive vice president, Hill Holliday

Source: Retrieved December 3, 2013 from www.boston.com/business/articles/2010/01/10/you_have_your_foot_in_the_door_how_to_keep_it_there_1263010162/?page=1

BEHAVIORAL-BASED INTERVIEWS

Behavioral-based interviews are based on the premise that past performance in a similar setting is the best predictor of future performance. Before a behavioral interview, hiring managers identify specific competencies or abilities needed to succeed in the available position.

A list of questions is designed to prompt candidates to talk about how skills acquired in one job can be applied to the new job. Based on this knowledge about the candidate, the interviewer's confidence that the person will do well on the job may be substantially increased. There may be one or more steps to a behavioral interview. Step one is usually the face-to-face interview. A second step could include a standardized test administered in person, online, or by telephone.

GROUP INTERVIEWS

Group interviews pair one or more interviewers with several job candidates at the same time. Group interviews may be held for two reasons. Some companies may find it faster and more economical to interview a group of candidates at the same time. The other purpose of group interviews is for the employer to observe how individuals conduct themselves in group settings. For example, employers can observe how well you interact with others. They may also want to observe how well you are able to compete with other candidates and what strategies you use to stand out among the group. Some things you can do to stand out include:

- Participate in discussions.
- Do not dominate the conversation.
- Ask questions.
- Disagree tactfully.

Some group interviews place candidates in smaller teams and lead them through problem-solving or decision-making exercises as a group. Here the employer may be looking to see who has the best ability to persuade others in the group or who emerges as the leader.

No matter how group interviews are conducted, they are usually an opportunity to show how well you handle pressure and still stand out, in a positive way, among the group.

One last thought. Everyone does not need to be the leader and not all positions require those skills. If you are the type of person who will emerge as a good team contributor or individual performer, that can work as well. This will help the interviewer know which type of role you are best suited for.

Real Life Stories

Ken's Group Interview

Ken successfully completed his first interview with Magnus Resort and Entertainment Complex. He was applying for a job as a promotions coordinator for the group conventions division. The next steps in the process consisted of a candidate profile assessment and a group interview.

The group interview consisted of two parts, beginning with questions asked to the entire group that individuals could volunteer to answer. Each time Ken and others were about to respond, Tony spoke first. Toward the middle of the session, Ken decided to appropriately assert himself before Tony could jump in. Ken stood up, signaling he was about to speak, and proceeded to respond to some questions. It worked. Others began to participate more once Ken broke the pattern Tony set. Ken was recognized for the quality of his responses and his ability to manage a dominant group member.

In the second part of the interview, Ken was placed into a smaller group for a group exercise. One person role-played a client presentation, and others were asked to provide feedback. Ken listened to his presenter and then asked questions to ensure he understood some key points. He had some good ideas about how to improve the presentation, but thought it best to encourage other team members to provide their input before he spoke. The trainer for his group noticed Ken's ability to lead each member to participate in the discussion.

During the group interview, Ken demonstrated leadership, teamwork, and self-confidence. He stood out among the group without being domineering, earned the respect of the group, and proved to the trainer that he was well prepared for the promotions' leader position. In his first interview, Ken showed an ability to answer interview questions well. In the second interview, he demonstrated interpersonal and communication skills in a real-life situation. His performance on his group interview and the results of his assessment confirmed the first interviewer's impression that Ken was a good fit for the job and company.

TELEPHONE INTERVIEWS

Occasionally, you may be in a situation where your interview will be conducted by telephone. This can happen when there is not enough time to wait to interview in person or when travel expenses are too costly to bring the interviewer and interviewee together in the same place. Although most job candidates are not hired after having a telephone interview only, this type of interview often precedes or follows a face-to-face interview. It can be challenging to make a positive first impression through a telephone interview because in this case, the employer does not have the benefit of observing your physical appearance or your body language, both of which play a major role in creating an impression of you. To make your telephone interview successful, focus on these three things: voice quality, preparation, and attention to detail.

Voice Quality When speaking on the telephone, be sure to project your voice, speak slowly, enunciate clearly, and sound enthusiastic. Speaking slowly shows you are in control and helps manage your stress.

Preparation Try to be where you know you will be uninterrupted during your telephone interview. Have any important documents stored on your iPhone or iPad ready to send if asked. Have a copy of your resume with you to refer to as you describe your skills, experiences, and employment dates over the phone. You should also prepare some notes of keywords or key points about yourself that you want to be sure to interject during the interview. A current version of your career networking card would be a perfect tool. Have your list of questions available. Being well groomed and in business casual dress for a telephone interview helps you feel like and communicate as a serious candidate.

Attention to Detail Because you are not in the interviewer's office, you cannot be handed copies of information or business cards that give you the correct spelling, title, address, and telephone and e-mail address of your interviewer. You need this information for follow-up communication. You can ask the interviewer to forward what you need by e-mail or if you feel more comfortable, ask the administrative assistant. As a follow-up to your telephone interview, send a thank-you letter immediately and stress your willingness to meet in person.

WEB-BASED INTERVIEWS

In a Web-based interview, the candidate is asked to reply to preset questions using computer software. Responses are recorded and evaluated to determine if the candidate meets the criteria for either a telephone or face-to-face interview. The Walt Disney Company is an example of a company that uses Web-based interviews as part of its screening process. The Web interview consists of two parts; each is time based and can be multiple choice, with a rating scale of one to five. At the Walt Disney Company, the next step for a candidate who passes the Web-based interview is a telephone interview.

VIDEO INTERVIEWS

Video interviews are a cost-effective way to interview out-of-state candidates. If you are asked to participate in a video interview, practice first. Be well groomed and dress professionally. Use a room with a clean background and good lighting. Sit at a desk or table with a clean surface except for a copy of your resume to refer to, your list of questions, and a notepad and pen. Try to appear relaxed and feel free to take notes during the interview. Turn off your cell phone!

SOCIAL INTERVIEWS

Sometimes it just happens. A conversation turns into a spontaneous interview. You are in a professional or social situation, and before you know it you are talking about your career goals and experience. The other person probes a little and asks for more details. The person might say he can refer you to a job he knows about, or better still, say he is hiring and would like your resume. You lucked out, but will you say to yourself, "What just happened?" or "Go for it!" If you recognize an unexpected opportunity while it is happening, you can pave your way to a formal interview.

INTERNAL INTERVIEWS

There might be a time when you would like to pursue an interview for another position at the company where you are currently employed. Maybe you are a part-time or temporary employee or an intern and think you would like a full-time position. You may want to change departments, be considered for a promotion, or continue working for the company after relocating. Let your boss know you are interviewing for another position. In the interview, focus your comments on your ability to do the job and how this change fits into your career plan. Avoid negative comments about your current boss or job. A few questions you may be asked in addition to general questions include "Does your manager know you have applied for this job?" "What don't you like about the job you are in?" "How will you handle it if you don't get the job?"

In your answers, talk about good professional relationships you have within the company and how you are already familiar with the company culture and operating procedures. Having a good reputation at the company will help you be seriously considered for the job. Most employers prefer to hire from within.

12.2 INTERVIEW QUESTIONS

"Applicants should sit down and think 'What are they going to ask me when I'm in that interview?'"

Kent Kirch, global director of recruitment for Deloitte

Source: Retrieved December 5, 2013 from http://mycareer. deloitte.com/ie/en/students/ careers-corner/interviews

The types of questions an employer may ask during an interview range from general to specific. Behavioral-based questions are targeted to learn more about your ability to apply previously learned skills to a different job or how you respond to a variety of workplace situations. Questions covering 21st century skills are an example of one way an employer may probe for transferable skills. Personal ethics questions probe personal values and can help determine fit with the company culture and trustworthiness. You can deflect illegal inquiries during an interview by first staying current on what constitutes discriminatory questions. Most interviews will include some of the following general questions.

GENERAL QUESTIONS

The following general questions are typically asked by interviewers to learn about your background and career goals.

1. What kind of company or work environment are you looking for?
2. What kind of job or duties and responsibilities are you looking for?
3. Tell me a little bit about your professional training and/or your college experience.
4. Describe some of the part-time or summer jobs you've had.
5. What is your academic and school record up until now?
6. Describe some of your extracurricular and student activities.
7. What do you consider to be some of your strong points?
8. What are some of your short- and long-term job goals?
9. Tell me about your past employers.
10. What do you know about this company?
11. What led you to choose your major field of study?
12. Why did you select your institution for your education?
13. What are the three most important accomplishments?
14. What is the most difficult assignment you have had, and how did you handle it?

15. Why should I hire you?

16. How would a friend, former employer, or instructor describe you?

17. Will you relocate and/or travel for your job?

18. Give an example of your ability to work with a team.

19. What are your salary expectations?

20. Are you willing to spend at least six months as a trainee?

There are not always right or wrong answers to interview questions. Practicing answers with someone else to be sure you have thought through your answers prior to an interview can be helpful. In a while you will have the opportunity to practice your own answers. Before you do that, complete the following activity with one other person or a group so that you can discuss different opinions about how to answer some general questions.

ACTIVITY 12.1

Practice Responses to General Interview Questions

The following are some examples of answers to some general questions. Review each option, and select the reply you think would be most effective. Discuss your thoughts with others, providing the reason for your choice. Your discussion might cause you to see things from a different perspective. In any case, this exercise will help you learn to develop thoughtful answers to some important questions.

1. What kind of company or work environment are you looking for?

   a. I do well working in a team environment. I can give you examples of some of my best work performed as part of a team.

   b. I enjoy working independently with little or no supervision.

   c. I think I would benefit from starting in a more structured environment until I am adjusted to my job and the company culture.

2. Tell me about your past employers.

   a. I'd rather not talk about my previous employer. I did not have a good experience with the company.

   b. I have learned something from my experiences with each employer that I think can help me in my next job.

   c. My internship employer taught me a lot about the industry and provided me great coaching on how to improve on some of my weaknesses.

3. Why did you select your institution for your education?

   a. It was close to home.

   b. I received the financial aid I needed to afford my degree.

   c. The alumni are generally following great career paths because of the quality of their education and the school's reputation with employers.

4. Why should I hire you?

   a. I am confident my qualifications match the requirements of the job.

   b. XYZ company has emerged as my first choice because of your reputation and the opportunities for me to learn and gain more experience.

   c. I don't have a lot of experience, but I am willing to learn.

5. Will you relocate and/or travel for your job?

   a. I would relocate to a warmer climate.

   b. I would be prepared to relocate in two more years. I currently have personal commitments that require me to stay in this area until that time.

   c. I can travel as often as needed for the job, but I need my home base to be here.

6. What are your salary expectations?

    a. I am open. What does the position pay?

    b. I need to earn a minimum of $40,000 to eliminate debt I have incurred. I think this salary is in line with my education and work experience.

    c. I am very interested in your company and the position. Can we continue to talk about the position requirements and how I might be the best match for what your company needs?

7. Are you willing to spend at least six months as a trainee?

    a. It depends on what is involved.

    b. Yes.

    c. Yes, I would expect to be required to participate in some type of training program. Is training done at the location I will be assigned to work, or will I need to travel to another location to complete the training?

8. What kind of job or duties are you looking for?

    a. I am willing to do anything to get my foot in the door.

    b. I am interested in the legal offce coordinator's position posted on Monster.com because it will allow me to get started in a law firm where, eventually, I can apply my paralegal degree.

    c. What jobs do you think I qualify for?

ACTIVITY 12.2

Prepare Your Answers to General Interview Questions

Choose five questions below, and write down some keywords or phrases that you will use to help deliver a strong response to the question or write complete answers, whichever is most helpful to you.

1. What kind of company or work environment are you looking for?

2. What kind of job or duties and responsibilities are you looking for?

3. Tell me a little bit about your professional training and/or your college experience.

4. Describe some of the part-time and summer jobs you've had in the past.

5. What is your academic and school record up until now?

6. Describe some of your extracurricular and student activities.

7. What do you consider some of your strong points?

8. What are some of your short- and long-term job goals?

9. Tell me about your past employers.

10. What do you know about this company?

11. What led you to choose your major field of study?

12. Why did you select your institution for your education?

13. What are your three most important accomplishments so far in your life?

14. What is the most diffcult assignment you have had, and how did you handle it?

15. Why should I hire you?

16. How would a friend, former employer, or instructor describe you?

17. Will you relocate and/or travel for your job?

18. Give an example of your ability to work with a team.

19. What are your salary expectations?

20. Are you willing to spend at least six months as a trainee?

Progress Check Questions

1. After practicing answers to general interview questions, do you feel better prepared and more confident in answering these questions on an interview?

2. Are there any answers that you modified from your original thinking after your discussions with others?

BEHAVIORAL-BASED QUESTIONS

Interviewers will often try to judge how you would respond to a variety of workplace situations. Behavioral-based questions enable employers to identify patterns often missed with general questions.

Sample Questions

1. Describe a difficult problem you tried to solve. How did you identify the problem? How did you go about trying to solve it? *Employers are evaluating your problem-solving skills.*

2. Give me an example of a time when you went above and beyond the call of duty. *Employers are evaluating your motivation.*

3. Have you ever had to sell your idea to your coworker or group? How did you do it? Was the coworker or group sold on the idea? *Employers are evaluating your communication skills and ability to influence others.*

4. Describe a time when you tried to persuade another person to do something that he or she was not very willing to do. *Employers are evaluating your leadership and persuasion skills.*

5. Describe a time when you decided on your own that something needed to be done and you took on the task to get it done. *Employers are evaluating your initiative and self-monitoring skills.*

A simple way to prepare for a behavioral-based interview is to use what is commonly referred to as the three-step STAR process, explained next.

STAR Process   Using the STAR (situation or task, action, result) process helps you focus your responses to your interview questions on providing the following types of information (Figure 12.1):

Situation or task: Identify and explain a particular situation or task you have had previous experience with that best demonstrates how you might respond or perform in a similar situation.

Action: Identify and explain the specific action you took in response to the situation or task.

Result or outcome: Identify and explain the business result or outcome of your action.

> "Past behavior may be the best predictor of future behavior. The behavioral style job interview is based on that premise."
>
> Chris Carlson, Associate, Booz Allen Hamilton
>
> Source: Retrieved December 1, 2013 from www.boozallen.com/ careers/48784306/42325716

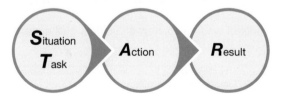

FIGURE 12.1
The STAR Process

TARGETED QUESTIONS: 21ST CENTURY SKILLS AND PERSONAL ETHICS

In Chapter 2 you learned about the importance of developing key skills employers have identified as important to succeeding in today's workplace. Some interviewers may choose to ask questions targeted to those skills. The following are some examples of the types of questions that employers might ask to probe how prepared you are in 21st century skills.[2]

[2]Society for Human Resource Management. Sample Interview Questions. Retrieved August 24, 2009, from www.shrm.org/TemplatesTools/Samples/InterviewQuestions/Pages/default.aspx.

NOTES   Interview Questions for 21st Century Skills

SAMPLE QUESTIONS

Communication Skills

- When do you think it is best to communicate in writing?
- When do you handle communication face to face?
- Describe a time you used your communication skills to negotiate with an angry person.
- What do you do when you think someone is not listening to you?

Creative Thinking

- What's the best book you read last year? Tell me what you liked about it.
- What was the most creative thing you did in your last job?
- Describe an ideal work environment or "the perfect job."

Diversity

- What kinds of experiences have you had working with others with different backgrounds than your own?
- Tell me about a time you had to alter your work or personal style to meet a diversity need or challenge.
- How have you handled a situation when a colleague was not accepting of others' diversity?

Interpersonal Skills

- How would your coworkers describe your work style or work habits?
- What do you do when others resist your ideas or actions?
- Describe a diffcult time you had dealing with an employee, customer, or coworker. Why was it diffcult? How did you handle it? What was the outcome?

Teamwork

- Tell me about a time you pitched in to help finish a project even though it "wasn't your job." What was the result?
- Tell me what role you play within work groups and why.
- Have you ever been in a situation where you had to lead a group of peers? How did you handle it?
- Tell me about any problems you had and how you handled them.

Time Management

- Describe a time you identified a barrier to your (and others') productivity and what you did about it.
- What do you do when someone else is late and preventing you from accomplishing your tasks?
- When you have a lot of work to do, how do you get it all done. Give me an example.

Source: Society for Human Resource Management. Sample Interview Questions. Retrieved August 24, 2009, from www.shrm.org/TemplatesTools/Samples/InterviewQuestions/Pages/default.aspx.

Personal Ethics Questions   Many employers are interested in knowing how you might react to ethical decisions you may face on the job. Your responses to these questions tell a lot about your own character and help an employer determine whether you are able to make decisions that are good for the company. Some of these questions do not always have clear-cut answers. You should be prepared to answer these types of questions.

The following questions are examples of interview questions that can be asked to probe your ability to make ethical decisions at work.

1. If you saw a coworker doing something dishonest, what would you do?

2. What would you do if someone in management asked you to do something unethical?

3. In what business situations do you feel honesty is inappropriate?

Discuss your thoughts about how to answer these questions in a group. You will probably learn that there are different ways to approach the answers. What's important is recognizing that employers are interested in knowing as much as they can about potential candidates' ability to make good ethical decisions that will uphold the image and reputation of the company.

Source: www.shrm.org/templatetools/samples/interviewquestions/pages/examplequestion.aspx

ILLEGAL QUESTIONS

In an interview, an employer cannot ask questions that are discriminatory. The focus of the interview questions should be on determining your ability to do the job. Illegal questions include inquiries about your race, color, sex, religion, national origin, birthplace, disability, or family/marital status. If you think you have been asked an illegal question, you have the option to respond or not respond. Deciding not to answer the question is certainly acceptable. The key is how you phrase the answer. You do not want to appear to be uncooperative, confrontational, or defensive. Your best choice is to answer the question only as it applies to the job for which you are applying.

NOTES | Handling Illegal Interview Questions

If you think you have been asked an illegal question, you have the option to respond in one of three ways:

- Answer the question.
- Decline answering the question.
- Answer the question only as it might apply to the job.

Here are some examples:

1. Are you a U.S. citizen, or what country are you from?

Answer: "I am authorized to work in the United States."

2. Who will take care of your children when you travel for your job?

Answer: "I am able to meet the travel and work schedule that this job requires."

3. How old are you?

Answer: "If I am hired, I am prepared to provide a copy of my birth certificate or other identification as needed to process my employment documents." Or, if applicable, "I am over the age of 18."

There are federal, state, and local laws that prohibit discrimination in employment to protect you from unfair or illegal hiring decisions by employers. There are many resources online that provide detailed information on how to avoid discrimination in the hiring process, while still providing an employer enough information about you to show you are qualified for the job. Most employers are well trained on how to conduct proper interviews. By being aware of and prepared to answer an illegal question, you will be in better control of this situation if it happens to you.

> "I am a big believer in visualization. I run through my races mentally so I can feel even more prepared."
>
> *Allyson Felix*, London Olympic athlete in women's running[3]

Progress Check Questions

1. What five interview questions do you think will present the greatest challenge for you and why?

2. What five interview questions do you think you will handle best and why?

PRACTICE INTERVIEWS

A practice interview can be conducted by an instructor, a member of your career network, or even an employer who is not the same as the employer you will interview with. Sometimes employers will help students with practice interviews during classroom presentations or at career fairs. Having your instructor demonstrate a practice interview with a member of your class can be very effective. If you have a portfolio, practice your portfolio presentation.

You can video a practice interview and observe what works well or needs improvement. Whether in person or by video, a practice interview is an excellent way to build confidence as you prepare for your actual job interview. A practice interview is also known as a mock interview.

ACTIVITY 12.4

Practice Interview

Ask someone to give you a practice interview: an instructor, a friend, a relative, or, of course, a member of your school's career services offce.

- Review the 20 questions typically asked by interviewers.
- Rehearse the answers mentally.
- Look over your resume.

Give the person who will interview you a list of questions most frequently asked on an interview. Let that person conduct the interview and evaluate you by using the following Practice Interview Evaluation form. Go through as many mock interviews as you think necessary to master the interviewing process.

Practice Interview Evaluation

Outstanding   Very Good   Good
Needs Improvement   Unsatisfactory

Communication skills _____

Appearance _____

Enthusiasm _____

Initial impression/clothing _____

Poise/confidence _____

Preparation _____

Comments and evaluation _____

Interviewed by _____

Date _____

---

[3]Retrieved August 1, 2013, from www.businessinsider.com/5-inspirational-career-quotes-for-your-career-from-2012-2012-12.

12.3 PREPARING FOR A JOB INTERVIEW

Now that you understand the different types of interviews and the questions you might be asked, it's time to prepare for your own interviews. To put your best foot forward, review your checklist, know the logistics, and ensure a winning attitude.

INTERVIEW CHECKLIST

✓ Review the company research.

✓ Research your interviewer on LinkedIn.

✓ Target and update your resume.

✓ Target and update your Career Portfolio.

✓ Update your social media profiles and/or personal website.

✓ Look the part.

What to Bring   Separate items in your Career Portfolio into two groups: your job search documents and your work samples.

For You

- Printout of the job posting.
- Sample completed job application for reference.
- One print copy of your resume.
- List of your questions.
- Notepad with two black pens or iPad.

For Your Interviewer

- Two print copies of your resume.
- Career Portfolio work samples.

You also will want to have on hand change for the parking meter or cash for the parking garage, and any last-minute grooming items. By the way, you may want to skip drinking your favorite coffee in the car while driving to your interview. The last thing you need to do is soil your clothing just before getting to the interview.

> To put your best foot forward, review your checklist, know the logistics, and ensure a winning attitude.

"One important key to success is self-confidence. An important key to self-confidence is preparation."

Arthur Ashe, professional tennis player[4]

LOGISTICS

Before leaving for your interview, make sure you know the answers to these questions:

- Do you know how to get to the right company location?
- Do you know how long it will take you to get there?
- Do you know where to park?
- Do you know what office to go to?
- Do you know the name and title of the person you will be interviewing with?
- Do you have the phone number of the company so that you can call if you are going to be late if you run into traffic?
- Do you know if you will be interviewing with more than one person?

[4]Retrieved May 13, 2013, from www.brainyquote.com/quotes/quotes/a/arthurashe109755.html.

Download driving directions, or program the address into your smartphone or GPS. Know potential routes and distance time. Take a dry run, not on the weekend, but during the same time that your interview is scheduled to check out the traffic pattern and check for detours or construction. You can check Google maps to see the building you are going to. You might think this is overkill, but having the logistics down will be very calming and put you in better control of the interview day! You have enough to think about; logistics should not be a distraction.

> *Practice answering difficult questions out loud several times. Your nervousness will eventually be neutralized, and you will project a calm demeanor addressing these topics on the interview.*

A WINNING ATTITUDE

Bring a winning attitude to the interview. Be confident and positive. Be conscious of what you are most anxious about, and develop your game plan for handling those issues confidently before and during the interview.

Confidence comes in many forms:

- *First, believe you are a successful person.* Part of convincing an employer you are right for the job is believing it yourself. Think of images that represent your greatest strengths, and visualize those images at the start of an interview.

- *Respect the unknown.* The unknown is part of most important experiences in life. Focus on what you can control, and don't let fear of the unknown derail you.

- *Listen to yourself.* Practice answering questions out loud, especially those you are most anxious about. Check your facial expression while you talk in a mirror. If you do this several times, your nervousness will eventually be neutralized, and you will be able to project a calm demeanor addressing those topics on the interview.

- *Focus on a role model.* Ask yourself what he or she would do to master the interview.

- *Don't apologize for shortcomings.* We all have them. Focus on portraying your whole package. Remember, in your career you will not be measured by one time at bat, but for a lifetime of achievement.

- *Be prepared.* Being well prepared for the interview tells the employer that you will likely handle important situations on the job with the same seriousness.

> *Bottom line—tell yourself you can do it!*

Maintain a positive attitude throughout the interview:

- Focus on a positive outcome.
- Anticipate making a favorable impression and not beating yourself up if something doesn't go the way you planned.

- Convey a positive attitude not just by what you say, but also through your body language.
- Communicate a "can do" attitude, an openness to new experiences, a willingness to learn, and genuine enthusiasm for the position and potentially joining the company.
- Come across as someone who is likable and can have a positive influence on others. Smile!

Confidence and a positive attitude can help overcome minor shortcomings and keep you in the running for the job offer. Positive self-talk and affirmations are powerful tools for building a winning attitude. Bottom line—tell yourself you can do it!

12.4 MANAGING THE FIVE STAGES OF AN INTERVIEW

To be successful at interviewing with prospective employers, it is important to know how to manage the five stages of an interview (Figure 12.2). The stages include the opening, questions and answers, observations, the closing, and the follow-up. Each stage is described in detail below.

THE OPENING

Before entering the room, turn off your cell phone. Walk in confidently. Give a firm handshake, make eye contact, and remember to smile!

The Icebreaker   The interviewer will start with some incidental conversation to break the ice. He or she might comment on the weather, a recent sports event, or big news of the day. The interviewer sets the tone. Will this be very formal or a more relaxed interview? A friendly tone is intended to help you relax, but be careful not to let your guard down. Always be professional throughout your interview. It helps to come across as approachable and likable if you can still maintain your professionalism. Proving your qualifications will come later in the interview. These early moments in the interview are when you make that important first impression.

Opening Questions   Questions such as "What do you know about our company?" or "Tell me why you chose (name of career) as your profession" signal the opening of the formal part of the interview.

"Sure it's a big job; but I don't know anyone who can do it better than I can."

John F. Kennedy, 35th president of the United States[5]

FIGURE 12.2

Five Stages of an Interview

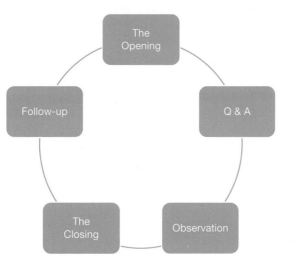

[5]Retrieved April 12, 2013, from www.brainyquote.com/quotes/quotes/j/johnfkenn135389.html.

QUESTIONS AND ANSWERS

Answering Questions   For the most part, you can expect to do well answering questions on an interview with preparation and practice. But how do you go a step beyond and be sure you leave a favorable lasting impression? Accentuate your best work, show how well you perform under pressure, and recover if you do stumble on a question.

> *Two ways to shine on your interview are to provide evidence of your best work and show how well you perform under pressure.*

Your game plan should be to not let the interviewer leave the room without remembering one or two key points about you that relate to the job you are applying for. Try not to leave the interview before making your important key points. The time might come in the course of answering a question asked by the interviewer or you may need to take the initiative.

Taking the initiative can be tricky because you don't want to appear to go off course, and you don't want to come across as arrogant or pushy. But you need to connect your key points to the general flow of the interview. So here's what to do.

- In advance, think about times when your performance stood out. Choose three or four major successes you would like to talk about. If you have only one or two, that's fine. They will probably be some of the accomplishments and results you listed on your resume.
- Don't just repeat what is on your resume, bring it to the next level in the interview. Give the employer more insight. Your resume said you did it, but not *how* you did it, the thought process involved, and what the major challenges were.
- Practice what you will say ahead of time about each one. If you can, during the interview find a way to include how these successes and related skills pertain to the job you are applying for.
- Take charge of this portion of your interview time. Don't be afraid to initiate interjecting your key points.

You can use your Career Portfolio to show examples of your best work or accomplishments.

- Incorporate portfolio examples into your answers. You can do this verbally to start.
- Tell or show the interviewer you have your portfolio with you (hard copy or online on your iPad).
- Have your strongest item ready to show as an example. It may draw in the interviewer to ask for more.
- Don't overwhelm the interviewer and start a complete presentation.
- Time constraints may not allow time for an interviewer to review your entire portfolio during the interview.
- You have put it out there. Wait for the interviewer to ask to see more.
- Refer to your digital portfolio link on your resume if it appears the interviewer does not want to view it then, or offer to send copies of selected work from your hard copy after the interview.

If you move on to a second interview, this may be a better use of time for discussing details of your sample work. You will likely be meeting with a department hiring manager who is more familiar with detailed position requirements. Your sample work could really add value at this stage of the interview.

Accentuate performance under pressure:

- Handle difficult questions confidently. How well you answer difficult questions during your interview is one example of how you perform well under pressure. One way to turn difficult questions into shining moments is to focus statements on what you have learned and what you will do moving forward. "I learned that . . . ," "In the future . . . ," "I can show you . . . ," "What will be different the next time. . . ."
- Major accomplishments are great, but it is just as important to show that you can meet the routine pressures of the job. Give simple examples of when and how you met important deadlines.
- Calmness in the interview is a sign of confidence.
- Incorporate examples of times you were able to overcome obstacles to achieve your goal and how you did it.

You know when you are going off course during your interview. You started at full attention, and now you are only half-listening. You stumbled on a question, and your mind is racing.

"I forgot to tell . . . " "Why did I say that?" "I made a mistake." "I forgot to ask . . . " "I didn't know what to say." "I just went blank." "Why am I so nervous?"

There is a strong comeback for every weak moment in an interview. Think on your feet, and don't let the interview run away from you. Look for the right time to say, "LET ME GO BACK TO . . . clarify, answer the question, add something I missed, ask a question."

There is a strong comeback for every weak moment during an interview. Think on your feet, and don't let the interview run away from you. Look for the right time to say, "Let me go back to . . . clarify, answer the question, add something I missed, ask a question." If you have trouble gauging the right time, you might have one last shot. Most interviewers will ask if you have any questions toward the end of the interview. If you can, taking the initiative to recoup before the interview reaches this point will impress. There is always time to briefly address any of these issues after the interview in a follow-up letter.

Asking Questions   Don't forget to make the interview a two-way conversation. Ask good questions. Use the following as a guide to what to find out during an interview.

- The exact job: title and responsibilities, as well as the department in which you would work.
- The fit of the department into the company structure: its purpose, budget, and other departments it works most with.
- Reporting structure: will you have more than one boss?
- Whether or not you would be working on your own or as a member of an official team.
- How skills learned on this job would prepare you for another position within the company.
- How your job performance is measured.
- Where the people who held this position previously are now.

Don't ask for infomation that you should have found on the company website. Do ask about something you read and did not understand.

Sample Questions to Ask on an Interview

1. How did this position become available?
2. What are the current challenges for someone in this position?

> "You want to have lots of questions to ask, so it's a two-way conversation and we can tell you're engaged."
>
> Mariana Bugallo-Muros, human resources director, Partners HealthCare System Inc.
>
> Source: Retrieved December 4, 2013 from www.boston.com/business/articles/2010/01/10/you_have_your_foot_in_the_door_how_to_keep_it_there_1263010162/?page=1

3. Is there a formal training program or is training informal? Please explain.

4. What type of technology is used in this job? Throughout the company?

5. What changes, if any, do you expect the next person to bring to this job?

6. What is the typical career path from this position?

7. How and when would I be evaluated?

8. Are there other graduates from my institution employed here? In what job(s)?

9. What is the employee retention at the company?

10. Who will make the final hiring decision?

Progress Check Questions

1. What two or three major successes can you focus on in your interview?

2. What are your own examples of how you have performed well under pressure?

CAREER PORTFOLIO 12.1

QUESTIONS TO ASK ON AN INTERVIEW

Review the list of possible general questions to ask on an interview. Make a list of five general questions you think you would ask on most interviews.

General Questions

1. _____
2. _____
3. _____
4. _____
5. _____

Targeted Questions

For each interview, once you have researched the company, jot down two questions that are targeted specifically to the what you read about the company.

1. _____
2. _____

Other Questions?

_____
_____

OBSERVATIONS

You can get a sense of how things are going before you leave the interview. Here are five telling observations you can make to size up your interview:

1. Were you asked to send more information about yourself after the interview?

2. Did either you or the interviewer dominate your time, or was there a balanced exchange?

3. Was there chemistry that made this feel like a right fit?

4. Did the interview go longer than expected?

5. Did the interviewer bring up next steps, or did you have to ask?

THE CLOSING

Closing Questions   The interviewer always takes the lead to close the interview. Two common questions signaling the close of the interview are, "If you were offered this position, when would you be able to start?" or "What questions would you like to ask me?"

Your closing questions should include asking what the company next steps are and what is expected of you next. Write down any specific dates or times mentioned. Be sure you have all the contact information about the person who interviewed you so that you can send a follow-up thank-you note.

Thank-You   The end of an interview can be a little awkward. Take a brief pause when you know the interview has ended. If you are nervous or disappointed about something, don't let it show. You want to leave the same calm and confident impression you displayed throughout the interview. Give that same firm handshake, make eye contact, and smile! The most important thing to do regardless of how it went is to say thank you for the time and information. Depending on how things went, you can state that you are very excited about the position and look forward to the next steps.

Regrouping   You did it! When it's over, take a breath. Stop somewhere for your favorite cup of coffee, and write some things down: additional infomation the interviewer needs, good points about your performance, things you learned, follow-up dates in your calendar, issues that arose, things you could have done better. Does this seem like a possible fit?

THE FOLLOW-UP

Once the interview is over, there are three simple steps to follow: send, read, and initiate.

1. *Send* a thank-you note, and complete and send any follow-up information requested during the interview (Figure 12.3). Send a thank-you note to the interviewer regardless of how the interview went. You may know you are moving on to a next step with the company, and that's great. But if you are unsure, or know it's not likely, you should definitely send a thank-you note.

    Show appreciation.   The "look see" process involved in an interview is definitely time-consuming. Both you and your interviewer expended a lot of energy getting to this point. No matter what the outcome, showing appreciation is common courtesy. Minimally, a thank-you note, should show your appreciation.

    Restate interest.   Unless you are no longer interested or know you haven't made it to the next cut, you should always restate your interest. You can benefit from details you learned in the interview to include comments targeted to the position and the company.

    Future contact.   If you have a follow-up date already, then reference or confirm it and state that you look forward to the next step. If you exactly know what's next, state that you are looking forward to the next steps and look forward to a future contact.

2. *Read* any information you were given during the interview.

3. *Initiate* further follow-up if the interviewer put the ball in your court. For example, you may be asked to contact the interviewer within a week, or to contact someone else in the company you were referred to. The interviewer may ask you to think about the interview and call to confirm your interest in the next steps. When the ball is in your court, run with it.

SHOW APPRECIATION

RESTATE INTEREST

FUTURE CONTACT

FIGURE 12.3
Thank-You Note

12.5 EVALUATING JOB OFFERS

The last step is evaluating a job offer for fit and the experience it can provide to help you reach your future goals.

KEY FACTORS

The key factors typically considered when evaluating a job offer are:

- Position
- Salary
- Location
- Work environment
- Company culture
- Growth

The type of position, salary, and location are the more practical things to deal with and the factors that we discuss in this chapter. Of course, if a job offer meets your expectations in all three areas, that's great. But the reality is that you will probably have to choose which of the three factors is most important to you.

NOTES | Practical Considerations

- Position
- Salary
- Location

Prioritizing these factors will help you make a decision you feel comfortable with.

Once you establish these priorities, you can factor in your feelings about the work environment, company culture, and growth potential. Activity 12.5 will help you think it through. Don't rule out the importance of your own "gut feeling" in making your decision. Your instincts might be right on!

ACTIVITY 12.5

Choosing the Right Job for You

1. Review the items in column 1, and in the blanks, add any other factors you might use in deciding about a job.
2. In column 2, check off the items that would influence your decision about a job offer.
3. Use column 3 to prioritize the factors you've checked off; give each a letter.

   a. I must have this (most important).

   b. I really want this (important).

   c. This would be nice to have (least important).

Column 1	Column 2	Column 3
Position		
Learn new skills		
Interesting work		
Responsibility		
Job importance to the company		

Column 1	Column 2	Column 3
Position		
Authority level	_____	_____
Challenging work	_____	_____
Career progression	_____	_____
Work hours	_____	_____
Working conditions	_____	_____
Relationships with customers	_____	_____
Salary		
Salary	_____	_____
Bonuses	_____	_____
Fringe benefits	_____	_____
Location		
Job location	_____	_____
Work Environment and Company Culture		
Formal or informal environment	_____	_____
Community involvement	_____	_____
Commitment to employees	_____	_____
Employee retention	_____	_____
Professional Growth		
Training	_____	_____
Educational reimbursement	_____	_____
Employee development	_____	_____
Other		
_____	_____	_____

Source: U.S. Department of Labor, Bureau of Labor Statistics. "Evaluating a Job Offer, 2009." Retrieved October 8, 2009, from www.bls.gov/oco/oco20046.htm.

BENEFITS

Benefits Checklist These examples of benefits will vary in importance to you depending on what stage you are at in your career, family considerations, and your current financial situation.

- Salary
- Health benefits
- Life insurance
- Education and training
- Seminars or conferences
- Housing, meals, and transportation
- Travel
- Financial counseling
- Time off
- Family care

Real Life Stories

Randy's Job Offers

Randy had two job offers. Both were in his career field with positions that were challenging and provided opportunities for career advancement over time. Altman Engineering, in his hometown, offered a competitive starting salary. The job at Scranton Planning and Design required him to relocate. The job offered a lower starting salary, but had better group health insurance. During interviews, Randy observed that each company had very different working environments. At Altman, his work would primarily be conducted from the office, and he would work under the direct supervision of a senior design engineer. Working in a closely supervised situation could provide some structure and a mentoring opportunity for Randy. If he took the job with Scranton Planning and Design, the company would pay his relocation expenses.

While he was not sure he was ready to move, he was attracted to the working environment at Scranton. After an initial orientation period prescribed by the company, much of his work would be done in teams. Part of his time would be spent in the field working on project plans with clients. Randy was leaning toward accepting the job with Scranton, but he was concerned about whether he could afford to move and work at a salary lower than what Altman offered.

Randy made a list of the pros and cons of each job offer. He researched the cost of living differences associated with each location. At Altman, he would need to contribute a significant portion of his salary to his employee contribution to the health care plan. At Scranton, the group health coverage was more comprehensive and paid by the company. Many of his friends suggested that health care coverage would be a more important factor in his job decisions as Randy grew older. In the process of computing his first-year budget, Randy realized that with the high cost of health care, even a small, unexpected medical emergency could be the one expense that he simply could not afford. Randy accepted the job with Scranton.

He was excited about the position, attracted to the work environment, and determined that the combined compensation and benefits were better. At first glance, the opportunity to stay and work in his hometown seemed like the obvious choice, but when Randy took the time to weigh many factors into his decision, the job with Scranton Planning and Design was right for him.

Seldom is a job offer perfect.

Salary   We all like to be paid what we think we are worth. But having accurate information about salaries beforehand should inform any communication you have about it with a prospective employer. The economy, education, experience, skill sets, geographic location, company size, and industry are all factors. The same salary does not always have the same worth in different parts of the country. You may be willing to relocate and decide to take a job because it pays more than another, but the American Chamber of Commerce Researchers Association (now known as ACCRA) recommends: Don't jump at a high salary unless you know what it is really worth!

Here are some dos and don'ts for negotiating a salary offer.

Salary Dos

DO: Research average salaries for your degree level, industry, and geographic area.

DO: Use your research to set realistic salary expectations based on degree level, industry, and geographic area.

DO: Know what you need to earn.

DO: Try to find out if the company has standardized salary ranges by job title.

DO: Set salary goals, but keep your career interests and goals first in mind. Stay committed to finding the job and company that best matches your career interests and abilities and consider the salary in this context.

DO: Try to hold off on salary discussion until you receive a job offer.

DO: Answer the question.

DO: Follow the interviewers lead and let him or her bring up the salary topic first.

DO: Act confident about the value you bring to the company.

DO: Be reasonable when discussing salary and stay professional at all times.

DO: Ask when and what the formal salary review process is at the company.

DO: Keep your career goal foremost in your overall discussion.

Salary Don'ts

DON'T: Use national averages if you can get good information at a regional or local level.

DON'T: Ask for a salary that is unrealistic and appear uninformed about your career field. Don't expect salaries between small and large companies with similar positions and titles to be the same. The scope of responsibility may be very different even though job titles are similar.

DON'T: Discuss your financial problems or situations with your interviewer.

DON'T: Expect the salary offer to be beyond standard ranges set by the company.

DON'T: Use salary alone to determine the right career decision.

DON'T: Consider any salary discussions final until you receive a specific offer.

DON'T: Say you are not prepared to discuss the question.

DON'T: Bring up salary until your interviewer does.

DON'T: Apologize for lack of experience and say that you will accept any salary.

DON'T: Show anger or disappointment that the salary does not meet you expectations.

DON'T: Ask the average percentage of increases typically given because this can vary.

DON'T: Give up a better career opportunity for a small difference in salary, if you can afford it.

"Many of us tend to focus on the salary, when in reality there are multiple—very important—components to the package."

Stacey Hawley, The Creedo Company

Source: Retrieved December 1, 2013 from www.businessinsider. com/a-step-by-step-guide-to-ruling-your-salary-negociation-2012-5

ACTIVITY 12.6

Practice Salary Negotiation

The following is a list of questions you might be asked about your salary expectations. Discuss the options for answers to salary-related questions your interviewer may ask, and discuss which answers that you think are most appropriate. Discuss whether answering the question with a question might be appropriate.

1. What salary range are you looking for?

   • My research has shown that the mid-30s is the average compensation for someone with my degree in this geographic location.

   • I am open.

   • I know that the mid-30s is the average, but I feel my work experience qualifies me for a higher salary.

- I am more interested in the position itself than the salary.
- What is the current salary range offered by the company for someone with my qualifications?

2. How do benefits play into your salary considerations?
   - Certain benefits are more important to me than the salary.
   - Tuition reimbursement to support my educational investment is my biggest priority right now.
   - I am more interested in the position than the benefits.
   - I need to consider the whole compensation package, that is, salary and benefits combined.
   - Are there opportunities to opt out of benefits that I don't need right now and keep those dollars as part of my salary?

3. Would you be willing to relocate for a position that pays more in another city at this time?
   - I would love to take advantage of that opportunity, but family and personal commitments will keep me in this area for another two years.
   - Yes, I am free and willing to relocate anywhere to have an opportunity to earn the salary I want.
   - It depends on how the larger salary compares to the different cost of living in that location.
   - I am more interested in the position than the salary.
   - If I take the job here, how long will it take and what is expected of me to reach that salary level?

4. Do you have an idea about how your salary might progress over your first few years on the job?
   - I expect to start at the entry level and then earn salary increases based on my job performance.
   - I would think that I would receive the average 4 percent increase each year that most companies are giving.
   - Not much, based on the starting salary you are offering.
   - I think my answer depends on whether or not your company has standardized salary ranges for different levels of jobs.
   - Can you tell me about career progression at your particular company and how that impacts compensation?

5. When you had your last salary review, do you know how your salary adjustment was determined?
   - I have had only temporary and part-time jobs so far as a student.
   - I have no idea; I was just happy to get a raise.
   - We don't have salary review meetings; we are just told what our raise is each year.
   - It was based on my performance review for the year. I received the company standard increase for the year and a 5 percent merit bonus for exceeding my goals.

Location   As the cost of living varies across the country, you should know how to compare a salary offer for a job in one state with a salary offer for a job in a different state. There are a number of websites that provide you the ability to do your own state-by-state salary comparisons. Use your favorite online search engine to search the phrase "salary calculator" and you will find several helpful results. The Salary Wizard on Salary.com is a commonly used tool.

YOUR DECISION

Accepting the right job for the right reasons is critical to your career success and your personal happiness. Your lifestyle considerations have a big impact on your decision. For example, normal working hours and vacation time may be important to you if you want to maintain a good work–life balance.

If you have family responsibilities, child care or elder care benefits may be important to you. With the rising costs of health benefits, you may choose a job with good health benefits over one with a larger salary. Early on in your career, frequent business travel may appeal to you, whereas you may prefer less business travel at later stages in your life and your career. Reassess your personal and professional needs each time you consider a new job offer. As your life's circumstances change over time, your priorities change.

Beyond lifestyle considerations, professional growth should play a major role in your decision. Evaluate the learning opportunities with a new position. Continuing to learn with each job you take will keep your career moving in a positive direction.

Communicating Your Decision   Once you have made your decision as to which job you will accept, respond immediately. Call the person who extended you the job offer. Tell the person you are pleased to accept the position, and ask what day and time you are to begin. If you are not sure of the location, ask for directions. Follow up by sending a letter accepting a job offer. Show your appreciation and enthusiasm (see Chapter 11).

If you are declining a job offer, call the person who extended you the offer and thank him or her for the opportunity. Remember that it is important to maintain a good relationship with all employers. There may be a time, later in your career, when you will reapply to one of the companies and you will want to have left a favorable impression. Follow up your phone call with a letter declining the job offer (see Chapter 11).

- -

The type of interviews you have may vary from industry to industry and company to company. By being aware of some different types of interviews and practicing answers to important interview questions, you will be prepared for a success in most interview situations. Beyond answering questions in an interview, you can take the lead to highlight your best work and ability to perform well under pressure, two key ways to distinguish yourself. The questions you ask on an interview give the interviewer insight into how much you know about the company, and what is important to you in evaluating a job offer.

Finally, always weigh the practical issues when deciding on a job offer in context to your career goals. Stay committed to your goal, and use your best judgment on a path to achieve what is right for you.

CHAPTER SUMMARY

SUCCESSFUL INTERVIEWS AND CAREER DECISION MAKING

Based on what you learned about interviewing in this chapter, answer the following questions:

1. What am I trying to decide? _____

_____

2. What do I need to know? _____

_____

3. How will it help me make a more informed decision? _____

_____

4. How can I obtain what I need to know? _____

_____

     People _____

     Experience _____

     Research _____

5. Who are my resources for the information I need? _____

_____

part **three**

Career Management

"Strivers achieve what dreamers believe."

Usher, recording artist and actor[1]

[1]Retrieved April 5, 2013, from www.brainyquote.com/quotes/authors/u/usher.html.

Growing Your Career

After completing this chapter, you will:

1   **Identify** the importance of transferable skills to career growth

2   **Understand** the impact of performance on career growth

3   **Recognize** the importance of positive relationships

4   **Learn** to manage change affecting your career

5   **Learn** to make successful career moves

In an ideal world, we have a job we love that puts us on a path to our career of choice and the path remains free of major obstacles. We grow our career by a planned set of experiences as long as we perform well and opportunities continue to thrive. But as we all know, there are no guarantees that the economy will thrive or that our work environment will remain constant and predictable. We are all too familiar with the saying that the only constant thing in life is change. Sometimes we grow the most when faced with unexpected challenges. This certainly applies to growing your career. Whether or not you are in the job you want, you can make your situation work in your favor. Getting off to the right start when beginning a different job at a new or current company can set you in the right direction. This includes making a good impression with solid performance and building positive professional relationships. Managing change can help you adapt to changes in your current work situation. When the appropriate step is to move on, knowing how to make successful career moves can help you seize the opportunity to grow your career in a new direction. Building the skills needed to succeed in difficult or changing situations can make your career resilient to most challenging times.

CASE STUDY

Amanda and Justin: Standout Performance

Amanda was hired by a large, multinational food service company based in the United States. She had just received her degree in food service management and thought she would be assigned to one of the company's food service operations. Amanda made a positive impression on her first day in the training program. She was punctual, dressed professionally, and was very attentive to the program. She participated in sessions and interacted well with other trainees. At the social functions she networked well with managers and operators. By the end of the program, she decided that she might like to work in college relations instead of a food service operation. She saw herself doing everything from company presentations at college campuses, training new hires, and presenting recruitment plans and results at staff and management meetings. When she had her six-month progress review, she told her supervisor what she was thinking. She agreed that Amanda had the interpersonal skills to do the job and told her that she needed to rotate through several different functions where she could also demonstrate her time management, planning, and organizational skills. In these rotations Amanda would interface with customers, operations managers at the units, potential hires, and coworkers in the college relations department. Amanda proved herself through this opportunity and continued to be offered different responsibilities based on her reputation and results.

Within six years, Amanda was director of college relations for one of the units. Her plan was to be promoted in a few years to assistant director of corporate college relations responsible for recruiting for all U.S. operations and then on to a director's and vice president's job. She was well on her way.

Justin joined a small, new Voice over Internet Protocol company. There was no formal training or mentoring program at the company. Training and assimilation to the company took place through informal training and mentoring. Justin was assigned a peer to shadow and spend time with. He learned about the company's culture and policies and about the different types of assignments that could be available to him if he did a good job and created a positive impression at work. By shadowing his coworker, he became familiar with different jobs. Eventually he started to fill in for his coworker and gained experience in different areas. In the process, Justin built relationships with employees at all levels of the company. He found that in this less structured environment he needed to focus on practicing his time management, planning, and organizational skills. His career path was less structured than Amanda's, but Justin enjoyed a series of successful career moves at the company, including two promotions.

Discussion Questions

1. What are some things you can do in a new job to make a positive first impression?
2. Can you think of a time when someone provided you informal training or mentoring?
3. Can you name the transferable skills that Amanda and Justin demonstrated on the job that contributed to their career advancement? Are these skills they could bring to another job if a recession caused them to lose their jobs?

Building a career that can still thrive during challenges times takes focus and a plan. Your career is less likely to be affected by change if you focus on three areas that matter most: transferable skills, standout performance, and positive relationships. This chapter discusses the three areas in detail.

> **CAREER RESILIENCE:** *the ability to thrive in difficult and changing situations, and to achieve career development and satisfaction despite the challenges at hand.*

13.1 TRANSFERABLE SKILLS

Transferable skills are the foundation to growing your career. Transferable skills are those that are acquired in one set of circumstances that can also be applied to a new set of circumstances. Examples of some transferable skills include organizational, budgeting, or interpersonal skills. Being able to show that you have talents to bring to a new situation and that you are willing to do so can help you keep your current job or be hired by a new employer.

Why are transferable skills important? With transferable skills you can:

- Apply previous experience to new situations showing you are adaptable and learn from experience.
- Create multiple career options. Transferable skills are critical in most career fields and jobs.
- Make career shifts along with shifts in the economy. Transferable skills can qualify you for new and emerging jobs and can protect you from job loss. When companies are reducing their workforce, you can be among the last to be affected, if you are affected at all because of your versatility.
- Strengthen your performance in your current position, making you more promotable.
- Indicate potential to grow and ability to change. You may even be identified as a key team member to help move change along at your company.

Assessing your transferable skills from time to time is important to your career growth. While you can update your list of skills you have developed, you can also identify an action plan for those you need to work on.

ACTIVITY 13.1

Assess Your Transferable Skills

Below is a partial listing of transferable skills that employers value. The more transferable skills you develop, the easier it will be to move to another job and perhaps even change careers during downturns in the economy.

People Management	Sales and Marketing	Operation Management
Supervising	Negotiating	Planning
Teaching	Selling	Organizing
Training		Budgeting

Communication	Leadership	Technical
Public speaking	Coaching	Computer literacy
Writing	Direction setting	Programming
Foreign language	Inspiring	

After reviewing the preceding partial listing of transferable skills, list the ones you currently have:

_____

_____

_____

Now review the list again, and list the transferable skills you would like to acquire:

_____

_____

_____

_____

Write out a plan to develop each of the transferable skills you want to acquire.

Skill	Plan
Example: Public speaking	I will volunteer to present our team capstone project and work on my specific areas of concern: organizing materials, engaging the audience, and handling questions and answers.
	_____
_____	_____
	_____

_____

NOTES | Factors That Enable You to Recession-Proof Your Career

- Broad responsibilities
- Many skills
- Flexibility

- Ability to deal with risk or uncertainty
- Transferable skills
- Positive attitude

"Prospective employees need to be able to set priorities and deadlines."

Janet McDougall, President of McDougall Scientific, Ltd.

Source: Retrieved December 4, 2013 from www.collegefortn.org/Home/Article.aspx?articleId=13yRY3FwQ8SOXAP2BPAXgitsBkbvAXAP3DPAXXAP3DPAX&level=3XAP2FPAX6J7I3kztATGuYyXAP2BPAXDahlQXAP3DPAXXAP3DPAXR

PLANNING SKILLS

Planning is the process of organizing work and related activities to achieve a desired goal. The most basic planning skills include prioritizing and scheduling work or activities to meet deadlines and monitoring progress toward results. Demonstrating the ability to plan your work and achieve results enhances your individual performance. You may also become involved with your company's strategic and annual planning processes. A strategic plan outlines the mission and future direction of the company. Annual plans outline how to get there, and include goals with specific action steps and deadline dates. Annual plans are monitored periodically to ensure progress and accountability of individuals responsible for the results. You or your department may be responsible for accomplishing part of an annual plan. Being clear on your individual or team's role and what results you will be evaluated on is important. Good planning skills are essential transferable skills providing focus and direction that can keep you and your company resilient during challenging times.

TIME MANAGEMENT AND ORGANIZATIONAL SKILLS

Time management and organizational skills go hand in hand with planning skills. Improving your ability to manage your time and organize your work will help you become more productive and effective. It can also help you be recognized as someone who may be able to assume more job responsibilities.

Assess your workload and schedule on a weekly, then daily, basis. Be sure to identify the most important things you must get done during the workweek. Then look at your schedule for any meetings or appointments that might take away from your time to work on important projects.

Reserve at least two days during the week to devote large chunks of time for individual work. Try to set aside 30 minutes a day to organize and complete some of your work. Keep your projects and important information organized in easy to get to files. Keep a daily calendar and to-do list, and check off tasks as you complete them. Be flexible enough to work through lunch, stay late, or follow up with work at home, if needed. Know when to say no!

There are great payoffs for being organized and managing your time well. Personally, you will reduce your stress and receive greater satisfaction from your work. Professionally, you will develop the image of a professional who is serious about getting things done and moving on to the next challenge.

13.2 STANDOUT PERFORMANCE

Many employers believe that past performance is an indicator of future success. There is no question that good performance will help you move forward in your career. This usually happens when good performance is consistent over time and not a one-time event. Good performance is generally expected if you want to maintain your position, but does not necessarily distinguish you from others. Standout performance is performance that exceeds, or stands out from, the performance of other workers and often is an indicator of your greater potential. Standout performance can help your career thrive if you are able to apply your skills to new situations. Following are examples of opportunities to demonstrate standout performance at work.

CAREER CRITICAL MOMENTS

There are critical times when your performance can stand out and leave a lasting impression about you. This can happen during routine situations at work or major milestone events such as a promotion. Recognizing those career critical moments when your performance counts most, and acting on them, is a skill most successful people develop over time. Those moments may come during your first few weeks on the job, during a presentation or meeting, or in your performance review.

During these critical moments your career can undergo a definite change that is either positive or negative (Figure 13.1).

First Day   Use the time between acceptance of the job offer and the first day of employment to maintain contact with the company. Be sure you have taken care of as many final arrangements as you can before your first day. For example, ask if any forms can be completed. Most often the company will provide you with literature that describes the company's benefits or otherwise welcomes you to the company. Read all this material carefully, and ask any questions you may have so there will be fewer questions on your first day. Know where and to whom to report on your first day. First impressions are extremely important because they leave a lasting impression on those you interact with for the first time (Figure 13.2).

> "Employees that routinely rise to new challenges and demonstrate a high degree of self-motivation, tend to get recognized when the opportunity for advancement is presented."
>
> Sara Nichols, Vice President of Finance, Kforce
>
> Source: Retrieved December 4, 2013 from www.kforce.com/Career-Resources/10-Ways-to-Meet-and-Exceed-Your-Boss-Expectations.aspx

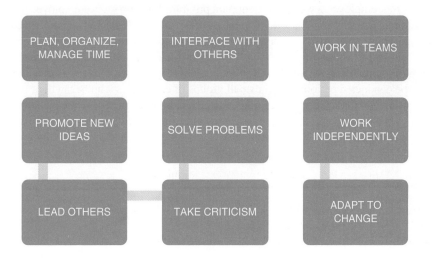

FIGURE 13.1
Standout Performance

FIGURE 13.2

Career Critical Moments

You can relieve the anxiety usually associated with your first day on the job by following some basic guidelines. Arrive a little early so that you are sure you are reporting to the right place. You may still have some paperwork to fill out before you start work, and an early arrival can give you more time to do this properly. Someone in the company will probably be responsible for guiding you through the day. While you should focus more on listening the first day, don't be afraid to ask any questions you may have.

Part of your day will probably be spent touring the area you are working in and meeting people in the organization. Focus on remembering the names of the people you will be working with most often. You may also be shown your work area and where and how to access the resources and supplies you need to get your job done. Someone may offer to take you to lunch as part of your welcome. If so, be sure to stick to your scheduled lunchtime. You will probably get a feeling for the company and the people who work there by the end of the first day. If something left you feeling unsure or uncomfortable, don't panic. This is normal. There is so much to get used to in a new job that you won't feel totally adjusted after your first day. While you should feel excited about all that lies ahead, be sure to keep your goals and expectations realistic and stay focused on learning.

Orientation and Training Programs Your orientation may last anywhere from a couple of days to a few weeks, depending on the company. Some examples of information communicated during an orientation include on-the-job safety and security information and an overview of the company and employee development programs and review of company policies. Be sure to understand the company's policy on the use of e-mails, mobile phones, and social media in the workplace. Your orientation period is focused mostly on getting you acquainted with your new environment and how it works. This differs from actual training programs, which may be longer (30–90 days) and are aimed at giving you the tools to perform your job better.

For your employer, a well-run orientation program can help reduce employee turnover. For example, Corning is a company that has successfully implemented an employee orientation program. Corning's primary objectives were to reduce early career turnover by 17 percent and to shorten by one month the time it takes a new person to learn the job.[2] Training programs may be administered individually for new employees as they are hired or may be conducted periodically for small groups of employees who began their new jobs at approximately the same time. Training may be hands on to teach or refine technical skills (drafting, machine operations), or classroom style to reinforce interpersonal skills (teamwork, customer service). The following box is a sample of a basic retail training program.

[2]Office of State Personnel. (2009). "From I Do to Happily Ever After: The Business Case for Onboarding." Retrieved September 1, 2009, from www.performancesolutions.nc.gov/staffinginitiatives/selection/Onboarding/fromido.aspx.

NOTES   Sample Training Program

Designed to help our management trainees achieve company objectives and identify individual store needs, our eight-month, three-phase training comprises the following:

- Phase I, II, and III participants manual
- Product knowledge manuals
- Supplemental videos
- Management resource books
- Support materials (tests and evaluations)
- Graduation certificate

PHASE I

This 30- to 60-day intensive program trains participants in the fundamentals of salesmanship, customer service, in-depth product knowledge, and basic store operating procedures. Trainees will learn skills ranging from the proper methods of greeting customers, determine customer needs, and overcoming objections, to the correct techniques for fitting footwear.

PHASE II

Reinforcing the basics begun in phase I, this 90-day period gives the trainee hands-on experience in various aspects of retail store operations. During this phase most trainees will attain the position of assistant store manager and will take an active role in sales floor management. Skills covered include recruiting and hiring techniques, coaching for improved sales productivity, visual merchandising, training techniques, and advanced store operating procedures, including loss prevention, bookkeeping, and accounting.

PHASE III

Under the guidance of our most experienced store leader, the manager-trainer, trainees receive 90 to 120 days of hands-on experience in managing a total retail store operation. The skills taught during this phase are deesigned to fine-tune the MIT (manager-in-training) in the areas of communication, customer relations, delegation skills, recruiting and training, leadership, marketing, merchandising, and maximising profits.

This program is divided into weekly lessons, each with clearly defined goals, discussion questions, and practice assignments. The objective of each lesson is reached through daily interaction on the sales floor and through one-on-one training with the sore manager. The lessons are outlined in the *Management Training Development Manual.*

Upon successful completion of this program, trainees can expect to attain a store management position in the near future.

Progress Check Questions

1. What do you think are the most important adjustments to make within a new company in the first 30 days? Why?

2. Are training programs only needed at large companies?

Presentations   Good presentation skills help you convince others of your ideas or communicate factual information clearly and concisely. Many people feel nervous at the thought of making a presentation even to a small group. You can reduce your anxiety about making a presentation and increase your effectiveness by following these guidelines: Decide on the main point you wish to convey and develop convincing information (articles, statistics,

etc.) to use to illustrate your point. This will help you address any questions. Prepare a brief outline on index cards. Do your homework. Spending enough time preparing your presentation will help you be more confident about what you say. Look confident. Dress professionally, look alert and well groomed, and show enthusiasm for what you say.

Meetings   How you interact at company meetings reflects an image of you to others. Among the actions you can take to help create a positive image are the following:

- Arrive on time. It is wise to arrive 10 to 15 minutes before the start of any meeting. This will give you time to become oriented to the room and the meeting agenda and to avoid having to sit at the perimeter of the room because all the best seats are taken.

- Introduce yourself to participants you may not know prior to the beginning of the meeting. Also, introduce yourself when you speak at the meeting if there are some attendees who may not know you.

- If the meeting is delayed, turn to someone and begin an informal conversation. You should be relaxed and prepared enough not to have to worry about any last-minute details by this time. This may give you an opportunity to communicate with someone you don't see on a regular basis.

- Arrive prepared. Don't count on being able to make last-minute copies or notes within 10 or 15 minutes before the meeting. Be prepared when you leave your own office.

- Rehearse your remarks well if you are to make a presentation. Bring a one-page list of key points you want to make at the meeting so you will be sure not to leave any out.

- Watch your body language. Look interested, alert, and ready to participate.

- Pay attention, even when topics don't relate directly to you; don't shift to converse with others when the topic shifts. You should always listen to everyone who is speaking. Not only is this professional courtesy, but you may learn something important. Avoid interrupting. If you have questions or comments when someone else is speaking, try to wait until he or she has finished making the main point.

- Don't monopolize the time. Be concise and to the point with your remarks. You will be more effective this way and will allow others the opportunity to speak.

- Ask for clarification if you don't understand something. Don't be afraid of appearing stupid. If you don't ask for clarification, you may base an important decision on the wrong facts.

- Be positive and tactful when disagreeing. Even though it is right for you to express your disagreement with someone, make sure you make it clear that you are attacking the issue, not the person.

- Use *we* instead of *I* when talking to a group; *we* signifies being part of the group.

- Think before you speak. It is more important to focus on the quality of what you say at meetings than on the frequency of times you speak.

- Be clear on follow-up assignments to be completed after the meeting.

- After the meeting, congratulate anyone who performed exceptionally well in his or her presentation.

Self-Monitored Work   Self-monitoring is a skill more employers look for in some employees. The need for self-monitored or independent work has risen with the growth of remote and virtual workplaces and telecommuting. However, most independent work assignments still occur on site. When assigning independent work to individuals or groups, employers need to know that the work will be completed on time and produce the desired results. Individuals or teams demonstrating the ability to monitor, define, prioritize, and complete tasks without direct oversight are usually the best choice for independent work assignments. These individuals are usually self-motivated and tend to show increased job involvement.

> **SELF-MONITORING:** *the ability to monitor, define, prioritize, and complete tasks without direct oversight.*

Performance Reviews   During your first three to six months on the job, it would be helpful to you for your employer to conduct periodic reviews and assessments of your job performance. This will help you know whether or not you are on the right track and give both you and the employer a chance to discuss your strengths and weaknesses so that you can set immediate goals for improvement. Periodic reviews and assessments can help you adjust to your job during the first few months by setting and keeping you on a successful course. If these are not formally planned by your employer, you might want to ask your immediate supervisor for feedback that might be helpful to you. When you do have a performance review scheduled, taking time to think ahead of time about key points that might be discussed can help prepare you.

> "I've learned that mistakes can often be as good a teacher as success."
>
> *Jack Welch,*
> former CEO of General Electric[3]

ACTIVITY 13.2

Appraise Your Own Performance

Using this sample performance appraisal as your guide to how you may be evaluated at your next job, rate your own work performance for the most recent position you held. In parts I and II, check all items relevant to your position. Using the following scale, rate each item on a scale of 1 to 5, and circle the number at the right.

Scale

1 Needs much improvement

2 Needs some improvement

3 Satisfactory

4 Very good

5 Excellent

PART I: GENERAL WORK HABITS AND ATTITUDES

A. Practices good attendance	1	2	3	4	5
B. Is punctual	1	2	3	4	5
C. Has a professional appearance	1	2	3	4	5

[3]Retrieved July 23, 2013, from www.brainyquote.com/quotes/quotes/j/jackwelch173306.html.

D. Meets deadlines	1	2	3	4	5
E. Cooperates with others	1	2	3	4	5
F. Accepts suggestions and criticism	1	2	3	4	5
G. Manages work schedule	1	2	3	4	5
H. Uses equipment properly	1	2	3	4	5

Comments: _____

_____

_____

PART II: JOB PERFORMANCE

A. Quality of work	1	2	3	4	5
B. Ability to solve problems	1	2	3	4	5
C. Original ideas	1	2	3	4	5
D. Communication skills	1	2	3	4	5
E. Time management skills	1	2	3	4	5
F. Technical/professional knowledge	1	2	3	4	5
G. Interpersonal skills	1	2	3	4	5
H. Aaptation to new duties	1	2	3	4	5
I. Ability to apply job knowledge	1	2	3	4	5

Comments: _____

_____

What are your greatest strengths and weaknesses?

_____

_____

What suggestions do you have to improve weaknesses?

_____

_____

What further training do you need?

_____

_____

What contribution have you made to the company, department, or division beyond normal requirements of your position?

_____

_____

What is your overall evaluation of your performance this past year?

_____

"A performance review is your time to highlight your accomplishments, hear what your boss thinks about your performance and to listen for the subtle clues."

Susan Davis-Ali, USA TODAY College

Source: Retrieved December 5, 2013 from www.usatoday.com/story/money/2013/11/14/make-your-next-performance-review-your-best/3525155/

Promotions   As you progress in your job, you may demonstrate the ability and desire to take on other responsibilities in the company. This is a great way to build your career, because assuming new roles makes you more versatile and more valuable to your company. These growth opportunities can involve a new job or more responsibilities than you have in your current job.

Job Enlargement versus Job Enrichment You may be asked to perform more tasks at the same level of difficulty; this is job enlargement. Or you may be asked to assume more responsibility (for example, supervising other people); this is job enrichment. Either of these two instances could be described as a promotion.

It is important to distinguish between these two different types of promotion because at some point, you need to decide which type of growth opportunity is best for you. If you enjoy the hands-on work you do and would be challenged by doing more of it, you may choose this as a way to grow professionally. Sometimes people who prefer to continue in their same job but expand on it a little more don't see these additional responsibilities as a promotion. A promotion does not always have to involve supervising others or moving up to the next-higher job title and level of responsibility. For some people this works very well, while others do better growing in the existing job. What is most important about either of these forms of promotion is that you feel properly challenged in a job that suits your skills and personality. You and your employer are the best judges of which route suits you best.

Real Life Stories

Karen Katz, Neiman Marcus

Karen Katz realized her career goal when she became the president and chief executive of Neiman Marcus Stores, based in Dallas, Texas. Her career path has been marked by a series of successful promotions that led her to her dream job with one of the most prestigious retail companies in the world.

Karen worked in retail positions during college. Her career goal was to be a lawyer, but her work in retail caused her to change her mind. At graduation, she applied to Neiman Marcus instead of applying to law school. She was not accepted and took a management position at another major department store in Dallas.

While developing her buying skills, Karen went on to earn a master's degree in business administration. She was promoted, and seven years later Neiman Marcus extended her an offer to join the company. She started as a merchandise manager. Her career sky-rocketed at Neiman where she went on to become vice president and general manager, then senior vice president and director of stores. Karen moved into the role of executive vice president and before long became president. Her time to accomplish all of this at Neiman Marcus was about 15 years, not a long time for such a strong story of career progress. Karen's first rejection from Neiman Marcus made her more determined to explore her passion for the retail industry. While she was certainly disappointed that Neiman Marcus had not hired her at that time, she stayed committed to her goals and eventually found success back at the very place that had challenged her along the way. Karen commented, "I have two rejection letters that I haven't thrown away: One is from Harvard Law School and the other is from Neiman Marcus."

Source: M. Halkias. (2007). "High End Resumes." *Dallas Morning News*, October 24, www.dallasnews.com.

13.3 POSITIVE RELATIONSHIPS

Throughout your career, you will be required to interact with people at different levels in your organization and with those outside the company. This interaction will range from dealing with your boss and associates to dealing with customers. Each of these situations always requires professionalism, but each requires a slightly different approach.

YOUR RELATIONSHIP WITH YOUR BOSS

A positive and productive working relationship with your boss can enhance your personal development as well as your professional growth. The following should help you:

- Loyalty sets the stage for trust. You can be loyal to your boss and to yourself even when you don't both agree. Be up front and discuss the issue honestly—with him or her only.
- Don't talk negatively about your boss or the company you work for to other people.
- Don't waste your boss's time.
- Be aware of your boss's priorities.
- Help your boss get promoted. It may help you in the same way.
- Incorporate the boss's point of view in your decision making. Try to see his or her point of view, and you may make better decisions.
- Accept criticism from your boss as a learning experience. Criticism should not be interpreted as a threat. It should be seen as a desirable challenge.
- Admit your mistakes.
- Ask for feedback.
- Don't ever upstage your boss.
- Avoid presenting your boss with bad news early or late in the day or week.
- No surprises—keep your boss informed.

Remember, you are part of the management team regardless of what position you hold. Your relationship with your boss should be mutually beneficial. You should foster an environment of cooperation so that you help each other achieve personal and company goals. Being a team player with your boss makes both your job and your boss's more productive and meaningful.

Handling Problems with Your Boss   Problems with your boss can stem from a variety of sources but most often will lie with your boss, with you, or a combination of both.

Common problems that lie with the boss include his or her inability to do the job, lack of experience with the job, poor communication skills, insecurity, or poor leadership skills. If you think your boss has one of these problems, you should be professional in your approach to resolving or improving the situation. First, you should avoid being disloyal and talking about the problem to others before you have the chance to talk directly to your boss about it. Before meeting with your boss, ask yourself what you expect from the meeting. Maybe you are looking for more direction, more authority, more responsibility, more involvement, or simply more support from your boss. Try to pin down the reason for your frustration so that you are able to tell your boss how the situation may be negatively affecting your productivity or morale. Also be ready to ask how the situation can be improved. Very often, differences between bosses and workers are the result of different expectations. Always take the high road, and let your boss know that you are eager to improve your relationship. Try to agree on a plan that will help both of you benefit from your meeting.

YOUR RELATIONSHIPS WITH MENTORS

A mentor is someone with more experience than you who is willing to provide helpful advice for your professional development. If at all possible, find a mentor early in your career. This person can be a big help in setting and achieving your professional goals.

Selecting both a role model and a mentor can keep you on the right track with your personal and professional development. The one thing both have in common is previous experience and success. Role models can be selected from any walk of life, can be living or dead, or can be famous or unknown. However, mentors are usually selected from within your career field, are living success stories, are usually employed within your own company, and are not necessarily famous people. You may or may not be able to consult with your role model, but you will be able to actually work with your mentor on an ongoing basis. In many ways your role model helps you believe in yourself and serves as your inspiration, while your mentor helps you develop hands-on strategies for success in the workplace and is a partner with you in your career success.

As you set goals for your own personal development, it will be helpful to choose a mentor. While a student, you may consider someone from the company where you have a part-time or summer job, an internship, or a cooperative education assignment. Think about some people who are possible mentors for you, and write their names in the space provided along with the reasons you would choose them.

ACTIVITY 13.3

Selecting a Mentor

As you set goals for your own personal development, it will be helpful to choose someone who can be your mentor. While a student, you may consider someone from the company where you have a part-time or summer job, an internship, or a cooperative education assignment.

Think about some people who are possible mentors for you, and write their names in the space provided along with the reasons you would choose them.

Names	Reasons Why

YOUR RELATIONSHIPS WITH COWORKERS

Imagine that you are at the top of your graduating class and are used to being number one. You've earned the job you have now, but something is different. You've been hired along with a lot of other "number ones," and suddenly, the skills and talents that once put you on top now put you in competition. Yes, there are other people who are smarter, who can do it better, and who will challenge you. Learning to work with others and to respect their opinions, talents, and contributions to your organization can be difficult. Perhaps one of the hardest things you will face in your career is having to work with people you really don't like. Learn to separate your personal feelings and preferences about people and situations from your professional life. The person you dislike the most might be an important link in your team. Tomorrow's jobs require the ability to get things done with other people. You will be measured on team efforts as well as your individual accomplishments. You will be treated the way you treat other people. The following tips should help you learn to become part of a team:

- Be a team player.
- Build working relationships with those at your level and in other departments.
- Realize the power of praise. Compliment people for a job well done.
- Say thank you.

Handling Problems with Your Coworkers   A large part of your professional development will depend on your ability to handle conflicts with coworkers. Problems with your coworkers are best dealt with immediately and professionally. You should focus on the person involved in the conflict with you. Go directly to that person, and ask for a meeting to discuss the situation. You may want to do this over lunch to avoid interrupting your work. Also,

being in a neutral environment usually helps diffuse a tense situation. In your discussion, take the initiative to state the problem between you and what you think the cause is. Do not place blame on the other person. Direct your comments toward the situation, not the person. Then ask for the other person's viewpoint. This is very important because if you listen carefully, you may learn that the other person's perceptions are much different than you thought. Active listening is critical in any conflict resolution, so work hard at it. After you have both explained your viewpoints, state that your goal is to come up with a resolution that is agreeable to both of you. Discuss what that might be, and resolve to make it happen. If the problem continues after you have truly tried to resolve it, seek the advice of your boss or another appropriate person at the company.

> "Winning is not always the barometer of getting better."
>
> *Tiger Woods,*
> *professional golfer*[4]

LEADERSHIP ROLES

If you are in the position to lead a team, then your human relations skills will determine your success. People want to be led, not managed. You *manage* projects, things, and your time. You *lead* people.

Leadership can be developed if you know its essential ingredients and have a real desire to lead. The strong desire is important because leadership requires much time, energy, commitment, and skill; and if you really don't want the responsibility, you will give up easily. If you don't want a leadership role, don't accept it. You won't do yourself justice, nor will it be fair to the people looking for leadership. If you do think the leadership challenge is for you, here are some qualities of a good leader that you should master:

Vision	Intelligence
Courage	Enthusiasm
Self-motivation	Character
Risk taking	Ability to motivate others
Positive attitude	Integrity
Energy level	Ability to plan and organize

Leaders create an atmosphere in which others can grow and develop their abilities. Effective leadership focuses on putting the people in your responsibility area first. Here are some guidelines for leaders:

- Recognize the power of people in your area.
- Empower commitment and loyalty by example.
- Recognize individual accomplishments as well as team efforts.
- Combine monetary rewards with other benefits such as free time, a new opportunity, or additional authority.

TEAMWORK

More and more companies are encouraging teamwork, as well as individual performance, as a means of professional development and as a technique for achieving company goals.

[4]Retrieved March 15, 2013, from www.brainyquote.com/quotes/quotes/t/tigerwoods465108.html.

A. Identify an influential leader whom you know or work with. Think about what traits this person has that makes him or her such an effective leader, in your opinion. In the first column of the following table, write down the traits.

B. Share your story about this person with one or more other people, and have them share a similar story with you. In the second column, list other leadership traits that result from your discussion.

In the third column, list the traits that appeared on both your own list and others' lists.

Use the information you have gathered to think about or discuss what makes a good leader.

Leadership Traits	Others' Leadership Traits	Common Leadership Traits
_____	_____	_____
_____	_____	_____
_____	_____	_____
_____	_____	_____
_____	_____	_____

ACTIVITY 13.4

What Makes a Good Leader?

As a member of a team, you are usually responsible for performing a specific role to help the team be successful. If one person on the team does not fulfill his or her role, the team will not succeed. Teamwork is important because it is a way of bringing together individual ideas and opinions to create new ideas or solve a problem. In some cases, teamwork is more effective than individual effort. Teamwork is also intended to foster relationships among the team members by opening their minds to different perspectives.

13.4 CHANGES IN THE WORKPLACE

Changes at work can occur for a variety of reasons. New technology, a new boss, a change in company direction due to a merger or downsizing, or new thinking by management are some examples.

No matter how big or small change is, it can disrupt normal work flow and can preoccupy thinking about what to expect. Wondering "What will happen to me?" is a natural reaction, as is the anxiety change often brings.

REDUCING STRESS FROM CHANGE

Why is change stressful? Everyone reacts differently to change. There is usually an upside and a downside. It seems to be a natural tendency to look at the downside first. It is common for worry and uncertainty to cause stress about the situation. The following are some examples of and simple tips for dealing with stress caused by change in the workplace.

- *Loss of networks.* Develop an expanded support network.
- *Loss of personal security.* Have a backup plan, especially a financial plan should you become unemployed.
- *Loss of confidence or feeling underskilled.* Make a list of skills you learned or used on this job. Make a list of your major accomplishments.

"Push through your uncertainty."

Marissa Mayer,
CEO, Yahoo[5]

[5]Retrieved March 9, 2013, from www.cnn.com/2012/07/17/tech/mayer-yahoo-career-advice.

- *Uncertainty—living outside your comfort zone.* Instead of focusing on what you can't control, make a list of what you can control and how to do it.
- *Lack of communication.* Find out what the channel of communication is for updates, and follow up with your supervisor with any questions you have along the way. Keeping informed helps minimize misconceptions.

FINDING THE POSITIVE SIDE OF CHANGE

Most often, there are some upsides to change to think about once you have some time to process what is happening. Depending on the situation, you may see change as long overdue and recognize the advantages up front. The following are some examples of the positive side of change at work.

- *New opportunities.* Perhaps you will take on new responsibilities.
- *New skill sets.* Find out if there are training opportunities to learn new skills needed.
- *Chance to stand out.* Become part of the solution, not part of the problem. Become part of the team helping others deal with changes happening to them.
- *Renewed motivation.* This is a time to become more involved and better engaged with your work.
- *Broader perspective.* Change can cause you to see situations and people in a new light if you are open.

MANAGE CHANGE

Attitude Counts		Action Steps
Adapt		Assess the situation
Resist negativity		Give it time
Embrace change		Plan next steps

MOVE ON

13.5 RESET YOUR CAREER

You have determined it is time to step up your career. Stepping it up may mean different things to different people. You may want to move into a new field or stay in the same field but with a different company. Perhaps you can make a successful career move within your current company. It's not always necessary to leave your current employer to start something new. Whatever your reason is for a change, before you press the reset button think about whether you can meet the challenges that come with your new career goals.

SELF-ASSESSMENT

Ask yourself some questions first to determine if bringing your inspirational goal to reality is a realistic move.

New Goals and Challenges

- Has my definition of career success changed?
- What are my new goals? (inspirational, SMART, financial, work–life balance)
- What challenges should I anticipate?

Promoting Yourself

- How will I promote myself?
- What updates do I need to make to my marketing tools? (social media profile, personal website, Career Portfolio, resume)
- What will be my biggest interview challenges, and what do I need to do to prepare?

New Beginnings

- How can my performance stand out in my new environment?
- How can I strengthen my professional relationships?
- What new footprint will I create?

> **"Do not go where the path may lead, go instead where there is no path and leave a trail."**
>
> *Ralph Waldo Emerson,* American essayist and poet[6]

NEW GOALS AND CHALLENGES

An updated self-assessment will help you reflect on your current values, interests, personality, and skills. These can change with time and experience and influence new career goals. Conduct career research to test whether your goals are consistent with the current realities of the economy. Use your research on career and job trends to write your new goals with realistic time lines and milestones.

Realizing new career goals usually means facing new challenges. Your ability to identify the challenges and create a plan to address them is key to any successful career move. Some potential challenges with realizing a new career goal might involve personal finances, work–life balance, new technology, child care, location, travel, and work hours. For example, a pay cut may be required to enter a field you have no experience in. Better check in with your family support network, and see if everyone is on the same page about spending adjustments needed to support the change. It may be worth the long-term gain of working in your field and being more satisfied with your career but have agreement on a plan to meet the challenges.

SELF-PROMOTION

The way to promote yourself during a career change is different than approaching your first job after college. While you need the same basic marketing tools, the way you use them may be different. The main difference is that if you are currently employed, you don't want to jeopardize your current job. Face-to-face networking is the best way to directly communicate your interest in a career change. Using social media, a personal website, and job boards online communicates your message to a much larger, more public audience, which can risk your current job. Use online tools to promote your skills, experience, and expertise without directly stating you are looking for a job. Some companies conduct passive searches online which means they source candidates they may be interested in without the candidate needing to express interest in employment.

In interviews, a challenge might be explaining lack of experience if you are entering a new field. Promote your transferable skills as follows:

- *Work your career network.* Face-to-face works best for career changers.
- *Update social media profiles.* Avoid mention of a career change if currently employed.
- *Update your resume and Career Portfolio.* Target them to specific employers and jobs.
- *Focus on skills, experience, and expertise.* Functional or combination resumes work best.
- *Emphasize transferable skills.* Give examples of applying them to new situations.

[6]Retrieved March 9, 2013, from www.brainyquote.com/quotes/quotes/r/ralphwaldo101322.html.

NEW BEGINNINGS

- *Achieve*—results count.
- *Aspire* to be better.
- *Affirm* your unique talents.
- *Believe in yourself*—how you see yourself is how others will see you.
- *Strive* beyond expectations.

As you move through your career, you will experience ups and downs and face unexpected circumstances. Not being prepared to handle them could sidetrack your career. In this chapter, you learned some techniques for keeping your career on course even during challenging times. A central theme is the value of transferable skills throughout your career.

Well-developed transferable skills drive standout performance and the ability to grow professional relationships, both cornerstones to a thriving career. The ability to recognize, and act on, those critical moments when your performance can make a huge difference will help you leave positive lasting impressions and keep you top of mind for new opportunities. The ability to anticipate and manage different types of change in your workplace will help you better adapt to the change and adjust to the new role you might play moving forward.

Deciding how to make a career move and considering the challenges that come with it is an important career management skill that can help you determine your next move whether it is planned or unplanned. No matter what happens, you can be confident knowing you have the tools to explore, brand, and market your potential and take yourself to the place where you can leave your next footprint.

GROWING YOUR CAREER AND CAREER DECISION MAKING

Based on what you learned about growing with your job in this chapter, answer the following questions:

1. What am I trying to decide? _____
   _____

2. What do I need to know? _____
   _____

3. How will it help me make a more informed decision? _____
   _____

4. How can I obtain what I need to know? _____
   _____

   People _____
   Experience _____
   Research _____

5. Who are my best resources for the information I need? _____
   _____

"Only you can control your future."
Dr. Seuss[1]

[1]Retrieved June 22, 2013, from www.goodreads.com/quotes/108615-only-you-can-control-your-future.

Contemporary Issues in the Workplace

After completing this chapter, you will:

1 **Describe** employee assistance programs

2 **Identify** how health-related issues affect you in the workplace

3 **Recognize** family care issues that affect you in the workplace

4 **Assess** the role of personal ethics in the workplace

5 **Explain** some laws that protect employees from workplace discrimination

The world of work is changing toward increasing integration between personal and professional aspects of life. For example, there is a trend for workers to value free time more than ever before. Changes in society also influence contemporary issues in the workplace. For example, men and women who want to raise families are faced with conflicts in work–life priorities. Unethical behavior by many business leaders is a societal concern that frequently disrupts the workplace. As a result, many corporations are implementing new codes of conduct for workers at all levels in a wide range of areas. Because contemporary issues in the workplace affect the way we live and work, you should be aware of some that will affect you during your career.

CASE STUDY

Jenny Gains Perspective

Jenny worked as an office manager for the local performing arts center for two years. She supervised four other employees and worked independently most of the time. Her boss came in one hour later than Jenny every day and then spent most of her time out of the office at meetings and community events, planning and promoting the center's work.

Jenny's morning routine started with organizing her work for the day. Within the first hour, she was sure to clean up any personal tasks that needed to be done. On any given day, this might have included paying some personal bills online, sending an e-mail confirming dinner plans with friends, ordering a birthday present, or checking airfares online for her vacation. Her boss was satisfied with Jenny's work and did not dictate how she managed her time at the office, as long as she got the job done.

Jenny accepted a new job as the assistant director of human resources at a large insurance company. She learned that the company had an Internet/e-mail policy that was published in the employee handbook and explained during the employee orientation program. She was aware of issues with employees spending time social networking at work, but never really thought about other abuses of technology at work.

The policy outlined specific uses of technology that were not acceptable during work hours. These included personal e-mails, sharing confidential company information, and sending e-mails that were potentially discriminatory. The policy prohibited the use of online activities during business hours including use of entertainment, sports, gambling, and online shopping sites. One of her assignments was to provide reports to the legal department for an employee lawsuit. The employee was suing the company for allowing e-mails containing discriminatory jokes about her ethnic background to be circulated within her department. As Jenny was preparing to hire a job candidate, she learned through a friend in human resources at another company that the person had been dismissed from a previous job because of sharing confidential information about the company's new product line to a friend who worked with a competitor. At her previous job, she never realized how serious misuse of the Internet could be for a company or its employees. While the company had an Internet policy, there was not a system to formally monitor it. Jenny's boss was now considering monitoring employee use of the Internet and had her research several computer and Internet monitoring services. When she worked at her previous job, she would have thought this type of oversight by her employer to be unnecessary, but now she saw things from a much different perspective. Jenny learned how to prepare written policy to spell out exactly what was acceptable and unacceptable for that company so that each employee knew what was expected of him or her. This created a company system for communicating and monitoring technology abuse at work.

Jenny came to realize that managing Internet use would benefit individual employees as well as the company.

Discussion Questions

1. Do you think Jenny was wrong to use the Internet for personal use at her job at the performing arts center? Why or why not?
2. Do you think that companies should monitor employee Internet use at work? Why or why not?
3. Was it right for Jenny's friend in human resources to tell her why the job candidate Jenny was about to hire was fired from his last job? Why or why not?

14.1 EMPLOYEE ASSISTANCE PROGRAMS

The many types of employee assistance programs (EAPs) that companies offer serve as a benefit to employees and a retention tool for the company. Employee assistance programs provide help to both supervisors and employees in responding to personal problems that could affect job performance. The extent of these programs may vary substantially by company. Most include assistance to employees with issues that range from substance abuse, family care, and stress management to financial planning and legal assistance.

14.2 HEALTH-RELATED ISSUES

By being better informed on these issues, you can understand why certain company policies are in place and what assistance is available to you to help you deal with these issues personally or with coworkers.

Health-related issues affect employees in the workplace in many ways. Substance abuse may affect an employee's productivity and attitude and can result in increased absenteeism. Laws requiring more accommodations are opening up new career opportunities for employees with disabilities. As a result of the emergence of these health-related issues, more companies are committed to formal health education programs for their employees.

SUBSTANCE ABUSE

Overuse of some drugs and alcohol can produce behavioral problems for employees that disrupt either their own productivity or the environment they work in.[2]

Employers report a higher incidence of problems with productivity, accidents, medical claims, absenteeism, and employee theft among employees with substance abuse problems. These all result in higher costs to the employer. As a job candidate or an actual employee, you can be affected by these problems whether you are a substance abuser or not. Drug and alcohol abuse costs U.S. businesses as much as $140 billion a year in lost productivity. As a result, drug-free workplace policies are more common.

If you test positive for drugs when looking for a job, you will almost certainly not be hired. Once you are employed, detection of drug or alcohol use can cause you to be fired if you show any kind of work-related problem because of it.

STRESS MANAGEMENT

Nearly one-third of employers report that high stress levels cause conflict between their work responsibilities and personal priorities. The same report cited other factors that contribute to work-related stress:

- Long hours 25%
- Fast-paced environment 14%
- Inflexible schedule 13%
- Personal values conflict with my company's core values 9%
- Highly competitive environment 7%[3]

There are many ways employees can learn to manage their own stress by developing better discipline for healthier lifestyles. Four basic lifestyle tips are helpful in managing stress:

- Maintain a healthy diet and weight.
- Maintain a daily exercise routine.
- Prioritize your schedule every day.
- Ask for help if you need it.

In addition to these lifestyle practices, EAPs may offer the assistance you need to get back on and stay on track at home and in the workplace. Some companies are even more committed to promoting healthy lifestyles than others and offer employees lifestyle benefits that may include memberships to health clubs, fitness centers, or weight-loss programs. Education and assistance with managing debt, buying a car, or planning savings and investments are other examples of assistance companies may provide to help employees manage the stress that is a natural outcome of daily living.

[2]Abbott Laboratories Diagnostics. (2005). "Drug Abuse." Retrieved July 14, 2005, from www.abbottdiagnostics. com/YourHealth/Drug_Abuse/.

[3]Deloitte & Touche. (2007). "Leadership Counts." Retrieved from www.deloitte.com/dtt/cda/doc/content/ us_ethics_workplace2007a.pdf.

HEALTH EDUCATION

"The health and well-being of our families and communities concern everyone."

Lisa M. Borders, Chair of The Coca-Cola Foundation

Source: Retrieved December 6, 2013 from http://www.csrwire.com/press_releases/36291-The-Coca-Cola-Foundation-Awards-8-1-Million-in-3rd-Quarter-Benefitting-3-8-Million-People-Worldwide Retrieved December 6, 2013

Many employers have implemented health education programs to help employees with how to prevent or manage health issues that could affect them in the workplace.

Health education involves wellness programs to promote overall good nutrition and exercise as a way of life. These wellness programs instruct employees on how to keep fit and may recommend individual fitness programs as well. Wellness programs are cost-effective (their cost often is outweighed by savings in health care costs), responsive to employees' needs, and offer a sense of social responsibility. For the employee, participation can result in reduced absenteeism because of improved physical health and assurance that one's work life can be a positive factor contributing to an overall healthy lifestyle. For example, Coca-Cola adopted its Active Healthy Living strategy focused on employee physical activity, nutrition, and local collaboration with its communities.

ACCOMMODATIONS FOR EMPLOYEES WITH DISABILITIES

The Americans with Disabilities Act (ADA) has required employers to make accommodations for employees with disabilities. The act bars employment discrimination against workers with disabilities and mandates access to public spaces. Companies that fail to meet these standards are subject to civil actions for noncompliance. The Americans with Disabilities Act makes it easier for job candidates and employees to get to and from work and move about safely in the workplace.

14.3 FAMILY CARE ISSUES

Labor force participation is significantly higher among women today than it was in the 1970s, particularly among women with children, and a larger share of women are working full time and year round.[4] The U.S. Census Bureau projects that the number of people aged 55 to 64 will increase to almost 40 million in 2014 and to 42 million in 2024.[5] More employees will become members of the so-called sandwich generation, who are caring for both young and elderly family members simultaneously. According to the National Alliance for Caregiving, an estimated 65.7 million people in the U.S. have served as unpaid family caregivers to an adult or a child, and an estimated of 36.5 million households have a caregiver present.[6] Parental leave for child care and leave for elder care are the two fastest-emerging work–family conflicts. Caring for the family often means taking care of older parents as well as children. This, coupled with job demands, puts tremendous pressure on many workers, who often experience stress trying to keep everything balanced.

PARENTAL LEAVE

The Family and Medical Leave Act (FMLA) requires companies to allow eligible employees up to 12 weeks' leave during any 12-month period for childbirth, adoption, or foster child care; serious illness of a spouse, child, or parent; or a personal serious health condition. Many leaves are nonpaid, although employees are entitled to continue their company-provided medical coverage during their leave. Despite the strong interest many men and women have in staying home to care for their children, many of them simply cannot afford

---

[4]U.S. Bureau of Labor Statistics. BLS Reports. (February 2013). Women in the Labor Force: A Databook. Retrieved December 6, 2013, from page 1, www.bls.gov/cps/wlf-databook-2012.pdf.

[5]SHRM Workplace Forecast The Top Workplace Trends According to HR Professionals. (May 2013). Retrieved December 6, 2013, from page 18 www.shrm.org/research/futureworkplacetrends/documents/13-0146%20 workplace_forecast_full_fnl.pdf.

[6]SHRM Workplace Forecast The Top Workplace Trends According to HR Professionals. (May 2013). Retrieved December 6, 2013, from pages 12 and 14 www.shrm.org/research/futureworkplacetrends/ documents/13-0146%20workplace_forecast_full_fnl.pdf .

to. The trend of men taking leave or reducing hours has been slow to surge, experts say, since most employers do not offer paternal leave. Accounting giant Ernst and Young provides two weeks of paid paternal leave.[7]

CHILD CARE

Working mothers and fathers continue to struggle with child care decisions. Balancing quality and cost of care is harder now, as child care costs have nearly doubled since the mid-1980s.[8] The quality of day care programs varies widely. Licensed programs better control learning activities and caregiver–child ratios, but they cost more. More families are turning to more affordable options including care provided by relatives and after-school programs. Local child care resources and referral agencies are a good source of information on programs providing financial support.

Companies also struggle with deciding best ways to support child care for their employees. Companies supporting child care solutions benefit in the recruitment and retention of employees. Child care issues can spill over into performance and absenteeism at work. DuPont surveyed its employees and learned that 80 percent would have missed work if not for its emergency/backup care program. One year, that program saved nearly 1,500 employee days.[9] While some companies offer on-site child care, the expense and oversight has discouraged most companies from following suit. Many offer financial assistance for child care or child care referral services.

FLEXTIME, TELECOMMUTING, AND VIRTUAL WORKPLACES

As new workplace technology develops, there are more opportunities for flexible work arrangements such as flextime, telecommuting, and virtual work. All of these are efforts by employers to respond to employees' work–life balance issues. There are different perspectives on their impact on work productivity and satisfaction. Each has advantages and disadvantages for employers and employees.

Flextime   Flextime allows employees more choices in managing their work schedule by working a full-time schedule, by adjusting start and end time to accommodate personal needs or commitments. Some consider job sharing as a form of flextime. Job sharing is an arrangement in which the responsibilities and hours of one job are carried out by two people.

> "From 2005 to 2011, the number of remote workers grew 73 percent according to the Telework Research Network."[10]

Telecommuting   Telecommuting replaces the physical commute to the office with telecommunications. Telecommuting is based on the idea that employees work successfully outside the physical

"We're becoming a workforce where the amount of time you spend in the [office] chair is not the issue. It's the results of the work. It's about what's been achieved."

Joyce Gioia, president and CEO of The Herman Group

Source: Retreived December 7, 2013 from www.devry.edu/know-how/the-new-concerns-of-an-evolving-workforce/

[7]B. Torres. (2005). "Dads on Leave." *Mail Tribune Online.* Retrieved April 21, 2005, from www.mailtribune.com/archive/2005/0421/life/stories/01life.htm.

[8]Retrieved May 3, 2013, from www.nytimes.com/2013/04/04/us/child-care-costs-are-up-census-finds.html?ref=opinion.

[9]Work Options Group. (2005). "Workplace Impact—Child Care." Retrieved July 14, 2005, from www.workoptionsgroup.com/Default.aspx?tabid 157#child.

[10]Retrieved June 30, 2013, from www.forbes.com/sites/danschawbel/2013/03/29/david-heinemeier-hansson-every-employee-should-work-from-home/.

office setting—if goals are established and results are monitored and achieved. Those in favor of telecommuting argue that an employee's physical presence in an office does not mean that they are producing work during all of their hours present and that managing work through attendance does not guarantee results.

The Telecommuting Debate

"To become the absolute best place to work, communication and collaboration will be important, so we need to be working side-by-side."

Marissa Mayer, CEO Yahoo[11]

"Bottom line, it's 'all hands on deck' at Best Buy and that means having employees in the office as much as possible to collaborate and connect on ways to improve our business."

Matt Furman, Best Buy spokesperson[12]

"Some people are capable of self-managing and can be far more productive working remotely."

Susan Gunelis, president and CEO, Keysplash Creative[13]

"Working from home affords many an extra ordinary boost in quality of life."

David Heinemeier Hansson, partner, 37signals[14]

Debates over the effectiveness of flexible work arrangements are ongoing. Perhaps the previous comments indicate a larger trend that telecommuting works better in certain industries such as high tech, international, or small business than in some larger corporations. These are evolving issues that will continue to impact how many businesses offer these options to employees moving forward.

Virtual Workplaces   A virtual workplace is not located in any one physical space. Mobile technology and other visual communication tools, like Skype, mean that work can take place anywhere there is Wi-Fi. The Web-based service firm, Automattic, is an example of a virtual workplace, where almost all employees work from home. Virtual workplaces are a trend to be watched. They may take a similar path as telecommuting, finding the industry and company niches they fit best.

NOTES | Top Three Positive Influences of Overall Job Satisfaction

- Compensation
- Flexible work
- Benefits

Progress Check Questions

1. What advantages and disadvantages do you see to telecommuting?

2. Do you think that you, personally, would be a more productive or satisfied employee working with a flextime arrangement at work? Why or why not?

---

[11]http://money.cnn.com/2013/03/05/technology/best-buy-work-from-home/index.html.

[12]www.dailytech.com/Best+Buy+No+Longer+Allows+Corporate+Employees+to+Telecommute/article30054.htm.

[13]www.npr.org/2013/02/27/173069965/presence-vs-productivity-how-managers-view-telecommuting.

[14]www.forbes.com/sites/danschawbel/2013/03/29/
david-heinemeier-hansson-every-employee-should-work-from-home/.

🔵 14.4 WORKPLACE ETHICS

The prevalence of unethical behavior in the workplace, and in society, requires stricter enforcement of laws against such behavior to stop it. Many individuals or companies have become comfortable with behavior with which they should be uncomfortable. Theft, fraud, discrimination, and harassment are a few examples of unethical behavior that exist in today's workplace (Figure 14.1).

PERSONAL ETHICS AT WORK

Being an ethically responsible employee involves consistently making good choices with both big and small decisions on a daily basis. Here are some behaviors that show a general lack of concern about ethics at work:

Misuse of company finances

> Stealing petty cash
>
> Cheating on an expense report
>
> Improper accounting

Using company technology for personal use

> Personal e-mails
>
> Social networking
>
> Online activities: shopping, gambling, entertainment

Misuse of company property

> Telephones
>
> Copy and fax machines
>
> Stealing supplies
>
> Company vehicles

Misuse of company benefits

> Calling in sick when you are not sick
>
> Applying for disability without eligibility
>
> Approving employee vacations beyond their eligibility

If you observe someone at work demonstrating unethical behavior, you should report it to your supervisor or to the human resources department. It might be unproductive to confront the employee directly, since, in all likelihood, that person will be defensive with you and put you in an uncomfortable situation. Doing nothing is even more nonproductive. Take some responsibility, and arrange to speak appropriately to someone who can take appropriate action with the company.

> "Real integrity is doing the right thing, knowing that nobody's going to know whether you did it or not."
>
> **Oprah Winfrey**
>
> Source: Retrieved December 7, 2013 from http://humanresources.about.com/od/inspirationalquotations/a/integrity.htm

Real Life Stories

Isabella and Max

Isabella was a working mother and part-time student at the local community college. She had a flextime arrangement at her current job that allowed her flexibility in the morning and at the end of the day to juggle getting her daughter to and from day care and attending her 4:00 p.m. class on Tuesdays and Thursdays. When she was offered a promotion with an attractive salary increase, she had a lot to think about. Her husband, Max, had just received word from his employer that because company revenues were declining, a decision had been made to cut the hours of one-third of its workforce, while keeping salaries level, instead of cutting people from the payroll.

Many companies were doing this to try to preserve people's jobs during the ongoing recession. Max's schedule was cut from 40 to 25 hours per week for an undefined period of time. His boss worked hard to convince Max that the company valued his work and wanted to ensure he would still be one of its employees once the economy improved. Max obtained a temporary position to fill in the hours he would be losing because he wanted to keep his job.

Isabella's new position would require her to be at early morning meetings and occasionally attend social events a few nights each month. She felt conflicted as she processed her decision to stay in her current job or accept the promotion. After all, her goal for furthering her education was to advance in her career, and this seemed like a perfect opportunity. She asked herself, "Should I delay my education to concentrate on a new job?" "Would the salary increase be offset with the additional hours per week I will have to spend on day care?" "How will the extra time needed to invest in the new job affect my personal life?" "If I refuse this offer, will there be a similar opportunity down the road?" Isabella talked with her family and with two of her teachers about her option. While everyone was excited for her, both her family and her teachers advised her to stay with her current job and finish school. Max agreed. Right now, Isabella felt she had a good balance with her family and work life and she was doing well in school. While the increase in salary certainly would make her family's financial situation easier, she was worried that if she accepted additional responsibility at this stage in her life, that she would add stress to herself and to her family. She also might become too distracted from completing her college degree, which was key to achieving her career goals. She decided she could make her best contribution, at the current time, to her family and to her job by keeping her current position.

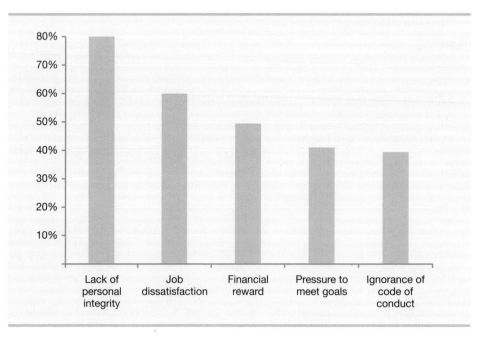

FIGURE 14.1

Why People Make Unethical Decisions

MISUSE OF TECHNOLOGY AT WORK

Misuse of technology at work is a major concern for employers and employees. Gartner Gray reports that non-work-related Internet surfing results in up to a 40 percent loss in productivity at American businesses each year.[15] Employers have valid reasons to monitor employees' activities online and on mobile devices that pertain to protecting their business. Employers need to clearly communicate the company's technology policy. Employees have valid concerns about their privacy at work. The best defense for employees is to be mindful of the digital paths they create at work every day with the use of technology.

Employee Monitoring   If the company owns the system, the employer can monitor the employee's use of it including personal files and communication. This mainly includes computer and phone monitoring.

On company-owned computers, employers can monitor the use of the Internet, including Web surfing and e-mails, as well as idle time on the computer. Keystroke monitoring can be done when an employee's main function is word processing or data entry.

Company phones can be monitored to track telephone calls, call locations, text and e-mail messages, Web usage, photos, and videos.

Just because employers have the right to monitor these things doesn't mean they will. When they do, it may be surrounding a specific event or person as opposed to a general policy. Web surfing might not be banned, but limited to 30 minutes a day. A little personal use of e-mail might be acceptable. Most employers will publish policies with guidelines the company considers to be reasonable.

SELF-INTERRUPT *verb*

To break off briefly from work to check e-mail, Twitter, Facebook, etc.
Office workers are interrupted, or self-interrupt, every three minutes.[16]

Employee Protection   Employees have the right to know if they are being monitored at work and should know the company policy. Employees are usually informed of policies through memos, the employee handbook, meetings, orientation programs, or employee development programs. Be proactive to learn about and better understand the policy. Once informed, following the policy should take care of protecting your privacy in most situations. There are simple steps to take to protect online privacy at work.

Tips for Protecting Online Privacy at Work

- Surf the Internet wisely.
- Use personal phones for personal calls.
- Try to conduct personal business during lunch and break times.
- Use privacy settings.
- E-mail wisely: always assume that they may end up in the last place where you would want to see them.

"For the employee who is doing the right thing and focusing on work and using technology moderately for personal use, electronic surveillance will have no impact."

Manny Avramidis, senior vice president of global human resources, American Management Association

Source: Retrieved December 7, 2013 from http://humanresources.about.com/od/technology/a/surveillance_2.htm

---

[15]Links on SpectorSoft. (2009). Retrieved September 2, 2009, from www.facebook.com/posted.php?id_44523071199&share_id_127034967288&comments_1&ref_mf.

[16]Retrieved May 20, 1013, from http://dictionaryblog.cambridge.org/2013/06/03/new-words-3-june-2013/.

ABUSE OF PRIVILEGE

Abuse of privilege occurs when someone takes a privilege that is given to her or him, such as a company expense account, and extends its use beyond what is acceptable or expected by the company. In this case, an individual may use a company expense account to be reimbursed for personal expenses that are not company-related.

Most companies have policies prohibiting the removal of company property without written permission from the supervisor responsible for the property in question. Company property can include tools or equipment; confidential literature; computer disks, tapes, and other storage media; or information identified as proprietary or a trade secret. Removing or attempting to remove company property without permission can be grounds for disciplinary action.

CONFLICT OF INTEREST

"Honesty and integrity are always in style."

The TJX Companies, Inc. Global Code of Conduct Guide

Source: Retrieved December 7, 2013 from www.tjx.com/files/pdf/coc_june_2010_distribution.pdf

Conflicts of interest sometimes occur between company and personal interests or goals. A drafter who has a private consulting business outside of the job with his or her employer may experience a conflict of interest if trying to consult during the employer's work hours.

Most companies expect all employees to avoid activities that create conflicts of interest with their responsibilities to the company. Employers may ask employees to refrain from activities that may conflict or interfere with company operation or with others with whom the company does business. Conflicts of interest include, but are not limited to, the following:

1. *Outside employment.* A second job with a competitor is usually prohibited because of the danger that exists for sharing procedures, business plans, and product development techniques, especially if the second company is competing for the same customers.
2. *Gifts and entertainment.* Some companies have strict policies prohibiting employees from accepting gifts of more than nominal value from people or companies that do business, or want to do business, with the company.
3. *Legal issues.* All companies prohibit employees from doing anything in the conduct of business that would violate any local, state, or federal law.
4. *Fair competition.* Companies generally encourage their employees to conduct business fairly and ethically, with consideration given to the needs of customers, fellow workers, and suppliers.

PREFERENTIAL TREATMENT

Preferential treatment is when an employee shows special treatment to certain groups of people or takes shortcuts for one person and not another. An example would be an account representative at a bank who processes a loan for a friend without following the prescribed waiting period for approval or without checking all the necessary references.

These are just some examples of how day-to-day work activities can lead an individual into an ethical dilemma. When faced with an ethical decision, most people follow their own personal code of behavior, as opposed to the behavior of others or any formal company policy. Ultimately, you are in control of your own actions.

Progress Check Questions

1. What would you do if you knew a coworker constantly used online entertainment sites during working hours?
2. How would you handle an e-mail sent to you containing an ethnically discriminatory joke?

14.5 NONDISCRIMINATION LAWS

The U.S. Department of Labor is charged with the responsibility of regulating workplace activity to ensure fair treatment of individuals and groups of employees in a wide range of areas. The following are some of the more commonly known laws that are in place to accomplish this goal.

EQUAL EMPLOYMENT OPPORTUNITY

Fairness in hiring practices is the goal of the Equal Employment Opportunity Act. Companies that maintain a policy of nondiscrimination in all phases of employment must also comply in full with all applicable laws. The following practices ensure that companies properly implement their nondiscrimination policy. The company will:

- Recruit, advertise, hire, transfer, and promote without regard to race, religion, color, national origin, physical handicap, sex, age, or any other legally protected classification.
- Base all employment decisions on candidates' qualifications to do the job.

AFFIRMATIVE ACTION

The affirmative action law was instituted to improve the participation of more minority and female workers in the workplace. Today, attitudes about affirmative action range from supportive to opposed. Those in favor believe that because of affirmative action, women and members of racial and ethnic minority groups play a larger role in the workplace. Those opposed say that as affirmative action has evolved, there is now too much emphasis on meeting "goals and timetables" for hiring or promoting women and minorities.

Most employers are engaged in some sort of affirmative action program. As they implement these programs, employers must be careful to maintain a balance in their hiring practices for first hiring the most qualified candidates and then ensuring there is a good mix of workers from all backgrounds in their workplace.

SEXUAL HARASSMENT

Sexual harassment issues in the workplace are costly to employers. It is reported that sexual harassment has cost some Fortune 500 companies up to $6.7 million a year in absenteeism, lower productivity, and turnover.[17] Legal fees for defending a sexual harassment charge average $250,000, and judgments routinely exceed $1 million. As a result, employers openly publish policies to make it clear to employees that sexual harassment is inappropriate workplace behavior that is not tolerated.

These policies exist so that all employees can share a work environment free of potentially harmful comments or actions. Employees who feel they have been harassed usually have the option of complaining to someone in the company (human resources department, supervisor's boss, etc.) other than the harasser. This provides them a more comfortable form of communication.

"Harassment may be physical or verbal, and may be done in person or by other means (such as harassing notes or emails)."

Source: Retrieved December 7, 2013 from www.pg.com/ en_US/downloads/company/ governance/Policy_Worldwide_ Business_Conduct_Manual.pdf

---

[17]J. E. Johnston. (2005). "Dear Human Resources Professional." Retrieved July 15, 2005, from www .workrelationships.com/site/awb/awb.php.

Tips for Dealing with Sexual Harassment

1. Tell the harasser to stop the offensive behavior.
2. Document all incidents of harassment.
3. Notify your supervisor or other appropriate person of the harassment.
4. Know your company or school policy on sexual harassment, and follow its procedures.
5. Consider filing a formal grievance or complaint if the preceding steps do not remedy the situation.
6. Stay on the job.
7. Find support from family, friends, or other groups to help you through the situation.

CHAPTER SUMMARY

As you navigate your career, there may be times when you feel some conflict between work and personal priorities. As you try to maintain the right balance between the two, take advantage of resources that your employer may offer. Employee assistance programs vary from company to company but basically are there to provide you support in a number of ways, ranging from financial advising, educational assistance, to advice on child care and stress management. Think of the employee assistance program as your safety net at work, providing you tools to achieve your goals and maintain work–life balance in the process.

Part of the services available to you might be advice on health and wellness and family care–related issues. Support to help you reduce stress and maintain healthy habits at work vary from a fitness club membership to health assessments with advice on a variety of health-related issues. Staying healthy at work is important to being productive and enjoying your work. There are many support programs to help you balance family responsibilities at the same time.

A major part of your career success will depend on how well you can bring your good judgment and common sense to ethical decisions you may need to make. Making sound ethical decisions is important to your personal reputation and can impact your company's reputation. Having a sense of fairness in the way you deal with others and avoiding behavior that is discriminatory will help you develop strong working relationships, including the trust and respect of people in your company.

Managing yourself and your family and building a solid reputation as an ethical and fair professional will improve your chances of success in your career, while balancing other important aspects of your life.

REFLECTION EXERCISE

CONTEMPORARY ISSUES IN THE WORKPLACE AND CAREER DECISION MAKING

Based on what you learned about contemporary issues in the workplace, select a topic that represents an issue that you think will impact your career decisions the most. Think about a career decision you are trying to make and how this issue might influence you.

1. What am I trying to decide?

_____

_____

2. What do I need to know?

_____

_____

3. How will it help me make a more informed decision?

_____

_____

4. How can I obtain what I need to know?

_____

_____

     People _____

     Experience _____

     Research _____

5. Who are my best resources for the information I need?

_____

_____

Credits

Part 1 opener, p. 2: © Brand X Pictures/PunchStock RF; **6:** © Ingram Publishing RF; **9:** © Beathan/Corbis RF; **Chapter 2 opener, p. 18:** © Dave and Les Jacobs/Blend Images LLC RF; **23:** © Jupiterimages RF; **28:** © Stockbyte/Getty RF; **Chapter 3 opener, p. 38:** © Digital Vision RF; **41:** © Brand X Pictures/PunchStock RF; **43:** © Getty RF; **45:** *(top left)* © Stockbyte/Getty RF; *(top center)* © Pixtal/AGE Fotostock RF; *(top right)* © Chris Ryan/age footstock RF; **Chapter 4 opener, p. 52:** © Chris Ryan/age fotostock RF; **57:** © Sam Edwards/age footstock RF; **61:** © Image Source/Getty RF; **69:** © Image Source/Getty RF; **71:** © Image Source/Jupiterimages RF; **75:** to come; **Chapter 5 opener, p. 82:** © Thinkstock/Jupiterimages RF; **86:** © Pixtal/AGE Fotostock RF; **87:** *(top right)* © Ingram Publishing RF; *(right center)* © Don Carstens/Brand X Pictures RF; *(bottom right)* © Thinkstock/Getty RF; **88:** © Digital Vision/Alamy RF; **96:** © Flying Colours Ltd/Getty RF; **98:** *(top left)* © C. Sherburne/PhotoLink/Getty RF; *(bottom left)* © Sam Edwards/age fotostock RF; **99:** © Don Farrall/Getty RF; **Part 2 opener, p. 104:** © Yuri Arcurs/Cutcaster RF; **Chapter 7 opener, p. 124:** © David Malan/Getty RF; **Chapter 8 opener, p. 140:** © Digital Vision RF; **150:** © Altrendo Images/ Getty RF; **Chapter 9 opener, p. 156:** © Comstock/PunchStock RF; **163:** © Digital Vision RF; **165:** © Rainer Holz/zefa/Corbis RF; **Chapter 10 opener, p. 168:** © Big Cheese Photo/JupiterImages RF; **175:** © Polka Dot Images/Jupiterimages RF; **198:** © iStock Exclusive/Getty RF; **Chapter 11 opener, p. 204:** © BananaStock/PictureQuest RF; **220:** © DreamPictures/Getty RF; **227:** © The McGraw-Hill Companies, Inc./Jack Holtel, photographer; **Chapter 12 opener, p. 230:** © Tom Merton/age fotostock RF; **235:** © Getty/Comstock Images RF; **235:** © Ingram Publishing RF; **243:** © McGraw-Hill Education; **244:** © McGraw-Hill Companies, Inc./Mark Dierker, photographer; **245:** © Comstock/PictureQuest RF; **Part 3 opener, p. 258:** © Big Cheese Photo/JupiterImages RF; **265:** © Sam Edwards/age fotostock RF; **265:** © Stockbyte/Getty RF; **266:** © Steve Cole/Getty RF; **269:** © Corbis RF; **271:** © Design Pics/Don Hammond RF; **274:** © Corbis RF; **Chapter 14 opener, p. 276:** © BananaStock/Jupiterimages RF; **279:** © Erik Isakson/Blend Images LLC RF; **281:** © Matthias Tunger/Getty RF; **285:** © Corbis RF.

Index

Page numbers followed by *n* refer to material found in notes.